IT AIN'T HEAVY, IT'S MY STORY

IT AIN'T HEAVY, IT'S MY STORY

MY LIFE IN THE HOLLIES

BOBBY ELLIOTT

Simon,
Thanks for your help
over the years.

Here it is, at last...
Enjoy!

Bobby Elliott

OMNIBUS PRESS

London / New York / Paris / Sydney / Copenhagen / Berlin / Madrid / Tokyo

Cover designed by Ruth Keating
Picture research by the author
Artistic liaison: Steve Lee Vickers

ISBN: 978-1-91317-220-6

Designed and Typeset by Evolution Design and Digital Limited, Kent
Printed in the Czech Republic

A catalogue record for this book is available from the British Library.

Contents

Sue

You rescued me when I was down, your smile lit up the room

At last I saw the future, sunlight cutting through the gloom

You caught me as I fell and we floated on the breeze

Life is just so easy now we can do as we please.

B x

Introduction

I stood in front of New York's world-famous Paramount Theatre and drank in the sight. Here we were, right in the heart of theatreland in Times Square, about to perform in the theatre designed to showcase the best of Paramount Pictures and now a top-notch live performance venue. We had made it to the States.

Stars like Ginger Rogers, Rudy Vallée and Bing Crosby had performed in this theatre. It was here that the crowds had danced in the aisles to Benny Goodman's music, with the great Gene Krupa on drums, and here that the bobby soxers had squealed and cried over Frank Sinatra.

As the heavy stage door closed behind me, I skipped up the short flight of concrete steps leading to the elevator. It was then that I heard raised voices. The sight of a group of theatre staff fronted by a tubby New York cop, pistol drawn, stopped me in my tracks.

'Those little white girls out there love me.'

It was Little Richard. And he was in real 'Tutti Frutti' tantrum mode.

The police officer appeared agitated and was now sticking the loaded weapon into my hero's neck. It was tense.

'Hold still or I'll blow your fuckin' head off!' ordered the officer.

Undaunted by the cold steel being poked into his jugular, Little Richard's outpourings continued in a sort of running-on-the-spot fashion. I was witnessing a serious incident, a surreal tragicomedy. Was I on a film set? Would someone shout: 'Cut'?

CHRIS WAINWRIGHT AGENCY LTD.

Directors :
C. F. Burton
K. W. Fisher

RECTORY CHAMBERS
204 WATERLOO ROAD
BURSLEM
STOKE-ON-TRENT

Telephone Nos.
Stoke-on-Trent 84052/3

№ .. 856

IN ASSOCIATION WITH :

MIDLAND ENTERTAINMENTS LTD.
CHRIS WAINWRIGHT PROMOTIONS LTD.

ROCKSTAR ENTERPRISES LTD
BRY MARTIN AND THE MARAUDERS LTD.

THIS AGENCY IS NOT RESPONSIBLE FOR ANY NON-FULFILMENT OF CONTRACTS BY PROPRIETORS, MANAGERS OR ARTISTES, BUT EVERY REASONABLE SAFEGUARD IS ASSURED.

An Agreement made the......10th.........day of...April.......
19.....63. between ...Mr Bob Wooler...

hereinafter called the Management of the one part and ...Alan G. Cheetham.........
.....................................hereinafter called the Artiste/s of the other part.

Witnesseth that the Management hereby engages the Artiste/s and the Artiste/s accept

an engagement to {
Present ....The Hollies..
Appear as Parlophone recording artists.........

(or in his usual entertainment) at the Dance Hall/Theatre and from the dates for the periods and at the salaries stated in the schedule hereto.

The Artiste/s agrees to appear at : {
......TEN..Evening
......TEN..Performances
.... Matinee

At a Salary of ....£200-0-0 (20 in cash after each evening performance)

SCHEDULE

12 Day(s) at.. The Cavern Club	on	Wed 24th Apl'63	Eve.+ Lunch.
Liverpool.		Sun 19th May'63	Eve only
Day(s) at..............................	on	Mon 20th May'63	Lunch only
		Tue 28th May'63	Eve + Lunch.
Day(s) at..............................	on	Wed 12th Jun'63	Eve + Lunch.
Day(s) at..............................	on	Wed 26th Jun'63	Eve. + Lunch.
		Sun 30th Jun'63	Eve only.

ADDITIONAL CLAUSES Mon 1st Jul'63 Lunch only. ***

(a) Playing times to be decided by the Management. But it is agreed that the Artiste/s will not be required to play for more than a total of......1½......hours, in.......—...........sessions.

(b) All financial settlement to take place with.....The Hollies after each date.

(c) Artiste/s to arrive not later than......11am lunch sessions, 7pm evening.

(d) Times of Performances ....as required by the management.

(e) The Artiste/s shall not without the written consent of the Management appear in any place of Public Entertainment within a radius of......5...........miles at any of the venues stated herein for ....weeks prior to engagement.

*** cont.

Fri 12th Jul'63	Eve + Lunch
Tue 23rd Jul'63	Eve + Lunch
Fri 2nd Aug'63	Eve + Lunch
Tue 6th Aug'63	Eve + Lunch

I/We the undersigned acknowledge that I/We have read the above clauses and agree that they will be adhered to in detail.

Signature .....Alan G. Cheetham.....

Address .. "THE TOGGERY.
HERSEY SQUARE
STOCKPORT.

~~PLEASE SIGN AND RETURN THIS COPY~~

The Hollies' 1963 Liverpool Cavern contract for lunchtime and evening performances.

CHAPTER ONE:

Pearl Harbour

Britain had been at war with Germany for over a year. My father, Bob Elliott, and his best friend, Ted Shaw, approached the saloon bar in the Talbot pub and ordered a couple of pints of locally brewed Massey's ale. There were many similar watering holes dotted around Burnley, a small cotton mill town which nestled, along with Nelson and Colne, in the shadow of Pendle Hill in Lancashire, not far from the Yorkshire border. Tall chimneys, each of them close to 300 feet high, dominated the landscape, belching smoke and cloaking the town in smog and grime. Far below were thousands of clog-wearing weavers, each of whom operated eight or sometimes sixteen clattering looms in the mills. The noise was deafening and they communicated with one another in sign language. Despite this, they were a cheery bunch of folk who lived mostly within walking distance of the stone-built mills –

known locally as sheds – in street after street of small terraced houses.

In the pub that night there was a modest celebration. I had just been born at the nearby nursing home and my dad and Ted had been to see mother and baby. As the beer flowed, the pub wireless crackled out the news that Japanese torpedo bombers had attacked the US Pacific fleet lying peacefully at anchor in Pearl Harbour, killing thousands of US sailors and servicemen. It meant that the Americans had been drawn into the conflict, resulting in a full-blown World War II. Throughout his life, my dear father would remind me of this fact every time war in the Pacific was mentioned.

'Pearl 'arbour – that's when you were born, Robert.'

Actually the attack happened on December 7, Pacific time, but the news reached the British public the following day.

As the evening ended the two revellers drank up and made their way up Ormerod Road, past the College of Knowledge (as Burnley College was always known), over the Leeds to Liverpool canal by way of Godley Bridge, along the iron railings that skirted Thompson Park and Queens Park, and along the Ridge that looks down onto Turf Moor, the town's football ground.

Those railings are still in place today, but sadly most of the ornate Victorian metal fencing had been cut down in 1940 to be turned into tanks and guns to fight the Germans. Well, that was the plan. The good folk of Burnley watched helplessly as fences were torn from their little terraced gardens by men armed with oxyacetylene torches. Throughout the country, churches and public buildings were shorn of their wrought iron glory. At the time the people of Britain were told that the metal would be melted down to build war-winning munitions. But their sacrifice was in vain. Part-way through this act of vandalism, our leaders were informed that it was the wrong sort of metal. What the arms industry really needed was quality Sheffield steel, not wrought iron. The nation had been duped but, keen not to lose face, the authorities carried on picking clean our crafted heritage, even though they knew it was not fit for the purpose. In a final desperate act of deception, the national stockpile of plundered railings was secretly dumped at sea under cover of darkness and the general public, none the wiser, carried on proudly believing that they had helped to win the war by donating their ironware.

Dad and Ted couldn't see much as they headed for Pike Hill, an elevated suburb on the town's outskirts. It was the age of the blackout. Hitler's Heinkels and Dorniers were in the skies looking for somewhere to drop their lethal high-explosive bombs. To thwart this threat, every streetlight in the country had been turned off. Vehicle headlights were covered and blackout cloth was fitted to the windows of every household in the land.

Home was 13 Chiltern Avenue, a modest semi-detached house where Dad lived with my mum, Edna. I was to be their only child. Dad was thirty-two when I was born and Mum was five years younger.

Dad and his brother, Jack, were master cabinet makers; they crafted hand-built furniture. Their company letterhead proclaimed: 'H. Elliott Furniture Manufacturer'. It was a family business, inherited from their father, Hartley Elliott. I never knew my grandfather. He died, penniless, eight years before I was born, leaving his two sons in debt and saddled with a crumbling rented building that dated back to the industrial revolution and was equipped with ancient woodworking machinery and not much else. It seems that Hartley had been a colourful character, always immaculately dressed, who spent most of his life playing chess with local, wealthier businessmen in the Mechanics Institute. He had grand ideas and he liked to show off. As a young man, he'd had a furniture factory built in nearby Nelson, complete with a high-mill chimney. When the work was completed, rumour has it that Grandad performed a headstand on top of the newly erected smokestack.

Hartley had been married twice and had sired nine children – Jack and Dad being the final two from his second wife. The old boy was an early riser and at dawn he would enter young Jack and Bob's bedroom, throw back the curtains, open the windows and bellow: *'Waken lords and ladies gay, to the mountain dawns the day; all the jolly chase is here with hawk and horse and hunting-spear.'*

In the early days of the war, Britain was fighting for its life against Hitler's hordes, and my father and uncle were doing their bit. By night they kept the family business going by making chests of drawers and sideboards for local customers.

By day they made parts for the Horsa troop-carrying gliders and, later, plywood sections for the twin-engine Mosquito fighter bomber at the local joinery firm of Earnshaw Brothers and Booth. The wood and canvas flying machines would be used in the invasion of mainland Europe. The plan was that they would carry British soldiers across the channel to France, hauled by obsolete RAF bombers or American DC-3 Dakota transport aircraft. On reaching their target zones, the gliders would release themselves from the tow plane's cable, and the soldiers at the controls would, hopefully, land safely on a flat, smooth field in pitch darkness, praying that the Germans hadn't seen them.

Unknown to Herr Hitler, hidden away in towns throughout Britain, workers were beavering away manufacturing whatever was needed to keep the Third Reich at bay. Probably the best example was at nearby Barnoldswick, where, tucked away in old cotton mills, Rolls-Royce was quietly making aero engines for Spitfires and Lancasters while Frank Whittle and his team were secretly developing the jet engine.

My dad was also a fine motorcyclist and was recruited as a dispatch rider for the Home Guard. He held down three jobs in the grim days of World War II.

In the 1940s the view from our front garden on Chiltern Avenue was quite impressive. The hillside sloped down to the pastoral expanse of Towneley Holmes, with the grand 500-year-old Hall and woodlands to the left contrasting with the dozens of smoking mill chimneys to the right.

I remember hearing the distant clank of the steam-powered freight trains as they coasted down the valley behind the old Hall, sounding like a wheezing old man with a wooden leg walking down a passageway. The locomotive would later return from Rose Grove sidings hauling a rake of fully loaded wagons, struggling and snorting, wheels spinning, as driver and fireman attempted to get it up the steep incline, heading up to Copy Pit, Windy Bridge and beyond.

As for me, I was safely tucked away in number thirteen. One of my first memories is of my Auntie Irene – who was actually my cousin, the daughter of Mum's sister, Margaret – singing 'I'll Be Your Sweetheart' or 'Bicycle Built For Two' as she rocked me in her arms. Who knows, maybe those mesmerising lullaby moments sparked my lifelong craving for melody and music – and rhythm? I vaguely remember the roar of something overhead and I was later told that it was a low-flying German fighter plane making a dash back to its Luftwaffe base in Europe.

At an early age I was sent to Todmorden Road junior school in Burnley. It was a brief, unhappy experience. The big stone building seemed scary and far too full of people and, as soon as I got inside, I knew I had to get out of there. When playtime ended, I decided to escape from the playground by climbing over the surviving iron railings, and I set off in search of Auntie Irene. I knew that she worked near Towneley Holmes in the Co-op laundry about a quarter of a mile away. I made it but I only used that trick once or twice, as Irene

6

would, duty bound, walk me back to my classroom or escort me home. Another ploy was to leave home for school as normal in the morning and then hang around the streets, waiting until the other kids were going home, at which point I'd board the same bus, arriving back at number thirteen as though nothing had happened. It was a long, lonely day.

Once I went up to Chiltern Avenue and concealed myself round the back of our house, planning to make an entrance at the appropriate time and pretend that I'd had a full day in class. Meanwhile, a worried teacher had walked up Pike Hill in search of the runaway pupil and arrived at our door. My mother insisted that I had gone to school like a good boy and was most definitely not in the house. But, unbeknown to my poor mum, I had come in quietly through the back door and was peering round the corner, in full view of the bemused teacher.

Around that time Sally's grocery shop at 1 Brownside Road, Pike Hill came up for sale. It was just round the corner from Chiltern Avenue and Mum reckoned she could run the shop and make some extra income, so my parents bought it. Our new home was a semi-detached bungalow with a dormer bedroom above, ideal for me and my train set and later my Meccano 'drum set'. The shop, in the front, was a compact confectioners and grocery store. We moved in at the end of the war. At that time there was no refrigerator to keep food fresh. During one summer's heatwave, Mum suspended a huge block of butter over a bath of cold water to prevent it from melting.

Mum's father, Alfred Precious, lived next door at number three. Alf was the local plumber and was assisted by his son, Tommy. The pair of them would be seen pushing their two-wheeled flatbed handcart around the parish, fixing this and that or replacing broken windows – a very useful neighbourhood service, especially when I had been playing football on Thornton Road or throwing snowballs at other kids. Grandad Alf was a good clog dancer; he had rhythm in his old bones. He looked like Buddy Ebsen's character, Jed Clampett, in *The Beverly Hillbillies*. He wore a battered hat and sported a moustache that I joked was for filtering tea leaves from his mug as he supped his brew. Alf's wife Florence, my Grandma Precious, had died when I was very small, so I don't really remember her, but I do remember the house going very quiet at Christmas when she died. Alf never slept in their bedroom again, choosing instead to sleep in the small back storeroom.

I liked to quietly observe him as he sat in his armchair listening to music on the radio, hands on the chair arms tapping out the beat with his arched thumbs. Thumbs like mine. He was a lovely man who often neglected to send bills out for jobs that he and Uncle Tommy had done. Mum heard from one of her customers that Alf and Tom had completed work on their property months earlier and yet they had never received a bill.

Each evening when she closed the shop at 7 p.m., Mum would be off next door to reprimand her dad and then set about sorting out his business affairs. Every Wednesday her sisters, Margaret and Nelly, who had been cotton weavers but were now dinner ladies in one of the mill's canteens, would come up to Pike Hill after work and cook fish and chips for their dad. Next door Mum would be busy serving in the shop, while trying to make my dad's evening meal in the family kitchen. I would take a tin of beans from the shop, pop next door and join Alf, Nelly and Margaret to happily dine on my favourite dish of Heinz baked beans and chips.

Back at Edna's – as the locals now referred to Mum's shop – one of the customers heard about 'Robert's running away problem' and recommended that I be sent to St John's Church School at Holme in Cliviger, about three miles away. It was a good move. Now I was settled in a much smaller school, and I was happy there.

The old BCN, the Burnley Colne & Nelson Joint Transport AEC single-decker bus, number 149 or 150, would whisk me from Pike Hill right to the front door of the school. At first I went home for dinner (or lunch as we call it now), but Mum was usually busy serving behind the shop counter and it was difficult for her to cook food for me and look after her customers. It was decided that I would stay for school dinners. I didn't really mind as I was now happy in my surroundings with my new-found friends.

There was no kitchen at our school, so the freshly made dinners had to be brought from the next village of Cliviger. The food was put into containers and loaded onto the Burnley to Todmorden bus that would then transport the dish of the day – which might be mashed potatoes and mince followed by rice pudding, topped with a blob of jam – a couple of miles up the road to us hungry kids.

Being chosen for dinner duty was the highlight of my school day. It was a carefully organised event that had to run like clockwork. I would stand by the bus stop with a classmate, and we'd be craning our necks for the first sight of the big green and cream corporation bus as it rumbled up the incline en route to Todmorden. As the double-decker approached, we'd hold out our arms to make sure that our mash and gravy didn't end up in the wrong hands. When the bus had stopped, the conductor would signal permission for us to board the rear platform. Once aboard we'd lift the food from the luggage area under the stairs and place each large circular canister carefully by the roadside. There was a handle on each side of the containers, so we would carefully synchronise our lifting technique to ensure that no food was spilled. Sometimes the odd folded pram or suitcase got in our way, but we were skilled operators. Once the deck was clear, we would give the bus conductor the nod and, with a cheery 'ding', the diesel-powered omnibus went on its way. After that we had to make several journeys on foot until all the containers were inside the school, ready to be served when the bell rang signalling lunchtime.

Next came Dog Dinner Duty. This was a means of disposing of the unwanted scraps left over from lunch. The Ram Inn across the road was also a working farm. Round the back of the pub lived a sheepdog in a kennel. We would take it in turns to carry the bowl of leftovers across the busy road and round to where the dog lived. He had a length of chain attached to his collar and the other end fixed to the kennel. There was an art to this. Get too close and Shep could nip you – too far away and his chain wouldn't allow him to enjoy his grub. You had to place the container as close to doggy as you dared, then carefully toe-end the food into his comfort zone. Good dog. Bon appetit!

A large field served as an extended playground and had been marked out with 'roads' by generations of kids' feet, but we also had the freedom of the village during our lunch break. One of the main railway lines from Lancashire to Yorkshire ran down the valley just across the fields from school. On a hot summer's day my pals and I would adventure down the lane and up to the path that crossed the tracks. We'd place pennies on the steel rails and wait for the Todmorden to Burnley train to run over them. The wheels of the heavy locomotive would compress and contort the copper coins, then we'd retrieve the bent discs of metal, dash back to school and gleefully show our spoils to the other children.

Mrs Clarkson was a fine headmistress. She lived just down the road from mum's shop in the 'bottom' bungalow. Each Wednesday she and the other two teachers would shepherd the whole school up the pathway, past the tomb of General Scarlett and into St John's Church, where Canon Edwards would preach and we would sing a few hymns.

I don't remember the sermons, but the sound of the voices of my little school chums filling the old place with haunting melodies served as an early stepping stone as I started out on my musical journey. Mum and Dad would select long-playing records, now known as LPs, from Burnley Library, just like borrowing a book. The works of Gilbert and Sullivan, Grieg's piano concerto and even the opera *Merrie England* would spin on our radiogram turntable after Mum had cashed up the day's takings and put the closed sign on the shop door. I still have Rachmaninoff's piano concerto on twelve-inch 78s that my parents bought, and Litolff's scherzo on two sides of a ten-inch 78; the latter jigged along merrily, enabling me to join in and funk it up on a Cadbury's Roses tin armed with my makeshift drumsticks. These forms of music were important in young Robert's musical development and helped map my way forward to the next port of call: the soon to be discovered land of jazz.

Pike Hill was surrounded by farmland and rambling expanses of moorland. The River Brun ran down from the peat moors above the hamlet of Hurstwood and in summer, along with the other lads, we would construct dams to form swimming pools. In winter we had the Brownside sledging tracks, the Big Dipper and the Skeleton, where we would test our skills to see who had the fastest sleigh. I was lucky – I had a dad who could make things out of wood, and I still have the sledge that he built for me all those years ago. Many a time, intent on being the fastest, I would be unable to stop at the bottom of the icy slopes and end up in the freezing river. Being very young, I was wearing short pants and wellington boots as I travelled head first – no hard hat protection in those days – down the snowbound track. My wellies would scoop up snow so that at the end of each run I had to empty them out. After a few speedy descents, I'd trail up Brownside Hill, dragging my iron-shod conveyance homeward. Once inside, I'd stand in front of the blazing coal fire and squeal in pain as my mum rubbed Snowfire ointment on the red, raw rings of flesh caused by my flapping boot tops.

SESSION DETAILS

ARTISTE	DATE	TIME	STUDIO
THE HOLLIES (Vocal)	11th October '63	8 - 10 p.m.	2
	TYPE MONO/STEREO	No. of SIDES	DJ/NP LAQUERS

COMPOSITION OF ORCHESTRA/CHORUS

Acoustic Guitar
Electric Guitar
Bass Guitar
Drums

RECORDING INSTRUCTION

Matrix Nos/Artiste(s)	TITLES	Publishers
	Titles to be selected	

Cheque No. 3048

Date 14.10.63

Amount £114~10~0.

Signed

Counter Signed

Items marked * are non copyright.

CHEQUE	COST DETAILS	CASH		
	Orchestra 4 men @ £5. 5. 0. each:	21.	0.	0
	Doubling			
	Porterage			
	Secretarial Fee			
	Chorus			
	Booking Fee			
	Conductor			
	Orchestrations			
	Royalty The Hollies ld.			
	Charged to E.M.I. RECORDS LTD.			
	Type of Contract Period			
		£21.	0.	0

DATE 10th October, 1963.

AUTHORISED BY For: George H. Martin

DATE ....

CONTRACT CHECKED BY ....

EMI's Abbey Road job sheet for the recording of The Hollies' first Top Ten hit, 'Stay'. Signed by Wally Ridley for George Martin and produced by Ron Richards.

CHAPTER TWO:

Nights at the Turntable

During the war an American B-24 Liberator bomber had crashed up on the moors and some of the villagers had collected souvenirs. I was told by one of the older boys that shortly after the crash a local character had managed to get the radio out of the aircraft, and the guy was seen sitting in a ditch shouting into the microphone: 'Hitler, you bastard!' One boy, prompted by his dad, organised us into a ragtag group of scrap dealers. We took it in turns to saw off the exposed propeller blades, or smash off a cylinder head on the Pratt & Whitney Wasp radial engines. The scrap was diligently carried across the moors and loaded into Eric Lord's handcart, which rode on two aircraft rear landing wheels. The plundered metal alloy was then pushed all the way down to Readers scrap yard in Burnley. It was a long way so I peeled off at Pike Hill, more interested in getting home than in the few shillings on offer when the metal was sold.

The war ended in 1945, and I can vaguely remember the Pike Hillers lighting a bonfire and burning an effigy of Hitler on open land off Delma Road near John Driver's farm. Food was rationed and each weekend Mum had to perform the time-consuming, unpaid task of counting every coupon that she'd taken from each customer's ration book. This went on until the early 1950s, when I remember the locals queuing across the road at Green's the greengrocers for the first bananas to arrive. None of us kids had ever seen one before.

Auntie Margaret and Uncle Fred lived on Glebe Street in Burnley, and when my parents were going out to a late dance, or 'do', I would sleep there. I must have been about five or six years old. I can remember the rat-a-tat on my bedroom window in the early morning from the knocker-upper, a chap who carried a long pole with a springy piece of tin fixed to the end. He woke the workers of Burnley Wood by tapping on their upstairs windows. Most of the cotton weavers paid him a shilling or so a week to be woken in this way, and a few minutes later I would hear the sound of doors opening and closing and the click-clack of folk in their iron-soled clogs, hurrying down to the mills to operate the noisy cotton weaving looms.

By the 1950s television had arrived in Britain, but for some reason or other we didn't have a TV set in the family living quarters behind the shop. One of the neighbours got one, and I remember Mum closed the shop so that she could pop round to watch the Queen's coronation at Jessie Hindle's. The Hindle brothers owned some disused mills stuffed with war surplus equipment, and I would go to play there with my chum, Alan Hindle. His dad, Clifford, would drive us to Cornholme in his American Chevrolet convertible. While he took care of business, Alan and I would explore the old buildings, finding pile upon pile of wooden US Army boxes. Some contained radar spares, clock gauges or tools. One section consisted of tins of foot powder. We'd unscrew the caps, pretend they were hand grenades and bomb one another as we hid behind the stacks of surplus war gear. As the canisters hit, plumes of white powder would explode and we'd stagger out of the warehouse looking like a couple of ghosts.

In another building sat an abandoned American Allison aeroplane engine. The US Mustang fighter was first fitted with the Allison and it was a poor performer. Then someone suggested the plane should be fitted with the latest British Rolls-Royce Merlin motor and arguably the best fighter escort plane of World War II was born.

I was about eleven years old when I joined the Burnley ATC – Air Training Corps, 352 Squadron. We would meet on Thursday evenings at HQ in Burnley in our little RAF-style uniforms, berets set at a jaunty angle. I was good at aircraft recognition and was picked to go to summer camp at RAF St Athan in south Wales. The highlight of the week was a ride in a piston-engine Chipmunk trainer, during which the pilot would give his lucky passenger the thrilling experience of looping the loop.

Auntie Irene's husband, Terry Flynn, had been a member of RAF ground crew during the war. His job was to keep the

Lancaster bombers in airworthy condition. I loved to listen to his stories in their home in Dall Street, Burnley. He had built, with incredible precision and skill, the perfect model of a Spitfire out of bits of wood and scrap while he waited for the aircraft to return from their German bombing missions. With a wingspan of just nine inches, the little fighter plane sported the same camouflage paint as those World War II machines, and every time I was in Terry's house, I would look at it in wonder. As I write this, that same Spitfire is still with me, suspended over my desk. When Terry passed away, Irene insisted I have it.

I developed a passion for steam trains and aircraft. Tagging along with some of the older boys from Pike Hill, I would catch the train from Burnley Central to Preston, where we could see the big west coast LMS locomotives, *The Royal Scot* or *The Mid-Day Scot*, as they cruised through the mainline railway station. Beautiful blinkered big beasts with names like *Duchess of Montrose* and *City of Carlisle* hauling maybe a dozen crimson or strawberry-and-cream liveried coaches.

Dad was a keen ornithologist and he and Mum would set off in our maroon MG saloon to nearby beauty spots like the Yorkshire Dales, the Trough of Bowland, Leyton Moss or the Lake District. I thought the bird lark a tad boring, so I would ask my parents to drop me off at the small station at Hest Bank on the busy London to Glasgow line where I would happily spend the day jotting down the names and numbers of locos until Edna and Bob collected me on their way home.

If we holidayed at Llandudno, they would drop me at Llandudno Junction. In Torquay they would leave me overlooking Newton Abbot Station and I would enjoy a feast of steaming Great Western green goddesses. We also had September holidays in a static caravan near Bournemouth, so I persuaded Dad to drive down by way of the Farnborough Air Show. In those days test pilots would show their flying machines with great skill, using every trick in the book to sell their companies' aircraft. Back then it was a showcase only for British-manufactured planes. Dozens of glistening silver shapes would take turns trying to impress the huge crowds in the days when British aircraft technology led the world.

On Saturdays I would go to Auntie Margaret's to watch her TV. I'd stay for tea and then catch the bus that came down from Townley and into Burnley. Under the Culvert – the aqueduct that carries the Leeds to Liverpool canal – I'd hop off, dash across the road and catch another BCN bus that was heading to Worsthorne by way of my home at Pike Hill. Once upstairs I'd head for the front seat. Every time I made the journey from my auntie's I would see Joan Parker, a pretty girl of thirteen, sitting at the back of the bus. It was 1956, I was fourteen, and that was the first time I realised I was strongly attracted to the opposite sex. As the weeks went by I plucked up the courage to ask Joan if she would go to the Odeon cinema with me one Friday night after school. She agreed and we sat in the expensive seats downstairs on the back row. The feature film was *Pardners* starring Dean Martin and Jerry Lewis and, as we watched, I actually built up enough courage to put my arm round Joan. In my innocence, I thought it was the best feeling ever. I felt proud and grown-up. I still remember her sweet smell and soft skin.

After that we would go for walks in the countryside around Worsthorne, and sometimes her friend Eileen Whitehead would come along. After a while Joan and I drifted apart and I became besotted with Eileen. Both girls were at Nelson Grammar, making it easy for me to meet up with Eileen and walk her home after class. The first time I took her to the movies we went to the Palace Cinema in Burnley centre. The film was a comedy, *You Can't Run Away From It*, starring Jack Lemmon and June Allyson.

Eileen lived above her parents' chip shop on Clayton Street in Nelson, but she spent some of the week at her grandma's in Worsthorne. She was cheeky, confident and horny. I was totally hooked. We went out together for about three months and I was heartbroken when she dumped me and began seeing a more mature guy, who was a painter and decorator.

I had passed my eleven-plus, a contentious exam that decided at the age of eleven whether or not you would go to a grammar school. If you 'failed' then it was a comprehensive school. I got my green and yellow uniform, cap and leather satchel and travelled on two buses in order to get to Nelson Grammar School. There was a ten-minute wait in Burnley centre before the school bus arrived. This gave me the chance to pop round the corner and look in the window of the Electron record shop. There I would excitedly view the latest LPs on display. From 1953 to 1957 I watched the fast-changing face of modern music displayed in that window – from Frankie Laine and Doris Day through to Bill Haley and Elvis, with a touch of Mel Tormé, Gerry Mulligan and, one of the most striking LP sleeves of all time, *The Atomic Mr Basie*.

Before I found jazz, at the age of ten or eleven, my exposure to music had been a mixed bag. My parents loved classical music, and they would borrow records from Burnley Library. They loved piano concertos by composers like Rachmaninov, Grieg and Litolff. There would be a sprinkling of Gilbert and Sullivan and songs from the shows. I knew most of the music by heart. Mum would la-la her current favourite in the car or around the house and shop, and Dad would join in with a cheery whistle.

When I was still quite small, they took me to the King George's Hall in Blackburn to see the Liverpool Philharmonic and the great concert pianist Benno Moiseiwitsch perform Rachmaninov's piano concerto. Dad reckoned that concert was a pivotal moment for me. He was right. It wasn't just the gifted soloist that took my eye, it was the percussionist playing the crescent of tuned tympani. We were sitting round the back of the orchestra, right next to him, and I remember watching his every move, enthralled by the constant adjusting and damping of the tymps.

Around that time my Uncle Terry would play Glen Miller 78s to me. 'The St Louis Blues March', 'American Patrol' and the trumpet solo from 'A String Of Pearls'. He also had several wacky comedy records by Spike Jones & His City Slickers, which featured cowbells, gun shots, washboards and tuned pots and pans. 'Cocktails For Two' and 'Der Fuehrer's Face' are absolute classics.

The other early influence in my life was the Rushton family. They lived round the corner from Mum's shop in a humble semi on Thornton Road. The two sons, Gordon and Donald, would play records, and I would stand in their open doorway and listen. They were older than me, and I would ride to their house on my little maroon BSA pushbike. On Sunday mornings, their dad, Roy, would strum away on his ukulele with Mum on the piano and the boys joining in on anything that sounded vaguely like a drum.

Uncle Terry Flynn, along with the Rushtons, sparked my interest in jazz and drums. Donald and Gordon would play modern jazz records on their radiogram, and on a hot summer's day the sounds of Gerry Mulligan and Chet Baker, Stan Kenton, Shorty Rogers & His Giants, and Oscar Peterson would hit Thornton Road and reverberate around Pike Hill. Gordon had made a pair of brushes by getting some lengths of copper wire, splaying them out and wrapping insulation tape around the end to form handles. He would use them to play along to the Gerry Mulligan Quartet on top of the family radiogram.

'Sing, Sing, Sing' from the soundtrack of the film *The Benny Goodman Story* with Gene Krupa on drums was the first EP I bought from the Electron. The second was the Mulligan Quartet's 'Nights At The Turntable', a ten-inch 78 rpm disc on the Vogue label. Drummer Chico Hamilton's brushwork on the snare drum lured me into a life of percussion. I'd emulate Chico, swishing away on the daily newspaper atop our treasured French-polished sideboard that my dad had made. Mum would say: 'Robert, get off that sideboard. Your dad will go mad if he sees you doing that.' So I resorted to biscuit tins and progressed to long paint brush handles that I had borrowed from the art department at school.

My first drum kit was the aforementioned Cadbury's Roses tin, an Oxo tin and an upside down baking tin from Mum's oven. There was a big square biscuit tin in the shop that was used for storing raisins. I commandeered it and stuck a Meccano leg into the dried fruit and voila – I had a cymbal stand. I'd seen that most jazz drummers at the time had a 'sizzle' cymbal. No problem; I drilled two holes in the baking tin, inserted two little nuts and bolts that dangled loosely and stuck it on top of the Meccano leg in an ingenious fashion. Now I was a bebop drummer.

In the evenings I tuned into Voice of America, broadcasting from Tangier. It was on the shortwave and reception was poor. Lying on the floor next to our Bush radiogram, I'd note down the records and jazz artists that were played that evening.

Then one day when I was tapping on my desk with a couple of wooden rulers, my school friend Bob Palmer told me there was an old drum, with sticks and brushes, in a junk shop on Leeds Road selling for the grand price of £2. I rushed home and emptied out my savings. Auntie Margaret used to give me half a crown every week when she came to see Grandad, and I would put the money in my piggy bank. To my joy I had £2, so the next day after school, I went to see the drum and bought it on the spot. At last I had a real snare drum, and I spent every spare minute playing it.

I would be clattering away upstairs in my little rooftop bedroom, and Mum would come up and say: 'Mrs So-and-So came into the shop today with a long list of groceries, and then you started banging and crashing and she said, "I think I'll just take a loaf today, Edna."' Although my drumming was getting on their nerves, my parents were pretty good about it. We had developed a system. In the evenings they would turn my bedroom light on and off using the switch at the bottom of the staircase leading to my room. The light was the signal that their nerves were beginning to fray. It was time for me to desist.

I had settled into the grammar school quickly and was reasonably happy in Mr Crowthers' form. It was a very strict school by today's standards. There was a girls' and boys' side to the school. In charge of the girls was a pompous headmistress who went by the name of Miss Jump. She had a network of informers who, at weekends, would spy on pupils. If a boy and girl sat together in the local cinema, Miss Jump would get to know. The girl would be called into her office on Monday morning for a ticking off. She was a nightmare. I still remember the instruction posted on the girls' side of school: *'Girls must not run along the lower corridor.'* It was signed: *'I Jump.'*

I was doing well in most subjects until Dad decided that our annual holiday at Burnley Fair in the first two weeks in July was too late. 'All the birds have stopped singing. We need to go away the last week in May and the first week in June,' he said. I had to take a letter to Mr Brown, the boys' headmaster, for special permission to miss school. Mr Brown was not happy, but Dad persisted, and over the next two or three years, I was taken away from school in term time. I had some fantastic holidays down in Devon at the Waterside caravan park in Paignton. While Mum and Dad went looking for the red-backed shrike, I could drool over the beautiful Great Western Railway's locomotives. But there was a serious price to pay: I'd missed a lot of lessons and after the holiday I had to try to catch up at home and copy all the work I'd missed from a classmate's exercise book. That task proved to be impossible and I was soon left trailing behind and at the bottom of the class.

Our music teacher was Miss Pamela Johnson. During one lesson, she played a piece of classical music on the record player. 'Now class,' she said, 'I want you to listen and mark time.' Bob Palmer and I smiled and nodded knowingly at one another as we laid down a strong backbeat, while the rest of our classmates gently tapped around. Miss Johnson was shocked. She stopped the proceedings, shouting: 'Elliott, Palmer, stand up!' We did. 'Class take note,' she continued, 'these two can't keep time.'

STAY

Words & Music by MAURICE WILLIAMS

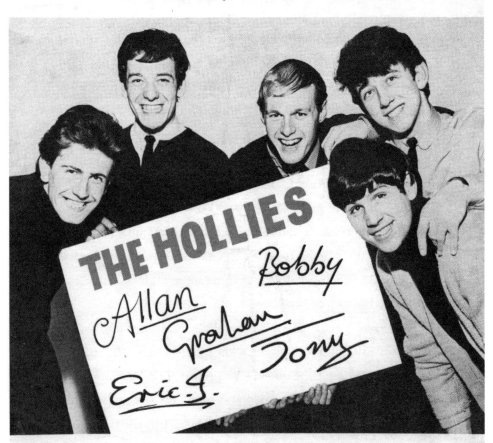

Recorded on
Parlophone R 5077

Photograph by BRUCE FLEMING

LORNA MUSIC CO., LTD.,
5, DENMARK STREET, LONDON, W.C.2
SOLE SELLING AGENTS :
MILLS MUSIC LIMITED,
MILLS HOUSE, 20, DENMARK ST., LONDON, W.C.2.

2/6

CHAPTER THREE:

Drummer Boy

I left Nelson Grammar School in the summer of 1958, aged sixteen, with one O level GCE in Art. But by then I was focused on only one thing – playing the drums.

Bob Palmer had a friend who would drive us round in his dad's old Standard Vanguard. On Sunday nights we'd visit the Hodder Bridge Hotel in the Ribble Valley. Wilf, the landlord, had been a professional musician, and he had a Premier drum kit for sale for £60. I borrowed the money off my dad, and I was good to go. Now I was the proud owner of a proper drum set.

My parents were tolerant of my drumming, which was just as well, because I would practise for several hours a day. I was basically self-taught as there were no instructional videos or YouTube demonstrations in the 1950s. I had to do it by ear by listening to records, the Voice of America or by watching other drummers play whenever I got the chance.

My pal Bob played double bass in George Buckley's six-piece band at the Sefton Club in nearby Colne. My Burnley friends couldn't understand why I would sacrifice my Saturday nights of boozing in the Talbot to sit in a smoky working men's club with old people I hardly knew. But I loved to watch the band and hang out with the seasoned musicians during their break and have a pie and a pint and talk about music. As the evening of merriment progressed, George would get up from behind his drums and head for the microphone at the front of stage. Once in crooning position, he would point to his vacated stool and say: 'Bob'. Quick as a flash, I would spring onto the bandstand and make myself comfortable behind the old Carlton drum kit. I was now part of a band and would accompany the ruddy-faced bandleader as he launched into the breakaway blues, Fats Waller's 'On The Sunny Side Of The Street', 'Ain't Misbehavin'' and 'I Can't Give You Anything But Love'. Although bebop and modern jazz were my first love, I followed George's guidance and laid down a groove like his idol, American drummer Sid Catlett. For three songs I was one of the lads and in seventh heaven.

I would sit in on drums anywhere I could. I met trumpeter Bob Price when sitting in at the Borough Band Club in Nelson. He invited me to join his combo, the Bob Price Quintet. The venue was the Queens Arms Hotel in Rawtenstall. As I didn't drive, my dad would kindly transport me and my drums from Roughlee to Rawtenstall each Thursday in his little Austin A35 van. The trio of piano, bass and me would accompany guest soloists. Don Rendell, Harold McNair, Eddie Thompson, Ronnie Ross, Joe Temperley and others would travel up from London to jam in the Rossendale Valley pub. I didn't earn much, just enough to cover Dad's petrol, but the money was not important. West Indian flautist and saxophonist, Harold McNair, impressed me the most. It was a privilege to have played drums for the great man; he made my job so easy. Ronnie Ross, the Scottish baritone sax player, was also a favourite. You can hear Ronnie's playing on Lou Reed's recording of 'Walk On The Wild Side'.

By that time my parents had retired. Dad was still only in his late forties. It's a sad tale. As their furniture was made by hand, Dad and Uncle Jack found they couldn't compete with mass-produced furniture. But all was not lost. The brothers had worked out that if they sold up they could, with care and prudence, invest the capital and live off the interest. So he and Jack auctioned off the business, and Mum and Dad sold our home and the little shop at Pike Hill, and bought a cottage in Roughlee for a few hundred pounds. Now they would be able to spend their days doing what they loved: bird watching and walking. Dad had swapped the maroon MG family saloon for the small cream coloured Austin A35 van, which was more economical to run and ideally suited for transporting my drums to and from local gigs.

When I left school, I had to get a 'proper' job. Back then it was unheard of for someone from the old mill towns of the north to think about becoming a professional musician. Not knowing what to do, I foolishly followed my Pike Hill chums and began work as an apprentice for the National Coal Board. The first year I studied mining engineering at the college on Ormerod Road, then it was a short distance to Bank Hall Pit to learn the art of overhauling mining machinery for the impressive sum of £4 a week. Over the next three years I learned to work a lathe and to repair or make anything to do with mining coal.

Bank Hall was a colliery with two vertical shafts, each about 1,600 feet deep. Sometimes I would work the afternoon on back-shift and be on standby for any breakdowns underground. At a moment's notice I'd be told to grab a bag of spanners and go alone and do whatever it would take to get the broken machine running again. I'd board the mine cage and be dropped like a stone until the banksman, seated in the engine house on the pit top, would apply the brake to his massive steam-driven engine and the steel cable would tense as we approached the pit bottom, and hopefully place the cage gently onto the landing stage. I would then be released from the solitary confinement of my steel cell to make my way past the underground offices, complete with glass windows – yes, window cleaners went down the pit – to the empty row of steel mine cars. They would be lined up ready to be hauled a mile or more back to the coal loading point where they would be loaded with more of the black stuff. There were no seats, you just had to clamber up the outside of the coal carrier and drop down onto the filthy cold steel floor for a long spine-jarring ride. A journey on foot followed, usually to an area known as Dip Three. Sometimes I would assist the amiable resident mechanic, Tommy McAleese, and when the machine was fixed, Tom would offer me the last half of the cheese sandwich he'd saved in his bait box.

The colliery had two ancient Thomas the Tank Engines: 'John' and 'Wasp'. These museum pieces worked on the pit top and were probably built in the late 1800s. It was the job of the Bank Hall mechanics to keep them running. One of the locos was leaking water from its rusting iron saddle tank that wrapped round the engine's boiler. As a lowly apprentice, I was subservient to a fully qualified pit top mechanic, in this case, the genial Freddy Large.

'Bob, I want you to mix some fibreglass and bung that leak up from the inside, but first make me a nice pot of tea,' Freddy said, peering over the top of his *Daily Mirror*. Tea brewed, I slid head first through the inspection hole and into the cramped rusty dampness and inched myself down towards the small hole that was emitting daylight into the pitch darkness. It was a tight squeeze, but as I tamped the sticky material into the fissure with my unprotected fingertips, I could hear Freddy shouting: 'Left a bit... down a bit... right... there!' The leak was sealed. Time to reverse the process and extract myself from the dank, rusty tomb before claustrophobia got the better of me. As I raised my head up through the cover of the water tank, I was relieved to see the inside of the engine shed and Freddy, who was holding out his empty pint mug. 'Right, cock. Now make me another brew and don't be so skinny wi't sugar.'

The following day, we needed to test the newly repaired old steamer. This time I was working with John O'Brien. 'Come on, Bob,' he shouted, 'climb aboard.' He expertly backed the Wasp, hissing and clanking, out of the engine shed and down to a waiting rake of National Coal Board railway wagons that had been filled with freshly mined coal. The loco's coupling was hooked up, and I was now on the footplate and feeling elated as the plucky little engine, wheels spinning and struggling to gain speed, bounced and rattled along by the side of the River Brun and under the Leeds–Liverpool canal aqueduct. John invited me to take control of the regulator, the locomotive's accelerator, and to open it fully. We had to build up enough speed so that the little loco could climb the steep incline to the mainline railway sidings by Burnley Central Station and deliver our heavy cargo of coal. Years before, when I was about eight years old, I'd looked on in admiration from the swings and roundabouts in Thompson Park as the Wasp struggled up this incline under clouds of steam and smoke. I never dreamed that one day I would be gunning that same old warhorse through the rhododendrons and bluebells where I used to play.

While the pit occupied my fixed working hours, at the end of a shift my thoughts turned to music. One day Bob Palmer told me that a local group called The Falcons were looking for a drummer. 'Might be worth a try,' he said. I went to the house in Nelson where the band rehearsed. We ran through a few Elvis and Eddie Cochran tunes and I had the job. The first gig was a Saturday afternoon bop session down at the massive Nelson Imperial Ballroom. I enjoyed playing rock, but what really hooked me was the sight of scores of girls bopping around and eagerly applauding our music – such a contrast to the more reserved reception the jazz quintet was shown over at Rawtenstall.

After a while I began to look into what other rock bands – groups as they were back then – were in the area. Ricky Shaw & The Dolphins were the most popular, along with the name Tony Hicks. So I went to see for myself when they were playing down at Nelson Imp. Tony was fourteen at the time and was already an amazing guitarist. I was impressed but kept my distance. They had three Truvoice amps and wore pale blue jackets and black trousers, white shirts and red ties. Cliff and The Shadows were obviously an influence, as was Eddie Cochran. Lead singer Ricky Shaw – known as Belsh because his real name was Pat Belshaw – sang and Tony featured on guitar, playing a couple of bluesy numbers between Shadows instrumentals.

I often hung out at the bar of the Talbot with my old pals from Pike Hill, all of us under-age drinkers. When I was eighteen, a gang of us went to Butlin's holiday camp at Pwllheli, north Wales for our annual Burnley Fair holidays. Rory Storm & The Hurricanes, a Liverpool group, played in the Rock and Calypso Ballroom with a then unknown Ringo Starr on drums. Rory Storm, the singer, was a bit of a poser and Ringo wasn't much of a drummer, but between

The Hurricanes' sets, records were played over the dance hall's PA. 'Shakin' All Over' by Johnny Kidd & The Pirates blasted forth. The record had just entered the charts, and on first hearing it, I realised that Brits could now rock in the same league as the Americans.

We'd drink in the Pig and Whistle where there were two guys from Atherton who played guitars and sang. They sounded good and I needed to play. Luckily, a drummer who was taking part in 'The People Talent Contest' lent me his basic drum set, and we became a three-piece for the rest of my holiday. We came second in the People/Butlin's talent competition.

A group of girls from Nelson sat near us Burnley lads at another table. I was struck by one of them but couldn't summon up the nerve to go and talk to her. At the end of the holiday I still didn't know her name. With the annual holidays over, I was back in the Talbot drinking with my friend Frank, when across the bar I spotted the same girl. This time I was on the case. I went over and offered to buy her a drink. She asked for a glass of cider. Her name was Maureen and she was eighteen, the same age as me. She told me she was a secretary at a local company called Salon that made hairdressing equipment. We got on well and at closing time I asked if I could take her home. We caught the Colne train to Nelson, and I walked her up to her family home in Bankhouse Road. She invited me in for a coffee, and as I sat down on the sofa, I noticed a Futurama guitar reclined in the corner of the room. 'Whose is that?' I asked. 'Oh, it's our kid's... he drives me mad playing it all day long,' she said. Turned out that 'our kid' was Tony Hicks. Maureen was his big sister.

Maureen and I agreed to meet again. A few days later I walked her home after we'd been to the cinema. As we were stood at the doorway of the family home, a young lad wearing a leather jacket pushed past us. As he was opening the front door, he turned and said: 'Hello, drummer boy.' It was Tony and that was our first meeting. We got on from the start. We both lived for music although at the time being a pro musician was a distant dream. Tony was at the local Catholic school, and he managed to get away with wearing his leather jacket rather than a school uniform. He was a keen cyclist, and Belsh would insist that Hicks was the only person in town who could ride his racing bike up the town's steepest street, which led to Jimmy Nelson's Sports Club.

I would visit the Hicks household at 22 Bankhouse Road most days. Maureen and Tony's mum, Peggy, served up generous portions of food followed by pudding, so one way and another their house was a magnet for me. I used to run and walk the three miles home at the end of the evening, speeding up Pasture Lane and over to Roughlee in the pitch dark.

Tony wanted me to join him in The Dolphins, and I was keen to switch because they were the best group in the area. They had a drummer, Alan Buck, but his father used to come along and offer his guidance. Tony, Belsh and Bernie could take it no longer. Happily, Alan found a job with The Four

Pennies. The Dolphins line-up then became Ricky (Belsh) Shaw on vocals, Tony on lead guitar, Bernie Calvert on bass and me, on drums. The Falcons weren't happy that I'd forsaken my drumming post, so much so that Ronnie Bullock's dad said: 'If I get hold of that Tony Hicks, I'll break his bloody fingers.' Thankfully, that didn't happen.

I played my first date with The Dolphins on September 30, 1961, at Wigan Palais. We played for two hours and I was paid thirty-six shillings.

That summer I went to Butlin's with Tony and Belsh. We were befriended by a chirpy Scouse Redcoat who went by the name of Jimmy Tarbuck. When we told him that we were a group, we all enthused about the current music scene and Jimmy told us about a new band called The Beatles. This was before they had made their first record, 'Love Me Do'. Tarby said they wore black leather jackets and had quite a following in Liverpool.

Fast forward four years and Tony and I would be carousing with megastar Tarby in the Scotch of St James night club in London's West End. He was now the 'cheeky chappie' compère of ITV's *Sunday Night At The London Palladium*. During one of our appearances on the show we performed our latest hit, and then Jimmy came on and joined Allan, Graham and Tony on The Hollies' front line as we performed 'It's In Her Kiss'.

In The Dolphins' early days, Tony and I couldn't really afford decent instruments. We used to set off on the Ribble bus from Nelson to Manchester on a Sunday afternoon when the shops were closed. When we got there, we would walk down Oxford Road on a window shopping expedition. Our oohs and aahs announced the sighting of Reno's shop window. We'd point at and discuss the merits of Reno's musical merchandise, stacked up on display. A few shops further along the street, we arrived at our favourite port of call, Barratts. Adrian and his father had the best selection of guitars and drums in town. Coupled with their friendly and accommodating service, the store became a hangout for any band worth its salt back in the 1960s. Having exhausted our enthusiasm and viewed every shop on the street, it was time to catch the red bus and head back to the hills.

The drum kit I dreamed of was a Chicago-built Ludwig, but there was no way I could afford one. I part-exchanged my Premier drums at Barratts and took delivery of a German-made, ruby-red Trixon set. At the time, British drummers Brian Bennett and Clem Cattini were playing Trixon and that influenced me to buy the drums.

The Dolphins forged a reputation across the north as one of the best bands of that period, and we started to make decent money, although we still had our day jobs. Tony had become an apprentice electrician and I was still at the NCB.

Bank Hall was a very dangerous, dusty coal mine. Many of the colliers would suffer from pneumoconiosis, or black lung, in later life. Highly combustible methane gas was always present on the coalface and in the tunnel. There was the constant danger of it being ignited by the slightest spark and starting a fatal firestorm, which could engulf the whole operation. I needed to escape from my indentured treadmill.

After completing a tricky repair during an underground shift, I remember thinking about the next Dolphins gig. At the time I was riding the scraper chain in order to exit the dangerous coalface. This moving, horizontal ladder was set in a long steel trough that traversed the length of the coalface. With my toes on one rung and fingertips gripping another, crouched, so as not to catch the arch of my back on the low roof, I remember thinking, if I lose my fingers, then my drumming dream will be over. Every few feet there was a sweating and blackened collier, shovelling the shiny black stuff onto the moving slats of steel. Usually the miner would pause to allow you to pass by. Dismounting at the end of the ride was fraught with danger, as you had to get off the chain or cascade down onto a conveyer belt to be dumped into a waiting mine car and buried in coal.

I played with The Dolphins for a couple of years, and minor professionals like Mike Sarne, Wendy Richards and later Billie Davis asked us to accompany them at various venues. Their manager was Robert Stigwood, who went on to guide the Bee Gees to international success. We even cut three tracks at Decca Studios in West Hampstead with backing singer Doug Sheldon.

All of us were really excited about the London-based bands like Johnny Kidd & The Pirates and Nero & The Gladiators.

Scottish musician Joe Moretti played the wonderful guitar part on 'Shakin' All Over'. The Krew Kats' recordings with Jim Sullivan and Brian Bennett had become quite an influence on us too. I'd seen Joe Brown & The Bruvvers with Brian Bennett on drums at Barnoldswick Majestic. That was shortly after drummer Bobby Graham had been fired by Joe for being drunk while riding an elephant in Glasgow. I had first met Bobby when The Dolphins supported Joe and co. at the Oasis in Manchester. After Joe fired him, Bobby went on to be the most in-demand session drummer in the country. He was Dave Clark – not literally, but it was Bobby's drumming on the DC5 tracks. And he played on the first two or three recordings by The Kinks, including 'You Really Got Me'. Listen to the fine drumming on P. J. Proby's 'Hold Me' – yes, that's Bobby Graham again. I look back on the period around 1964 as the glory days of British studio rock. I saw Johnny Duncan & The Bluegrass Boys down at the Nelson Imperial, known locally as th'Imp. The 'Boys' were Big Jim Sullivan on guitar, Licorice Locking on double bass and Brian Bennett, all three performing with great panache as a country band.

I now had a Ludwig Acrolite snare drum to complement my Trixon drum kit. At that time, Tony was using a very rare Maton guitar that I believe Beatle George Harrison later used on Granada TV's *Scene At 6.30* and Bernie had a nice Fender Precision bass. We were armed and ready to go. The Oasis was our favourite Manchester gig. Only soft drinks and frothy coffee were served in clubs back then. Between sets we'd hang out at the café bar and be served by Rose Eccles, a girl with a stunning figure who later married Graham Nash.

Pete MacLaine & The Dakotas were probably the slickest and best dressed of all the Manchester bands. They also sported the best instruments and equipment. I first saw them at the Oasis. Tony Mansfield had a new sky-blue-pearl Ludwig Super Classic. I'd never seen such a beautiful set of drums at close quarters. I just had to touch them and swoon. In austere post-war Britain, American drums were expensive and almost impossible to obtain. Some drummers knew musicians who worked the big transatlantic liners, but you needed to be in London where the pros were or in Liverpool, where friends or relatives were either in the merchant navy sailing on the big ocean-going liners or working on the docks.

Fellow musicians generally acknowledged that The Big Three was the best of all the northern groups. On a rare night off in Manchester, Tony and I saw them play the Oasis Club. Johnny Gustafson was the excellent bass player who sang, fronting Johnny Hutchinson on drums and Brian Griffiths on guitar. Their music was rough and ready and had to be experienced live. Apart from Johnny Gus's Fender bass, their equipment was cheap and decrepit, but they attacked each song like men possessed. Sadly the band is now overlooked in the annals of British rock. Their few inferior recordings are not a true representation of what I saw and heard on that night in 1963. It was pure unfettered Mersey punk.

One night The Dolphins were playing the Oasis. A guy by the name of Alan Cheetham introduced himself and without further ado went about trying to persuade Tony to join a new band, The Hollies. At first Tony resisted, but Cheetham kept turning up at Dolphins gigs when we played the Manchester area. He just would not take no for an answer.

Eventually Tony said: 'I'll join if Bob can come along.' Cheetham said that would be tricky. They had a drummer, and more importantly, he was the only one who was qualified to drive the group's van.

Tony, curious to know what he might be missing, caught the red Ribble bus to Manchester intent on listening for himself to Cheetham's group. On arrival in the city he made his way to a place that he knew well, the Oasis Club. Pauline Clegg was the co-manager of the club, and he asked her what she thought of this new band. Pauline said they were good and that they had the potential to make the big time. They weren't playing there that night, The Beatles were – The Hollies were in another prestigious Mancunian venue, the Twisted Wheel. Tony walked round there, but he didn't go in. He listened through the air vent on the side of the building: 'Just in case they were crap.' There he could hear the bass guitar. He was impressed. When they finished their set, Tony went inside and introduced himself. They were keen for him to join. He went home and asked his dad what he thought. Hicks senior said: 'Tell them you'll join if they pay you £18 a week.' None of the other Hollies were paid that much, but they agreed and in February 1963 Tony went to join Allan Clarke, Graham Nash, Eric Haydock and Don Rathbone. The original guitarist, Vic Steele, didn't want to be a professional, so Tony stepped in.

Tony's departure left us with a major problem. The Dolphins were contracted to play a couple of nights later at the Northwich Memorial Hall, backing singer Mike Berry, except we didn't have a guitar player. Alan Cheetham told us that Vic Steele, freshly departed from The Hollies, would fill in for Tony. He promised Steele would arrive for the afternoon rehearsal, but by 7 p.m. he still hadn't shown. At this point we were all anxiously pacing about. Steele finally walked in at 7.10 p.m., leaving no time to rehearse before the 7.30 p.m. start. Mike Berry gave us a list of the songs, but we never stood a chance. Tony had taken all his own equipment, including the power lead for Bernie's amp. We were gibbering wrecks before we even started playing.

We had our own van, a dark blue Ford Thames. We drove back via Manchester and stopped at an all-night café in Salford Docks, where The Lowry and Media City stand today. We sat round the table with our cups of tea and cheese on toast. The Dolphins were over, and we knew it.

I was heartbroken, as were Bernie and Belsh. On the plus side, The Hollies were all set to pass their Abbey Road recording test now that they had one of the most talented guitarists in the north of England. Oh well, I thought, I still have my jazz gigs.

A few weeks later, on my way to work on the back shift, I stopped off in Nelson to visit Tony's mum. Even with Tony away, I was often round at their house because Maureen and I were now going steady. Not many families had phones back then, but Tony's parents had one. 'He's phoned to say I must tell you Shane Fenton & The Fentones are auditioning for drummers,' she said. If I was interested, I had to be at the King's Hall, Stoke-on-Trent on Saturday afternoon. Of course I was interested. On April 6, Mum and Dad drove me down to the venue and I played two or three songs with the band. They enthused about my drumming, and I presumed that I had got the gig. The following day, I was over at Maureen's when the phone rang. Could I be in London tomorrow?

Excerpt from Dad's diary – Monday, April 8:
'Off to London about 6.30 a.m. Got to Russell Square at 2.30 p.m. Warm in London. Robert saw agent (Tommy Sanderson's assistant, Eddie Donohue) and made another date to see them at 11 a.m. Tuesday morning. So we had tea on Shaftesbury Avenue then we went and booked in for the night at the Arama Hotel, Sussex Gardens.'

Tuesday, April 9:
'Robert got the job with Fentones, and we set off for home at 6.30 p.m. and arrived home at 2.30 a.m.'

Wednesday, April 10:
'Took Rob to the National Coal Board to throw in his
job and after tea took him to Altrincham to meet the
Fentones and say goodbye to Robert and wish him well in
his venture into professional entertainment... then back
home to an empty house.'

Thursday, April 11:
'Edna happy now that Robert has left the Coal Board. He
will probably be fine at Mansfield. Gave Rob £20 with
his £7 making £27.'

This is how it played out: Mum, Dad and I stayed in a cheap
boarding house overnight when we reached London, and the
following day I set out, sticks in pocket, to find the action. It
took a while, but down a narrow street off Tottenham Court
Road I spied a queue of about ten blokes, all with drumsticks
protruding from their coat pockets. It was raining, and I was
late. The first candidate was coming up the steps from the
cellar having completed his test.

Eventually it was my turn. I descended into the rehearsal
room and met Shane and the guys again. I had to be judged
on my handling of 'The Breeze And I', 'It's All Over Now' and
maybe 'Sticks And Stones'. Lloyd Ryan, one of the hopeful
drummers who I'd been standing next to in the rain, later
told me that Keith Moon was number three in the queue
– but I got the gig, and I was about to become a Fentone.

Tommy Sanderson was Shane's manager and because he had a connection with record producer Ron Richards, who produced both bands, Tommy now handled The Hollies too. Alan Cheetham had been disposed of.

After five years working in the colliery, I was finally in a position to leave. Back home I walked into the office of Bill Walton, the boss of the central workshops at Bank Hall. I told him I wanted to leave my job. 'But you haven't served your time yet,' he said. 'Why do you want to terminate your apprenticeship?' I replied meekly: 'I've got a job as a drummer in a band.' He rocked back on his chair with laughter. 'Tell you what, lad, I'll keep your job open for two weeks, and I'll see you later.'

In the industrial north, back in 1963, working class youngsters were expected to know their place, to 'get a trade in your hands' and graft as generations had done before them. Even Mum and Dad once told me: 'Robert, this drumming lark is fine, but only as a hobby. You need the security of a proper job.' They were finally won over when they came, with Maureen, to see me perform with Shane and The Fentones at the Liverpool Empire.

I met up with Shane and co. at the Stamford Hall in Altrincham. It was the last gig for the then drummer George Rodda. I was told that he'd upset record producer Ron, and Tommy had decreed that poor George had to go. When I'd said my goodbyes to Mum and Dad, Bonney, The Fentones' bass player, said to my folks: 'Don't worry Mr and Mrs Elliott, we'll take care of him.' I found his reassurance quite moving. They kept their word, and I had some happy times performing with them in theatres and dance halls the length and breadth of Britain. When possible, after a show, the guys would drive to their hometown of Mansfield in Nottinghamshire.

Shane's real name was Bernard Jewry, although he later went on to become better known as Alvin Stardust. I lived at his family home, a large terraced house which doubled as our showbiz digs, run by his mum. One morning I got up to find Rolf Harris, singer Julie Grant and mind reader the Great Zarada sitting around the breakfast table. Dear Mrs Jewry had made me a steaming hot curry for breakfast. That certainly woke me up.

The following night we were on a star-studded bill at the Royal Albert Hall in London for a live Light Programme radio broadcast for the BBC. At the end of the show everyone linked up along the front of stage to take a bow. I was next to singer Susan Maughan, whose single 'Bobby's Girl' was a huge hit.

After-hours I would visit the Flamingo Club. In early 1963 groups of American GIs would hang out there to be entertained by Georgie Fame & The Blue Flames. What a contrast. It was hard to believe that a couple of weeks earlier, I had been working down a coal mine, 1,600 feet underground.

Years later I wrote these lyrics, and with my friend Mark Nelson playing guitar, the following song was created, which The Hollies and I recorded in 2009 for our album *Then, Now, Always*.

Dolphin Days

We came down from the hills, the land of millstone grit,
Escaping from tradition where our faces didn't fit,
People smiled and said: 'This ain't nothing but a phase',
But we knew different back in Dolphin days.

We played the big city, wowed the big smoke,
'You must be up for the cup,' the plebs they used to joke,
But when they heard the sound we made
There was nothing else but praise,
We sure knew how to cut it, back in Dolphin days

You get there you get it, so it was me all along,
The bus stops and the carousels, life's milestones here in song,
You leave them standing, they scream and shout,
The illusion in a haze,
We cracked the code, back in Dolphin days.

JUST ONE LOOK

Words and Music by D. PAYNE & G. CARROLL.

Recorded by **THE HOLLIES** on PARLOPHONE

T. S. MUSIC CO. LTD. 142, Charing Cross Road, London W.C.2.   2/6

Sole Selling Agents:— SOUTHERN MUSIC PUBLISHING CO. LTD. 8, Denmark St. London W.C.2.

CHAPTER FOUR:

Men in White Coats

'It was a lunchtime session, and it seemed as if the whole world had gone to see them. The walls of the club were dripping with water. You could hardly move. It was crazy. They were singing their hearts out. Graham Nash was really lamming into his acoustic guitar. At the end of the set he showed me his guitar... there weren't any strings on it! But nobody noticed because there was so much noise.' So said record producer Ron Richards on seeing The Hollies for the first time in Liverpool's Cavern Club.

Tony was just eighteen when he appeared with The Hollies at the Cavern Club. Humour featured greatly in the group's repertoire, both on and offstage. Allan and Graham introduced the young lad to the eager Cavern dwellers, joking that he would serenade them with the toddler's favourite, 'Teddy Bears' Picnic'. That humorous incident stuck with me, and a few years later, I plucked three words from the nursery rhyme which became the title of The Hollies' 1966 album *For Certain Because*.

By the summer of 1963 Tony was touring with The Hollies, and I was touring with Shane and The Fentones. We used to bump into each other when we all stayed at the Aaland Hotel in London, just off Russell Square. It was a cheap, clean bed with no breakfast. The Searchers and Jimmy Savile stayed there too. Savile had a bicycle in the hall, a bubble car out the front and an E-type Jaguar around the corner. He would come in waggling his cigar, make loads of noise, then disappear. At the time he was a flamboyant man of mystery.

One day outside the Aaland, as Tony and the guys were about to board The Hollies' van, and I was leaving for a gig with The Fentones, I said: 'When am I joining The Hollies?' To which Graham replied: 'Don't worry, we'll sort it.'

Soon after that Graham and Tony came to see me play with The Fentones. Tony later told me that Graham was raving about my drumming. Shane came onstage, and I counted in the Ray Charles classic 'Sticks And Stones'. That clinched it. Graham and Tony told Tommy Sanderson that they wanted me in The Hollies ASAP. Don, the current drummer, was a lovely, sensible bloke but quite a bit older than the others. Technically he struggled to give the band the emphatic foundation that was needed to elevate their music onto the world stage.

Don moved into management and took up a position in Tommy Sanderson's office. Mrs Jewry didn't want me to leave

50

her Shane, but I was driven and just had to pursue my true vocation and become The Hollies' drummer.

Although I was still officially Shane's drummer, I was measured for my first Hollies suit a week before I joined the band. It was made out of a dark burgundy material, but the jacket neckline looked like a girl's gymslip top. The Beatles' suits had round collars, The Hollies' suits had square collars – get the idea? We hated them. That jacket, with its shiny material and bizarre collar, was soon discarded. Next came silver-grey Tonic suits with black-edged jackets and a velvet collar trim, which I thought were the best looking of all The Hollies' togs.

The Hollies' suits were made by Michael Cohen's family business. Graham had been a trainee with Cohen before he went full-time with The Hollies, and Michael was now the band's manager, alongside Tommy Sanderson. Cohen's shop, The Toggery, was in Mersey Square, Stockport and it doubled as a trendy boutique as well as The Hollies' HQ where we'd hang out and often meet up with other musicians. Throngs of schoolgirls would congregate outside the door making it difficult for us to collect our wages. We had become walking adverts for Cohen's garments and soon he was making suits for The Beatles and Tom Jones. On one occasion Michael arrived at the *Ready Steady Go!* TV studios with five red leather waistcoats. Thinking that they were ours to keep, we posed for photographs for teen magazines and performed on live TV wearing them. Then after the show, he took them back to his shop to flog. He loved all the show business glitz, and he soon struck up a relationship with one of the female stars of *Coronation Street* when we were appearing on Manchester-based Granada TV.

After I'd done my last job with The Fentones, I travelled up to Manchester in The Hollies' van – a shiny new black Commer with a sliding door on the side for easy loading. Allan's brother, Frank, was now driver and roadie.

I joined The Hollies in time for their twenty-six gig Top Rank Tour, appearing in dance halls all over the country. Also on the bill were my old boss, Shane, with his Fentones; Frank Kelly & The Hunters; and The Marauders from Stoke-on-Trent.

My first gig with the band was on Wednesday, September 18, 1963. We'd had a bit of a knock around the day before in Stockport, so I was comfortable with the running order and after months on the road with Shane, I was a seasoned pro. But although I knew Tony well, I hadn't got to know the other three. Now in the dressing room at the Parr Hall in Warrington, it was my first chance to chat with bass player Eric. It wasn't easy; he was a man of few words. Showtime was fast approaching, and it was time to get changed into our stage suits, but there was no sign of our lead singer. I attempted to strike up a conversation with the enigmatic Eric: 'Where's Allan?' I asked anxiously. Eric mumbled: 'He'll be in the pub. If he don't want to turn up he won't… that's how he is, he's done it before.' Blimey, I thought, what have I got myself into? Was this a tease? In fact, as I was to discover, Eric would turn out to be the unreliable one.

Minutes later Allan arrived. The show was a breeze and included 'Memphis, Tennessee', 'What Kind Of Girl Are You', 'Fortune Teller', 'Do You Love Me', 'Lucille', 'Searchin'' – in fact, the bones of our yet-to-be-recorded first LP, *Stay With The Hollies*.

The Hollies had a special kind of chemistry. Perhaps, in part at least, because Allan and Graham had grown up together in Manchester, or more precisely, the neighbouring city of Salford, where they first met in primary school. They both came from very poor backgrounds. Think early *Coronation Street*. Graham used to make a bit of cash by collecting stray bits of coal in an old pram and selling them. Both were self-taught and passionate about music, and they became a childhood duo. With the arrival of Elvis and Little Richard, they modelled themselves on their idols The Everly Brothers and for a time performed as Ricky & Dane Young.

The two of them used to wait in the rain outside the stage door of the Free Trade Hall when the Everlys had been performing there. They'd get Phil and Don's autographs and walk back with the brothers to the Midland Hotel where they were staying.

A few years later we were appearing at the London Palladium when our tour manager Rod Shields took a backstage phone call. 'Hi, it's Phil Everly here, can I speak to The Hollies?' Graham took the phone and Phil said: 'We're in the Decca recording studios and wondered if you have any songs for us.' Graham said: 'We sure have.' As a result of that call the Everlys were able to complete their album, *Two Yanks In England*, and Allan, Graham and Tony wrote about three quarters of the songs under the name 'L. Ransford'. Two of the musicians on that 1966 recording session were Jimmy Page and John Paul Jones. As Tony recently observed: 'It was The Everly Brothers backed by Led Zeppelin.'

Back in the early Manchester days, Allan and Graham joined The Fourtones, then The Deltas. Eric Haydock, Vic Steele and Don Rathbone were already in place and The Deltas changed their name to The Hollies in December 1962, in a tribute both to Buddy Holly and to Christmas.

Tony and I also had a strong connection; we understood each other musically and were close friends – family even, since I was seeing his sister. That left Eric, who came from Stockport and who, in his quiet, sardonic way, got on with all of us. Eric was self-taught, and in 1963 he had a six-string bass guitar and was a joy to work with.

London was the place to be. It was also a world of sharp-suited, competitive music men, who at first didn't know what to make of us. We had come down from the dark satanic mill towns that, to them, were vaguely situated somewhere north of the Watford Gap. But we had something to offer and they wanted to harness it. Graham, known to all of us as Willy, could sing higher than anyone. No squeaky falsetto for him. Clarkey was the dynamic lead singer with a natural feel for rock 'n' roll. Tony completed the front line and by now had cleverly crafted a lower harmony, creating the famous Hollies three-way. The sound was irresistible, and we knew that we had hit on a winning formula.

Soon after becoming a Hollie, I got the drum kit of my dreams. I went to Footes Music Store in London and traded in my Trixon kit for a brand new, American-made, Ludwig Super Classic. The drums were finished in silver sparkle, and the legendary 400 snare drum was made out of solid brass. I loved that kit; it meant more to me than anything else I'd ever owned.

We spent a lot of time on the road. In the autumn of 1963 The Hollies' Famous Five adventure was well under way and our treasured van became our refuge and home on wheels. That vehicle had enabled us to escape the treadmill lives that we could have been destined for in the north of England, had we not been immersed in our beloved music. We tried to make the long journeys as bearable as possible, with equipment at the rear, band up front.

At that time our gear consisted of Eric's Fender Bassman amp and his six-string Fender bass, plus my drums in fibre cases and Tony's Vox AC30 or T60 amp. The Hollies' three-way harmony was heard by means of our humble PA system, consisting of three microphones amplified through a pair of small Vox column speakers. Our stage suits would be hung round the inside of the van, carefully positioned so as not to cover the windows.

Graham and Allan usually slept throughout those long pre-motorway journeys. The 'worm', a long, red, padded strip of seating, was fought over by the two sleepyheads and would be positioned below a plank of wood, one end of which was placed on an amplifier at the rear of the van, and the other end on a ledge behind the passenger seat. Allan would then slide under the plank and have a snooze on the worm, while a couple of us would sit on top of the plank in reasonable comfort. Sometimes the plank would slip off the supporting amplifier and drop onto our singer's head. He usually slept on, and we would jump up quickly to avoid waking him and place the plank back on top of the amp. Most journeys were accompanied by the sound of Al's empty cider bottles, as they rolled and clinked around on the van floor.

We tried to get back to our own homes as often as we could. Since Nelson was a bit far to get home every time, Michael found a flat for Tony and me on Corkland Road in Chorlton. It cost us six guineas a week and was damp and horrible. We didn't stay there long – I preferred to get back home to the family cottage whenever I could, and Tony would stay at Michael Cohen's flat in Manchester.

One night Frank Clarke was delivering us weary band members to our places of domicile in the early hours of the morning, and we were all asleep or dozing after a raving gig and a long road journey. Graham was laid out on the plank on the nearside of the van when we accelerated and the side door slid open. Whoever had been dropped off last had not closed it properly. One minute he was there, then no Hollies high-harmony bloke. Poor Graham had disappeared out of the van onto the road below. Fortunately, he had landed on his backside and bounced and slithered to a halt. He was bruised and shaken but thankfully not injured. Three things contributed to his lucky escape: he was relaxed and sleeping with his legs facing the front of the van, so he landed on the cheeks of his arse; he was wearing a pair of brand new, tough Levi jeans; and finally, it was raining and he aquaplaned along the smooth tarmac road surface.

The next day we flew to Scotland. In Dundee the weather was good and we played football in the park. Some local youths arrived and challenged us to a five-a-side. Unlike the athletic teenagers, we didn't have suitable footwear. We were kitted out in our Anello & Davide Cuban-style stage boots but, after an intensely fought game, we won. Maybe the high heels gave us an unfair height advantage.

On Friday, October 11, 1963, we appeared on ITV's *Ready Steady Go!* We were there to promote our second single release, 'Searchin''. Down in the basement studio, director Rollo Gamble instructed the five of us to walk line abreast, miming in time with the playback of our record, up and down the studio, right hands above our eyes, looking from side to side as if we were, well, searching for something. 'Gonna find her... Gonna find her.' We felt ridiculous but, as the new kids on the block, we didn't complain. Rollo was one of the old school; I imagined that he had probably put together quite a few damn good pantomimes in his time. I can still picture his ruddy, weather-beaten appearance; a rum-soaked old sea dog, dressed in an oversized tropical shirt. He gesticulated and directed his heart out. So there we were, a rock band with no drums or guitars, trooping up and down like five fish out of water.

In those early days there used to be a girl carrying a small pooch standing at the studio exit with the usual throng of autograph hunters. We'd chat to her as we signed autographs. She later ditched the dog, removed her shoes, and became Sandie Shaw.

After appearing on *Ready Steady Go!* that evening, we dashed up to EMI's studio in Abbey Road, St John's Wood. Walking up those steps to the front door and entering the imposing Georgian townhouse was quite a daunting experience. Sir Edward Elgar, Cliff and The Shadows, Johnny Kidd & The Pirates, Sophia Loren, Sir John Barbirolli and, more recently, The Beatles had all passed through those illustrious portals.

The Hollies' instrumental backing was sparse: two amps and my drum kit. That's the way we liked it. We were ready to rock and we wanted to impress. The red recording light went on, and we tensed up like greyhounds in their starting traps. Our A&R man in charge of the recording, Ron Richards, announced over the studio intercom: 'We're running.' I counted us in: 'One two three: "Oh well your mama don't mind…"' and we were off at full tilt. That night we recorded my first two tracks with the band, 'Stay' and 'Poison Ivy'.

The band had to sound just right. No overdubs or multitrack recorders in those days. It was a live performance, warts and all. Listen to that recording of 'Stay'. The atmosphere crackles with energy and excitement. Earlier in the session I had to plead with veteran engineer Peter Bown to put a mic on my bass drum. His response was: 'We find that one mic, correctly placed, is sufficient for drums.' I persisted: 'My bass drum figure needs to accent the vocals.' He reluctantly obliged and the result was the punchy Don Lamond kick sound I'd dreamed of. Because the extra microphone worked so well, I would now be remembered as the first drummer who made it the norm for Abbey Road's white-coated technicians to mic up the kick, or bass drum. We did two takes for 'Stay' and Tony played a different guitar solo each time. There was one particular section of Hicks' wizardry that Ron found appealing, and he wanted it to be inserted into the second superior take. Quick as a flash, engineer Peter Bown marked, then chopped out the length of the quarter-inch-wide tape with a razor blade, and skilfully spliced in Tony's hotter solo from our first attempt.

There was an air of BBC-ness at EMI. The whole operation was formal, correct and reassuringly British. The toilets were kitted out with Izal toilet paper. Every sheet of the shiny tracing paper-like rolls was stamped 'EMI' – just to let you know who was boss.

In case we got any ideas about being 'stars', our accommodation soon brought us back to earth. We were all sharing the same bedroom in the Sussex Gardens Hotel near Paddington. Five of us Hollies plus Frank, the roadie.

Our date sheet was crammed with gigs. On November 13 we flew up to Aberdeen while Frank drove the equipment in our Commer van. It was a long journey north and maybe Frank was tired because the van rolled over and crashed. Thankfully he was OK, though in my diary entry the next day, there was no mention of Allan's brother's well-being: *'Top Rank Ballroom, Aberdeen. Frank smashed van up – thankfully gear OK.'* That's how we thought back then. The music, the performance and our gear, the tools of the trade, were paramount in our thoughts. Not much else mattered. Every time we performed, we aimed to be better than the time before. We were all, in our own ways, perfectionists. We'd all spent endless hours teaching ourselves to play and then practising until our fingers bled and our arms ached. Now we'd got a chance to show the world what we could do, and we weren't going to blow it.

On Friday, November 15 our new 45 rpm single 'Stay' was released, and we played in Maryport, Cumbria. The next night it was Romford, Essex, after which we caught the sleeper train from London's Marylebone Station up to Manchester to play in Crewe that night. The following day we were working for Ferrari-driving promoter Fred Bannister, at Bath Pavilion. We'd managed to get through floods caused by heavy rains, but our equipment didn't arrive, so we borrowed the support band's stuff.

A few days later on Tuesday, November 19, we appeared on ITV's *Five O'Clock Club* with presenter Muriel Young – 'Aunty Mu' as the kids knew her – cheekily assisted by Fred Barker, a dog hand puppet worked and voiced by Ivan Owen, who later created Basil Brush. Wally Whyton operated Ollie Beak, a tatty looking owl, who was Barker's partner in crime. We mimed to 'Stay', which was climbing the charts, and then dashed off to play Wallington Public Hall in south London later that evening.

On Friday, November 22, President Kennedy was assassinated. We heard the news as we checked into the hotel after our gig in Gravesend, Kent. Like everyone else in the world, we were stunned.

HERE I GO AGAIN

By CLIVE WESTLAKE & MORT SHUMAN

Recorded by **THE HOLLIES** on PARLOPHONE

BELINDA (LONDON) LIMITED
Sole Selling Agents :
17, SAVILE ROW
LONDON, W.1

2/6

CHAPTER FIVE:

Lip-Sync – The Art of Deception

It wasn't unusual for The Hollies to play three gigs in a day. For example, we'd guest on the lunchtime Joe Loss big band radio programme, which was broadcast live on the BBC's Light Programme from London's Playhouse Theatre. Next we'd head for *Ready Steady Go!*, which was also live, followed by a dash up the A1 to the Stevenage Locarno dance hall for our third performance of the day.

As the black Commer had been written off, we now had a secondhand, red Ford Thames van. The new Hollies band wagon was faster than the Commer but not as roomy. On Boxing Day 1963, we travelled from Manchester to London on the midnight sleeper train. Our equipment went by road in the Ford van driven by Frank. We arrived in London at about 8 the following morning and made our way from the station to the BBC Playhouse Theatre. We'd been booked to guest on another live, hour-long, lunchtime radio programme, *Go Man Go*, featuring the Oscar Rabin Band. It was early and we were hungry. In the BBC café, situated at the very top of the Playhouse, Aggie, a small Scottish lady, greeted us with her squeaky, lilting: "Ello 'Ollies.' On offer were her exotic sandwiches, filled with goodies like sardine and marmalade, or banana and nut. It was a veritable 1963 Pret a Manger – Aggie was ahead of her time. Think of an unusual combination and she would make it for you. And as in the EMI canteen, tea or coffee was served in a ceramic cup and placed with a clink onto a matching saucer, making elevenses an event to savour with a truly great British brew. The Aggies of bygone times would turn in their gravy to see today's tea squirted from a machine into a disposable, chemically constructed, bendy container.

Refreshed and ready to set up, we went in search of Frank and our equipment. But our van, it seemed, had broken down somewhere en route. We had no amps or drums, not even a pair of drumsticks. Maybe a plectrum in a pocket somewhere, but that was it. Fortunately, the musicians in the Oscar Rabin Orchestra let us use their gear. At bang on 12.30 p.m. the 'On Air' sign glowed, and after some big band pop, a packed audience heard David Ede's voice deliver a cringe-making introduction that ended with: 'Spend your Christmas holidays the Christmas Hollies' way. Here are The Hollies!' The audience burst into life, girls screamed and the five of us ran onstage grabbing whatever instruments were on offer in order to get through the performance. Graham was singing lead on 'Candy Man', Allan was playing harmonica, I had jumped onto the Rabin drummer's kit, leaving me isolated somewhere between the saxophones and the trombone section, and Tony plugged into guitarist Laurie Steele's amplifier. I don't remember how Eric got by, but it all sounded good – and it was transmitted live. I was able to listen when I was back home, thanks to my mother's foresight in recording the broadcast on the reel-to-reel tape recorder that Maureen had bought me for my twenty-first birthday. Edna had become a dab hand at placing the microphone next to the radiogram and she had recorded most of my early radio performances.

A few days later we arrived outside an old boarded up church on Dickenson Road in Manchester. The BBC had converted the derelict building into a TV studio, and we were there to perform our single 'Stay' on the very first *Top Of The Pops*. The show aired on New Year's Day 1964, and we appeared alongside The Rolling Stones, Dusty Springfield, The Dave Clark Five, The Swinging Blue Jeans and The Beatles. It was hosted by the yet-to-be-infamous Jimmy Savile. Little did we know that *TOTP*, as it was always known, would become a BBC1 staple for the next forty years.

We started 1964 on a high. 'Stay' was in the prestigious Top Ten and we were ecstatic. The Hollies' first single '(Ain't That) Just Like Me' had reached number twenty-five, 'Searchin'' peaked at twelve, and now 'Stay' had hit the number eight spot: a steady upward progression.

My diary entry Sunday, January 12:
'*Bitterly cold – snowing hard. Played at the end
of Hastings Pier. Travelling back to London, the
van skidded into a low wall smashing the front
suspension.*'

We were stranded in the snowbound village of Robertsbridge, and it was late as we slithered around in the silent, icy snow. Fortunately, we had crashed close to a local inn, the Seven Stars, but it was closed. We managed to rouse the landlord, his wife and daughter, who welcomed us into their living quarters for a hot drink and a friendly chat. They recognised us from our regular appearances on TV and, despite their tales of the pub ghost, we all got a good night's sleep. The following morning our host alerted the local garage, which sent a truck to collect our broken Ford for repair.

If the pub was supposedly haunted, then the van was certainly jinxed. It was repaired and we set off again, only to have the head gasket blow just ten miles from London. We had to hire taxis to fulfil our commitment for the day: recording songs for the BBC's Light Programme and a radio show called *Easy Beat*.

The following week after our appearance at Manchester's Oasis Club, Jay Vickers took over from Allan's brother as our road manager. Frank was a nice guy, but he didn't enjoy the pressures of being on the road, so he went off to live with his family near Morecambe.

One of Jay's first tasks was to drive us from Manchester to London in thick snow. It took ten hours. The following day we played Birmingham Town Hall. Also on the bill was Screaming Lord Sutch, or as we knew him, David. During one of his numbers, 'Jack The Ripper', his Lordship dived on top of keyboard player Freddie 'Fingers' Lee, pinning him down on the electric piano and stabbing him with a rubber 'blood' filled dagger. The weight of writhing bodies proved too much for the old instrument and the piano's spindly legs collapsed, resulting in the stage being littered with a flat-pack of wires, keys and bodies.

On Monday, January 27 I bought an eighteen-inch Paiste 602 cymbal for £6. I gave it the Pike Hill baking tin treatment by drilling holes in the precious instrument and inserting bifurcated rivets. It had become a sizzle cymbal and can be heard on all The Hollies' records and performances throughout the 1960s. On the same day during an evening session at Abbey Road, we recorded 'Just One Look', along with a B-side that Tony and I wrote: 'Keep Off That Friend Of Mine'. Ron double-tracked the three-way harmony and, at the press of a button, we became choir-like. We'd been softened up. The future was set, and that simple process was to become addictive as we advanced along the lucrative road of making hit records.

I didn't make it home very often because the band was booked solidly. But when I could, I loved getting back to the peace and quiet of the cottage and one of Mum's home-cooked meals. I was still just Robert and more likely to have a conversation with friends about cars and the countryside than about music. And of course there was Maureen. With both her brother and her boyfriend in the band, she understood the world we were in, and she was happy to live at home with her parents and see me when I came home. From time to time she would catch the train down to London or come to our northern gigs. We usually managed to have some quality time together.

Looking back, I'm not proud of the fact that Maureen always came second to my drums. But that's how it was – music was my selfish passion, and I was lucky enough to have a girlfriend who didn't mind and who was happy to wait for me. From the moment I first met her, I loved Mo and I never wanted anyone else.

Our Scottish dates were great fun, with raving crowds and sold out venues. On February 10, 1964, we played to a packed, sweaty audience in the legendary Barrowlands Ballroom in Glasgow. During our performance, the screaming girls who lined the front of the stage began to faint. It appeared, to this cynical drummer, as though each lassie was trying to upstage her swooning sister. As we fired into our final songs, Tony, Allan and Graham teased the seething masses even more and the collapsing got more dramatic. The venue's bouncers came to the rescue, delivering each young lady safely backstage to be resuscitated. After the show we all made a quick dash to the van, clambered in and

I'll be your sweetheart – Auntie Irene and me by the River Brun near Worsthorne, Lancashire, 1944.

Mum outside her bungalow shop (known as Edna's) which was also our home, Pike Hill, Burnley, 1948.

Time for tea betwix the loch and our Ford Prefect, Scotland, 1950.

Me in my rubber bumbo, Blackpool, 1949.

On holiday in Llandudno with Mum and Dad, 1950.

In our garden behind Mum's shop at Pike Hill, 1953. I'd passed my eleven-plus exam and I'm ready for my first term at Nelson Grammar School.

352 Squadron, Burnley – me in the ATC, middle of back row, at St Athan, 1954.

My first bass drum, Newbridge Barrowford Nelson, 1958.

Guess Who – pre-Dolphins with Eddie Marten and The Falcons in Nelson, 1960.

I met these lads and borrowed that 'drum kit'. We didn't win. Butlin's, Pwllheli, Wales, 1960.

Robert (not quite Bobby yet) in my bedroom watched over by some of my drumming idols, in the village of Roughlee, Lancashire, 1960.

Maureen Hicks and me – both 18 years old, 1960.

Me and tenor sax star Don Rendell jamming at the Circulation Club in Burnley, 1961.

Ricky Shaw and The Dolphins outside Tony Hicks's house in Nelson, Lancashire, 1961.

Ricky Shaw and The Dolphins posing in Burnley Mechanics-Mecca, 1961. Tony Hicks with his new Maton guitar. That same guitar was later played by Beatle George Harrison.

Wearing my favourite Hollies suit and playing Ludwig drums, 1963.

(L-R) Shane, Mick Eyre, Bill Bonney, me and Jerry Wilcock – The Fentones in Soho, 1963.

Me with the Fentones in Cambridge Corn Exchange, 1963.

Here I am with Shane Fenton & The Fentones in the basement of Jennings, the Vox shop on Charing Cross Road, London, 1963.

Jay drove off. As we pulled away, there was a knocking on the steamed-up side window. I slid it back to come face to face with a guy shouting: 'Autograph, autograph, gee us yer autograph,' in breathless Glaswegian. We quickly obliged – his legs were going like hell as we passed the autograph book back to him. The unknown sprinter is remembered with great affection as a true 'Flying Scotsman'.

A couple of days later we played Stourbridge, followed by Kidderminster. We were moving upmarket from the boarding houses and shared rooms to quality hotels. Jay would book us into country house hotels, sometimes set in acres of beautiful grounds. Eric had acquired a .410 shotgun and would run from bedroom to bedroom opening windows and blasting the local crow population. Fortunately, that fad was short-lived and no one was injured. On Valentine's Day we recorded BBC TV's *Blue Peter* at Shepherd's Bush. After the show, Val Singleton travelled down to Gravesend with us in our old Ford van, happily perched atop the engine compartment between me and Jay.

In February 'Just One Look' was released. That night we played the Wimbledon Palais and after the show fans almost wrecked the van. They tore off the wing mirrors, daubed lipstick all over the windows and let down the tyres.

'Just One Look' made it to number two in the charts, and we were more in demand than ever. Screaming fans became the norm, and we began to be recognised, together and individually, wherever we went. For me and, I think, for the others too, it wasn't about the fame. I felt privileged and happy to be making a living through the music that I loved.

The gigs came thick and fast. *Thank Your Lucky Stars* was recorded in Birmingham, we featured on *Scene At 6.30* for Granada TV in Manchester, and a couple of days later it was another *Ready Steady Go!* Then we pre-recorded *Top Of The Pops* so that we could appear with The Rolling Stones at the Gaumont theatre in Bradford.

At this point The Beatles were starting to rack up number one hits, and the Stones had made number three in the charts with their third single 'Not Fade Away'. The early sixties was an amazing time to be in a group; we were doing something new and different and it was incredibly exciting. The news was awash with this new beat group phenomenon, dramatically illustrated with images of the vast crowds of screaming fans, which I found quite scary. This media circus wasn't what any of us had imagined when we started out, but our music was going around the world and that was a heady feeling.

Allan had met Jeni Bowstead, a hotel receptionist from Coventry, when she came to hear the band. Now they wanted to get married, but that was causing tensions. Graham and Rose Eccles had been together the longest, and they were not happy about Allan and Jeni getting married before them. Graham also claimed that marrying was selfish and could affect the band's image – what would the fans think? A meeting was called at Tommy Sanderson's place, and there was talk of Allan being thrown out of The Hollies and getting Frank somebody from Michael Cohen's new group The Toggery Five. Tony, Eric and I couldn't believe the fury with which Rose and Graham vented their opinions, but Allan stood firm. He was going to marry his girl – and he wasn't leaving.

I had more important things to think about. On Friday, March 13 my lovely grandad Alf Precious died, aged eighty-five. I wasn't there. That was the downside of our success – I couldn't just drop everything and go. Instead, I was playing the Morecambe Floral Hall where there was a riot among the fans. We had quite a few riots around that time, with the police out in force to keep control. We were all bemused by the kerfuffle. We just wanted to perform.

On Tuesday, March 24 Allan and Jeni got married in a little church near Coventry. The tiff put aside, Graham was best man and we were all there. Allan was twenty-one and Jeni was nineteen, and the best thing about it, at the time, was that when they went on honeymoon, we all got a holiday. I was able to head home to see my parents and Maureen.

Graham and Rose got married too, two months later on May 24. None of the other Hollies were there. Neither marriage dented the band's image in the least. Graham and Rose only lasted a couple of years and they divorced in 1966, but Allan and Jeni went on to have three children and a long and happy marriage.

Next on the agenda for us was the forty-date Dave Clark tour. The Hollies were special guests, and also on the bill were an unknown band, The Kinks, plus The Mojos and Mark Wynter, backed by The Trebletones. The compère was

Canadian Frank Berry, who had just appeared in the Peter Sellers film *Dr Strangelove*.

We liked The Kinks. Drummer Mick Avory would entertain us on the bus with his excellent impression of a tarmac tamping machine, complete with sound effects. One night after the show, Eric and I were looking out of the window of our hotel near the Coventry Theatre. Kink Dave Davies appeared across the road pursued by two or three girls. He seemed to shake them off. Then he came running by again. It dawned on us that he was looking to be mobbed but couldn't find any takers. He needn't have worried. By September The Kinks had a number one record and everyone knew who they were.

Early on in the tour we'd watched all the acts to see what we were up against. The Kinks included an unknown original song by Dave's brother, Ray, in their set, 'You Really Got Me'. We thought it was a little like 'Louie Louie' by The Kingsmen, but nevertheless, a strong song. I remember Graham and Tony enthusing to The Kinks' roadie, Hal Carter – who had previously worked with Billy Fury – about the song being a potential hit. Nearby, listening intently, were The Kinks' posh managers, Robert and Grenville. Sure enough, on the first available day off from touring, the boys were ordered into the recording studio. American record producer Shel Talmy had been hired. He didn't rate Mick Avory's drumming and had booked session drummer Bobby Graham. I mentioned earlier that Bobby had forged himself a career as a powerhouse studio drummer, and he was perfect for the track.

Topping the bill on the tour were The Dave Clark Five. The clattering drums on 'Glad All Over' and 'Bits And Pieces' propelled the boys to the top of the charts across the Atlantic Ocean and into the USA as they followed in The Beatles' boot tracks. But in reality, the smiling Dave was not the originator of the infectious percussion. The Musicians' Union later discovered that he was miming along on *Top Of The Pops* to the drumming of my mate Bobby Graham. He told me that he was paid a double session fee of £18 for the recording, on condition that he kept schtum and didn't blow Dave Clark's cover. The Union rightly perceived this as deception.

Unbeknown to us, Eric had started a one-man crusade against Dave and co. and their impressive stack of amplifiers. We quite liked Mike Smith. He had a good voice and would sit on a stool at his Vox Continental organ and deliver his distinctive vocals, but the rest were a pretty bland bunch. As the roadies were setting the stage for Dave's show, Eric would appear and assist with the positioning of the speakers. When no one was looking, our naughty bass player would push the stacks behind the theatre's proscenium arch so that they were facing into a brick wall. As the tour progressed, so did Eric's tactics. He took to cutting their guitar leads. I was adjusting my drums backstage when I saw a hand coming out from under the stage drapes holding a pair of wire cutters. Eric! Another time he was seen high above the stage throwing stink bombs onto the five as they performed.

All the artists and musicians travelled on one of Timpsons' coaches – apart from Dave Clark, who travelled in his E-type

Jag. A few dates into the tour, Dave stopped the bus, climbed on board and demanded to know who was sabotaging his show. Silence. I glanced sideways at Eric. 'They can't prove nothing,' he whispered, and he was right. He never did get caught.

On a rare day off from the two-shows-a-night tour, we went into Abbey Road's Studio Two. The date was April 13, 1964 and between 2.30 p.m. and 10 p.m. we recorded 'Here I Go Again', 'Baby That's All', 'Time For Love' and 'Don't You Know'. The following day we caught up with the tour bus outside the London Transport canteen near the Planetarium and hit the road again.

A week or so later at the Gaumont in Doncaster, the stage manager came rushing into The Hollies' dressing room: 'Scrivs has been hit in the eye by something. It's an emergency – Bob, can you take over?' It was fashionable at that time for kids to throw sweets and candy onto the stage and The Trebletones' drummer, John Scrivens, had been hit by a rock-hard humbug. I dashed onto the stage, stood behind the injured drummer, took his right-hand stick and continued playing along with the band. As Scrivs moved off his stool I slid on, relieving him of his left stick while continuing to accompany singer Mark Wynter. After a couple more songs, Mark looked round and with an astonished expression, mouthed: 'What are you doing here?' He'd been totally unaware of the changeover. I played drums for them for another six nights until Scriv's eye was fixed.

WE'RE THROUGH

Words and Music by L. RANSFORD.

Recorded by **THE HOLLIES** on PARLOPHONE

HOLLIES MUSIC LTD
37, Soho Square, London, W.1.
sole selling agents:
SOUTHERN MUSIC PUBLISHING CO.LTD., 8, Denmark Street, London, W.C.2.

2/6

CHAPTER SIX:

The Beat of a British Drum

Saturday, May 9:

The Hollies' new single got Four HIT votes on BBC TV's *Juke Box Jury*.

*J*uke Box Jury was a big Saturday night show, and each week the panel of four voted on new records – hit or miss. Four hits was as good as it got!

Roadie Jay Vickers insisted that we buy a massive American Ford Galaxy Ranch Wagon from Hampstead Motors and we succumbed to his wishes. Eric had christened Jay 'Freddie Flea' and the name stuck. I have fond memories of dapper little Freddie crooning Sinatra or Chuck Berry songs as he drove us along, sitting behind the wheel of the left-hand drive gas guzzler wearing his cool shades. 'Riding along in my automobile…' Meanwhile John MacDonald from Stockport, 'Johnny Mac', was hired as equipment roadie to drive the van and set up our gear ahead of time, so that it would all be there for us when we arrived.

In June Tony and I flew to Majorca for a holiday. We stayed at the Club Nautico in Palma right on the harbour, where Hollywood actor Errol Flynn's yacht was still moored by the hotel five years after he had died. We met a guy from Leeds who was the captain of Madam Renault's floating gin palace anchored out in the bay. A few days later Madam sent word via her captain that she would like to meet us. We were whisked across the bay in a beautiful speedboat and were soon standing before the old girl, who was sitting on some sort of throne. Very Miss Havisham. At that point we realised we had been summoned to entertain her. So, Tony strummed on a Spanish guitar, I faffed around on a pair of bongos, and after a few rounds of 'Olé' and stamping of feet, we were soon back in the bar at Club Nautico. In 1964 the Majorcan village of Magaluf was a quiet beach with a single wooden cabin and a couple of hotels. I noted that the taxi driver who drove us there and back had a pistol in his glove compartment. He was a Franco Special – one of the General's many secret police.

The break was fun but by July we were back on the road and in bonnie Scotland again, where we sailed across to Dunoon on an old steam boat.

The Wellington Hotel

Dunoon

Dear Mum and Dad

Just had supper and now I'm in bed. Played Hawick last night – it was a bit rough, but a good gig. Nice day today, although it's much cooler up here.

Passed through Selkirk, Peebles, Carstairs and Paisley – then on to Gourock. I think that's where we got the ferry to Dunoon – cost us 30 shillings. Could just see the Holy Loch submarines. Plenty of Yanks up here in Dunoon. I remember being here on holiday when I was young – it's the place where they unloaded the coal barges near the open-air theatre. I got my best jacket burned by Jay's cigarette today. He threw it out of the car window and it blew back in and onto my jacket.

We were getting to know our new roadie Johnny Mac. He was an entertaining character who liked to drink, and while doing so would recount tales of his days in the army. All very 'muck and bullets'. The following day we drove by Loch Earn where we hired some speedboats and had a great time racing and ramming one another. One boat sprang a leak, so we decided that we had better move on as we had a gig at the Dundee Palais that evening.

The summer of 1964 was easy and enjoyable. Gigs in Jersey and Guernsey were followed by a leisurely boat journey back to Weymouth on the mainland where we started a month's season topping the bill at the Gaumont theatre. We rented a large terraced house where I had a cosy bedroom on the third floor. Johnny Mac's room was up in the attic and everyone seemed happy. A lovely girl would cook for us, and it was a stroll along the sea front to the theatre. Graham's Rose and Allan's wife, Jeni, were also in residence, plus a couple of beautiful Afghan hounds, Missy and Sultan, who belonged to Eric and Graham. Travelling musicians owning sensitive, demanding dogs was not a good idea. I would come down from my room in the morning, barefooted and heading for the kitchen. One of the poor creatures would often deposit a wet or sticky welcome on the first floor landing causing my first brew of the day to be delayed while I cleaned up the mess.

After the first week, the routine was getting boring. With two short stage appearances a night, we were spending more time in the pub than onstage. And each night Johnny Mac would roll back to the house drunk and start a row, which usually ended with his party piece: throwing the van keys on the floor and offering his resignation.

Sitting in the kitchen late one night, Mac introduced us to the art of igniting farts. When the volunteer fartee was ready, the lights would be turned out and, as wind was being passed, the oven gas lighter was applied to the volunteer's tail pipe area. The ignition resulted in a lovely blue glow. For health and safety reasons, methane providers were advised to keep their underpants on, though the more daring would go for the flamethrower effect, which required bare-backed delivery. Though risky, the results could be quite spectacular.

One hot day Rose and Jeni had hired a rowing boat and went out into Weymouth Bay, relaxing. Eric came along and rocked the girl's boat so hard that it capsized and they fell into the deep water. Eric thought it great fun and he sailed away, laughing, leaving them floundering around. When Allan and Graham heard what had happened to their loved ones, they angrily confronted our bass-playing prankster, who shrugged off the episode as 'just a bit of fun'. They were not happy.

As tensions simmered in the summer heat, and we approached the end of our month-long stay, Graham had a major disagreement with Jay and Freddie Flea was no more. His replacement was Rod Shields. The first time I set eyes on Rod was when he entered Studio Two at Abbey Road. I was chatting to Eric when the heavy studio door on the ground floor slowly opened. 'Ah, what have we got here?' Eric said, rubbing his hands. 'I bet it's that new geezer that Coco [Michael Cohen] has sent down for the roadie job.'

After the recording session we had arranged to meet in the bar of the Carlisle House Hotel on Devonshire Terrace, where we were staying. We chatted to Rod and all was well, until Eric decided to buy him a drink.

'You a drinking man, Rod?'

'Well, er, I quite enjoy an occasional sherry,' Rod replied politely.

'I bet I can drink more glasses of sherry than you. Set 'em up barman, I'm paying,' Eric declared.

I tried to warn our new tour manager, but he seemed intent on trying to impress Eric and the assembled band of onlookers. Eventually, the sherry began to take its toll on Rod, or 'Doddy', as Eric now addressed him. It was time to rescue the inebriated one and help him up to his bedroom, which was a little stuffy and in need of ventilation. Eric slid the big sash window open: 'Here, get some fresh air,' he said, half walking, half dragging poor Rod to the window. With his victim's head and shoulders overhanging the street below, Eric then slid the window down, trapping his limp body. He then pulled down Rod's pants, shouting triumphantly: "Ere everyone, come and 'ave a look at Dod's arse!'

The Ford Galaxy Ranch Wagon had been an unreliable whale of a motor that had seen better days. New roadie Rod Shields stamped his identity on the job and chose a form of transport that suited his personality – in other words a conveyance that was upright, forthright and dependable. A grey-blue Austin Westminster fitted the bill.

Rod, always smart in his crisp shirt and tie, drove the Westminster at a sedate pace. During the journey, Eric would lean forward and quietly draw patterns on the back of Rod's white shirt collar with a ballpoint pen. Another of Eric's tricks was to pick his nose and put the crow on top of the gear stick and wait for poor Rodders to change gear. Around that time Rod would sport a three-quarter length padded, nylon car coat. When Rod protested at Eric's latest outrage, our bass player would taunt him with the phrase: 'Never trust a fella in a foamback.'

We had bought a brand new dark blue Ford Thames van to transport our gear. Fortunately for Rod, Eric decided to ride with Johnny Mac to keep him company, giving Rod a welcome break from Haydock's harassment.

In September we began a nationwide tour, supported by Freddie & The Dreamers, a band fronted by the wildly energetic Freddie Garrity. As usual the artists travelled on a Timpsons bus. The journeys were made more bearable by the presence of Marianne Faithfull and her companion, Mary. On September 22 our tour bus arrived at the Castle Hotel in Taunton. It was a beautiful English, autumn day, and almost everyone had decided to go to the local cinema as we had a rare afternoon off, but Rod, Marianne and I remained at the hotel. It was lunchtime, so we decided to eat in the hotel dining room. Marianne chose the wine with care and, after a leisurely lunch, we went outside, spread a blanket on the grass and lay out on the hotel lawn. Rod took a photo using my trusty old Agfa Optima, capturing the happy pair perfectly.

Another Hollies nationwide theatre tour followed. Also on the bill were The Dixie Cups, Heinz, The Tornados, and Jess Conrad. The only thing memorable about those sixteen dates was Ritchie Blackmore's guitar playing in Heinz's band. Ritchie was the best and, at the time, the fastest guitarist I'd seen. His onstage thrusting, devil-may-care showmanship exemplified all that was good about the British rock scene in the early 1960s. The lead singer was a sideshow. Blackmore was the one to watch.

That tour ended at Coventry Theatre on November 8 and the following night we played at the Royal Albert Hall on a *Top Beat* concert, supported by The Kinks and The Pretty Things.

Gerry's Christmas Cracker was quite a production. Gerry & The Pacemakers topped the bill, and the show opened at the Liverpool Odeon on December 26, 1964. As with all the rock tours of that period, there would be two performances each night at 6.15 p.m. and 8.30 p.m., apart from Sundays, which we had off. The following week it was the Leeds Odeon and the third week was the Glasgow Odeon. Along with The Hollies and Gerry & The Pacemakers were Cliff Bennett & The Rebel Rousers, The Fourmost, Tommy Quickly & The Remo Four, and Danny Williams.

At the beginning of each performance, a giant Christmas cracker would rise up out of the orchestra pit and part in the middle as the compère introduced each act. 'Who do you think of when I say "Moon River"?' Before the audience could answer 'Danny Williams', a Liverpudlian voice from inside the cracker chirped: 'Henry Mancini' (the writer of the song), prompting stifled laughter from everyone inside. The huge cracker trundled open and crooner Danny Williams stepped out, his thunder somewhat dampened. The huge tube then closed and the next performers prepared to exit on cue.

1964 had been an amazing year. High-octane, exciting, full of new experiences and people, and my first full year as a full-time pro musician. And 1965 looked set to be more of the same. On January 3, our Sunday off, we boarded the train from Lime Street Station and travelled down to London and Abbey Road to re-record 'Yes I Will'. We had already recorded the Gerry Goffin/Russ Titelman song on December 15, after hearing the demo acetate disc that featured Carole King's distinctive voice, but we weren't happy with our performance. Producer Ron booked the studio for an evening session, so that we could have another crack at the song. The session went to plan with Tony using a Phantom twelve-string guitar given to him by the makers, Vox. It was an improvement on our earlier effort and became The Hollies' first single of 1965, although EMI cocked up and included the scrapped version on our LP *Hollies' Greatest*, which was number one on the album charts for ten weeks in 1968.

After staying overnight at the Hyde Park Towers Hotel, we travelled back north on the Monday morning to begin our second week of *Gerry's Christmas Cracker*. The show's promoter, Beatles manager Brian Epstein, was also on our train, the plush Leeds Pullman, and before we had pulled out of King's Cross Station, he had invited us all to join him for lunch in the dining car.

He seemed quite shy and spoke in gentlemanly, soft tones. I don't recall any of the conversation over that lunch, but he paid the bill. Rumour had it that he was keen to sign The

Hollies, but we heard later that John Lennon had warned him off.

The third and final week of *Christmas Cracker* was at the Odeon in Glasgow. We stayed at the Central Hotel by the station. Sometimes Allan Clarke would provide the after-hours entertainment back in the hotel lounge, performing magic tricks. He was good, and you could see the joy that he got as he baffled his eager victims. When he'd exhausted his magical repertoire, usually around midnight, he revealed his newest pursuit, hypnotism.

I don't know how he learned the art, but on several occasions, usually north of the border, I witnessed susceptible young ladies falling under our lead singer's spell. An American by the name of Nancy, who worked for *Fabulous* magazine, on Allan's direction, seemed to drift back in time and act out her childhood, so much so that her voice would change to that of a little girl. 'Within this circle you will feel no pain,' he declared in his soothing Hollies' frontman voice, as he gently marked out an area on the woman's arm with his forefinger. Then, to demonstrate his powers, he pricked her arm with a pin. Silence. No recoil of the arm, not even the slightest squeak. Then, after counting down, with a commanding click of his fingers, Allan brought her back into the real world and she behaved as though nothing had happened.

Back in London in late January we appeared on *Ready Steady Go!* Our usual routine was to go back to the hotel and sleep for a few hours, then, when the time was right, assemble in the bar and, after a couple of Bacardis or brandy and Cokes, we'd make our way to the Ad Lib Club. This late night disco was one of the first 'in' places, where artists and celebs would hang out. In the early 1960s it served the best spare ribs in town. Towards the end of night, the chef would come out and dance among the punters, wearing his white outfit and the tall hat which seemed to defy gravity: a wobbly, rhythmic tower atop the beaming West Indian's head. Paul McCartney and John Lennon were often guests there, along with Paul's girlfriend Jane Asher and John's wife Cynthia. On this particular night it was very late and the staff signalled closing time. As the darkened atmosphere became illuminated by the cleaner's lights, Lennon got up and shouted: 'Let's all go round to Alma's for a pill!' Meaning the party-throwing Miss Cogan, at whose house The Beatles were regular visitors.

A few weeks later, rehearsing in the ITV studios for yet another *Ready Steady Go!* appearance, a chap by the name of Phil Frankland introduced himself as we hung around between camera line-ups. He said nice things about my drumming and ended up sweet-talking me into agreeing to use Premier drums exclusively. Within days I had signed a three-year endorsement deal, which stated, amongst other things, that The Hollies' drum set would display the Premier logo at all our performances, including TV appearances. In return, Premier would use pictures of Bobby Elliott and The Hollies in their drum adverts and shop displays. Being an Englishman, I was swayed by Phil's patriotic pitch; how could I be part of the pioneering British Music Invasion of the New World and not play British drums? We should march to the beat of instruments made by skilled British craftsmen. I should fly the flag and promote our country's exports. I was all for it.

They took my treasured American-made, silver sparkle, Ludwig Super Classic drums away and gave me two Premier kits. And although they kept their word on the adverts and PR, I soon realised that I had made a big mistake. The Premier drums were not a patch on the Ludwig. The snare drum was a disaster because the snare strings kept snapping. The patented 'disappearing bass drum spurs' kept disappearing during our live performances. It was depressing, frustrating and made me very angry. Fortunately, they didn't get my baby – the brass-shelled Ludwig 400 snare drum that was still in my spare traps case. After the failure of two Premier snare drums, my confidence in them was shot and I continued to use the L400, much to the Premier boss's annoyance. I would get phone calls after they had seen The Hollies on TV. 'You weren't using one of our snare drums on *Top Of The Pops.*' They were right. That Ludwig snare drum was heard on almost every Hollies hit record and album track throughout the 1960s and 1970s.

Both Keith Moon, drummer with The Who, and Mitch Mitchell, of The Jimi Hendrix Experience, told me that they too succumbed to the patriotic Premier sweet talk and surrendered their Ludwig Super Classics that were replaced by Premier equipment.

In my teenage apprentice days, I had designed and made a special spur system that would clamp to the old Premier lightweight flush-based hi-hat stand. My device was angled to dig into the floor, solidly holding the stand in position, thus preventing it from slipping away from the player. When I became a Premier endorsee, I naïvely thought that the company's research and development department would be interested in testing a useful modification to their product and I proudly sent my invention to the factory. Sadly, I didn't get a thank you or an acknowledgement. Was it lost or misplaced? Maybe they just couldn't be bothered to improve their obsolete product?

The best thing about Premier drums was the tough, gleaming chrome finish on the hardware and fitments. The company that specialised in that process was not Premier, but another firm based across the road in South Wigston near Leicester.

From 1965 to 1968, Hollies hits – 'I'm Alive', 'Look Through Any Window', 'I Can't Let Go', 'Bus Stop', 'Stop Stop Stop', 'On A Carousel', 'Carrie Anne' and all the albums in-between – were graced by the sound of the Elliott-tuned Premier percussion and a Ludwig snare drum. But maybe I'm being a little too critical. Listening to those classic tracks today, I think they sound pretty damn good. Armed with drums that were made in the heart of England, The Hollies played an important role in the musical invasion of America at a time when British bands began to rule the world.

YES I WILL

Words & Music by GERRY GOFFIN and RUSS TITELMAN

Recorded on PARLOPHONE R 5232 by

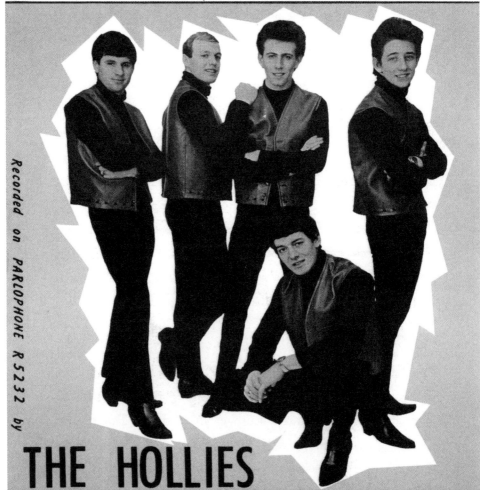

THE HOLLIES

SCREEN GEMS - COLUMBIA MUSIC INC.

SCREEN GEMS-COLUMBIA MUSIC LTD

Sole Selling Agents:- CAMPBELL CONNELLY & CO. LTD. 10, Denmark Street, London W.C.2.

2/6

CHAPTER SEVEN:

We Came, We Saw, We Partied

New York, Good Friday 1965, and backstage in the Paramount Theatre, I had happened upon Little Richard with a cop holding a gun to his head.

Our first time in the Big Apple, and I thought I was about to witness the tragic end of a world-famous star. But Little Richard seemed undaunted by the situation. Half in, half out of the lift, he quivered with rage. The stage manager was trying to calm him down, but to no effect. He was sweating and hollering and shaking his head, so much so that his wig tilted forward, jiggled around, and slipped over his eyes. I was frozen to the spot. Would the cop actually shoot? The pistol was cocked and I was next in line if the slug went clean through Richard's neck. I moved back a step, still riveted by the scene. A movie was being played out within touching distance, only there were no lights or cameras. Was it really happening? Had the transatlantic jet lag had a *Billy Liar* effect on me?

Eventually, the overwrought star was led away to his dressing room and ordered to pack his bags. It appeared that his stage performance had overrun wildly for the third time. After the first show, stage manager Bob Levine had warned Richard that if he went over his allotted time again, the sixteen-man King Curtis Orchestra would blast into action and play over his act. This had just happened, and the rock legend had gone ballistic. He'd run from the stage, arms outstretched, screaming abuse and going straight for Levine's throat. But Bob was prepared, and a couple of security guards stepped forward and grabbed Richard, who continued to shout and swear as his feet left the ground.

Sadly, he left the show along with his band, which included an unknown guitarist by the name of Jimi Hendrix. This eviction was possibly a blessing in disguise for Jimi since if Richard and his band had not been thrown off the show, he may not have had to find work elsewhere. Fortuitously, Jimi was spotted some nights later by The Animals' bass player Chas Chandler. The following day Chas came into our dressing room at the Paramount excitedly proclaiming in his Geordie accent: 'I've just seen this guy down the Café Au Go Go. He played the guitar with his fuckin' teeth.' Thanks in part to Chas's foresight, the seed had been sown and Jimi Hendrix was on his way to becoming a global giant of rock. A legend.

Chas took Jimi across the pond and introduced him to English musicians Mitch Mitchell and Noel Redding. Hendrix's time in London served him well; he was able to be more outrageous than the confines of his home country might have allowed. A touch of Keith Moon-style rock-daring had been added to his anarchic high-octane stage performance. I watched him set fire to his Fender Stratocaster during an early air-breaking performance at the Bag O'Nails on Kingly Street, a club located between Carnaby Street and Regent Street in London, after which the newly formed Hendrix Experience carried the torch back across the Atlantic. We had witnessed the emergence of Jimi Hendrix, superstar. Flanked by two pallid British musicians, he returned to his homeland to be lauded by the 1960s American rock aficionados.

British bands and musicians loved US blues, rock and modern jazz, which have been my penchant. We had been playing music influenced by Americans for most of our lives, unthinkingly and enthusiastically repackaging what we had absorbed and adding a twist of British flair and bravado just for good measure.

The British Invasion had begun in 1964, led from the front by The Beatles. They were the first with boots on the ground and the Limey landing craft followed, disgorging an assortment of groups and artists including The Dave Clark Five, The Animals, The Rolling Stones and The Hollies. About twenty years earlier, on the run-up to the Allied invasion of Europe, American GIs – 'Overpaid, oversexed and over here' –

had wooed the women of England by offering them stockings made of nylon. In the peacetime of the 1960s, the British key to the delights of the New World were hit records made of vinyl, crafted by an army of Rock Tommies.

The doctor had vaccinated me against smallpox in readiness for that first visit to the States. No jab – no entry. It was quite a palaver in the mid-sixties. The doctor's signed verification had to be carried in your passport. We all had the inoculations, the side effects of which could be quite debilitating. Eric and I were quite badly affected and we had to call the doctor while on the road up in Scotland. A couple of Hollies gigs were pulled – it was that bad. Eventually the sickness passed and after playing a gig in Tunbridge Wells, we travelled to Heathrow and checked into the Ariel Hotel for our departure to New York the following morning.

On Wednesday, April 14 we were all packed and ready. The excitement was building as we approached the airport check-in. Not so fast though. The rule was that we had to be exchanged for an American act coming to Britain, and there was no one available. Before The Beatles' incredible success in the States there wasn't really a problem. Although the Brits craved American talent, the Yanks weren't too keen on the musical fare on offer from old Blighty. Now that the US entitled 'British Invasion' was under way, the tables had turned, and it was pretty much one-way traffic from England to America. Hence the new rule. We had to wait at the airport, on standby, until an American exchange artist could be found.

Our agent Colin Hogg, from Harold Davison's office, kept us informed as we sat and waited. After two days of sitting around, shuttling between the Ariel Hotel and Heathrow, we had permission to fly. It seems that we'd been exchanged for the Count Basie Orchestra. Five Brits swapped for sixteen Americans! We were elated. Our work permits had been granted, and there was a huge sense of relief as we boarded the BOAC Super VC10.

On arrival at JFK Airport, re-named in honour of the assassinated President Kennedy, we were whisked straight to the Paramount Theatre. We were late, so we'd missed the thousands of teenagers circling the theatre, blocking traffic and breaking box office windows in their eagerness to get inside. They had started lining up for the Good Friday 9 a.m. show at midnight on Thursday. But all those kids weren't there for us, or any of the other rock acts and artists on the bill. They were clamouring for a comedian who went by the name of Soupy Sales. Milton Supman was also a TV personality, actor and jazz aficionado, famous for a children's lunchtime show called *Lunch With Soupy Sales*, which had been running for the past ten years.

Morris Levy, the theatre's new operator, welcomed us and we made our apologies for arriving late. He was a sharp, larger than life New Yorker with a tale to tell. Maybe he noted a refreshing innocence as we enthused about our first visit to the Big Apple and all the sounds and smells so different from home.

I remember Graham commenting on the bell ring on the American phones in our hotel rooms. 'They sound just like they do in the movies,' he said, as the two of us began exploring the vast backstage area of the theatre. Red-painted concrete steps led us down into the darkened bowels of the theatre. At the end of a passageway was a steel door which we dragged open. We couldn't see a thing. It was quiet. Chattering excitedly, we peered through the aromatic atmosphere, surprised when a lone voice drawled: 'Hey, where's Ringo?' It came from a member of the all-star sixteen-piece King Curtis Orchestra, which was assembled on the huge lowered stage. There was laughter all round. As the chuckling subsided, we realised it was showtime. 'One, two, three...' Curtis, resplendent in his shiny suit and holding his trademark saxophone, had counted in the horns and rhythm section. Nash and I ducked back as the huge platform jolted and was winched upwards to stage level. The orchestra was joined by a bevy of dancers for the opening production number. We dashed back up the steps to stage level to peer excitedly at the big band and hear the sound of King blowing improvised licks on his sax over the strident, uptempo barrage provided by the assembled trumpets, trombones and saxophones. I felt elated. The atmosphere in the Paramount crackled, leaving me tingling and exhilarated.

I was under the same roof as some of New York's finest jazz musicians, the likes of whom had inspired me since I was a twelve-year-old kid. I remembered doing my homework lying on the floor next to the radiogram in our modest family quarters beside the grocery shop. That was over a decade earlier. Back then I was listening to another opening fanfare, Duke Ellington's 'Take The 'A' Train', the signature tune for *The Jazz Hour* on the Voice of America radio station transmitting on the shortwave from Tangier.

The headliner Soupy Sales claimed to have been hit by 20,000 custard pies during his years in his children's show. Yet, surprisingly, his guests included stars like The Temptations, Sammy Davis Jr., The Supremes and Frank Sinatra.

Each day in the Paramount, Soupy entertained the Easter gathering with various song and dance routines. 'The Mouse' was his current record release, so during his performance, he bared his teeth in rodent fashion, raised his hands to his ears and wiggled his fingers in time with the music. This was enough to send the audience screaming and jumping. Soupy's most fervent admirers threw popcorn, shaving cream and apples at him.

The *Soupy Sales Easter Show* ran for about a week over the holiday period. The theatre doors would be opened at 8.30 each morning and at 9 a.m. a film would be screened, *The Wackiest Ship In the Army*, starring Jack Lemmon and Ricky Nelson. This would serve as a sort of intermission, to give the kids time to spend their money on popcorn and ice cream. The alternating film/live show formula would run through the day to late evening, which is why it was so important that none of the acts overran. Artists were only allowed to perform two numbers each. The Hollies, Shirley Ellis, The Exciters, Dee

Dee Warwick, Roddie Joy et al. obeyed the stage manager's directive… but not Little Richard.

The show's compère, Hal Jackson, would introduce us, skilfully building up tension in the audience and concluding with: 'And now, fasten your seat belts, from little old England, here come The Hollies!' On hearing that, I would scramble up a short ladder onto the elevated stage and Ray Lucas would move off his stool to allow me to get behind his drums. The rest of The Hollies would run onstage, Tony and Eric would plug in as fast as they could, and we were into 'Rockin' Robin'. As the week progressed, musicians from the King Curtis band, especially guitarist Cornell Dupree, would join in and subtly add to our performance. We loved the cool, uplifting, empathic feeling that those guys transmitted.

The Animals were in town and would join us in our dressing room where we'd exchange tales about our days in the Big Apple. They enthused about the famous Peppermint Lounge. A few years earlier the twist dance craze had started there. It was also an established celebrity hangout.

Our dressing room was upstairs next to King Curtis's room. Both doors were usually open wide, so I'd pop in and chat to King or his valet and KC's small son, Curtis. I remember seeing dozens of pairs of gleaming patent leather shoes lining the floor and a selection of cool suits carefully placed on hangers. KC was always welcoming, and we'd chat about music, his band and the behaviour of record companies. On the final day as we were saying goodbye,

I asked him to sign his photo in my theatre programme. He wrote: 'To my friend, Bob'. I still treasure that sweet memento, along with one of his albums signed by King and his drummer, Ray, who generously allowed me to play his black Ludwig drums during our allotted two songs. I liked to hang out with Ray between shows, and one day I suggested that we go for a cup of coffee in the stage door luncheonette. Ray gave me the impression that he couldn't go in there, and instead we walked further along the block to a diner. I realised later, much to my discomfort, that there was an unspoken colour bar in operation in the city.

We were all open-mouthed in wonder at being in New York. It had a certain smell. The buses roared noisily. 'Don't Walk' signs ordered pedestrians to halt at the kerb edge. The words 'please' and 'thank you' were rarely uttered. No time for niceties. The locals would snap: 'Give me a hot dog' or demand this or that. But there were also civilised pleasantries. On sitting down to eat, be it in a humble luncheonette (I love that name) or a serious restaurant, the waitress would give you the menu and at the same time pour you a complimentary glass of iced water. Throughout the meal your coffee cup would be regularly topped up. My notion at the time was that coffee was the reason why our New World cousins were sharper and could talk faster than your average Limey, who had probably been steadily tea-bagged from birth. After several shots of supercharged caffeine, I could bullshit with the best of 'em. A bit more stimulating than a cup of PG Tips.

The Metropole Café in Times Square was a venue that I'd heard of throughout my modern jazz-loving teenage years. So many world-famous musicians had played there. As I was walking from the Paramount Theatre to our hotel, the Americana on Seventh Avenue, my eyes did a Tom and Jerry cartoon pop out: Boing! There was the Metropole Café and the banner above the entrance shouted: 'Gene Krupa!' The very first vinyl EP that I bought from the Electron record shop in Burnley featured Gene. The 45 rpm disc would plop down from the Garrard autochanger on my parents' Bush radiogram. I would spring noisily into action, armed with my drumsticks – a pair of Nelson Grammar School paint brush handles – rattling along on a battered Oxo tin I had modified with knicker elastic and bits of my Meccano construction set. I was in full Krupa mode, driving along the swinging Benny Goodman band as 'we' performed the drum feature, 'Sing, Sing, Sing'.

Gene had been one of the most stylish and influential drummers of the thirties, forties and early fifties. There was no entrance fee at the Metropole, a cover charge was added to the price of your drink, so in I stepped. The fug of cigarette smoke hit me. Today, The Hollies' lighting technician strives for a similar effect with his fog machine in order to accent our light show. Here, it seemed that everyone inside was smoking a cigarette – no special effects needed and no health and safety in the sixties.

There he was, up on the long narrow runway of a bandstand, seated behind his white marine pearl Slingerland drum set, Mr

Gene Krupa. He was brushing away on his Radio King snare drum, seemingly oblivious to the throng of Bud-quaffing New Yorkers. I needed to get closer, so I edged towards the bar. By wafting a bunch of dollar bills, I eventually got the attention of one of the wonderfully grumpy, uniformed bartenders and ordered a glass of beer. Now I was directly in front of the ruddy-faced 'Drummin' Man' and could scrutinise my hero over the rim of my glass of Michelob. He still had a good head of hair, but there was just one sax player. They were a duo. Sadly, this was all that was left of the great sixteen-piece Gene Krupa orchestra. His matinee idol looks had been swooned over by boppers and bobby soxers alike. Now, a couple of decades on, the assembled guzzlers were more interested in talking and smoking. After watching him play a few tunes, I finished my beer and headed back to our hotel. Later I wished I had hung around. Maybe I could have chatted with the great man.

Standing before Gene had been something special. In my eyes, he was the figurehead of swing jazz. Only later did I realise that I had witnessed Krupa's Last Stand – the last gasp of the four-on-the-floor American music that I had loved and listened to when I was a kid in the little shop at Pike Hill. Mr Krupa and his contemporaries were the ones who had propelled me onto The Hollies' drum stool.

During that same trip to New York, I saw Gerry Mulligan and Dizzy Gillespie at the Village Gate, Cannonball Adderley at the Blue Note, Kenny Dorham with Billy Higgins on drums at Slugs. I witnessed a wonderful, intimate performance by the master of the tenor sax Stan Getz as he casually rested his butt against a high stool at the Café Au Go Go and flirted with an attractive blonde sitting by the bandstand. I also saw bebop drummer Max Roach at the same venue with his wife, singer Abbey Lincoln. But the coolest image from NYC, still etched in my memory, combines my favourite car of the period and one of jazz's most enigmatic bandleaders. Early one evening, as I was standing outside the Village Vanguard looking at the list of forthcoming jazz attractions, a black Chevy Corvette Stingray approached. The top was down and it glided to a halt right next to me. In the driving seat was jazz great Charlie Mingus. He climbed out, wearing a long black leather coat. Next to him, in the passenger seat, was his precious instrument, the double bass. The Mingus Quintet were going be performing that night. I followed the great man as he carried his instrument into the club and onto the low stage. No one bothered me, and it was early, so I just sat at the nearest table and watched as the quintet gathered together. The club was now opening for business and the punters were drifting in, ordering drinks in readiness for the Mingus onslaught. Eventually, the ensemble roared into life. I was almost within touching distance of the two horn players, and over to my right was drummer Dannie Richmond. At one point he added colour to his drum solo by bizarrely shouting: 'Goldfinger, Goldfinger, Double O Seven.' My evening was complete.

A year later, we were again working in New York and Tony and I had been to Manny's Music store, as we usually did when we were in town. I'd check out the drums, Tony the guitars. Walking through Times Square, we passed the Metropole to see which jazz great might be appearing. Instead, we were confronted by 'Tonite – Go-Go Dancers' backed up by life-size images of tasselled young women. Almost overnight, the jazz era had ended. Another year on, the old bartenders were gone and the Metropole banner now announced 'Topless Dancers'.

Morris 'Mo' Levy, the head of Roulette Records and owner of the Roundtable club, had an office backstage at the Paramount. He was the promoter of the current show. He seemed to like us and between performances we would wander into his den for a chat and maybe a cup of coffee. His bubbly blonde secretary, Karen, was chatty and welcoming. Although Morris was a larger than life character, we had no idea at the time that he was mafia, although the sign behind his desk – 'Oh Lord, please give me a bastard with talent' – should have provided a clue. More recently, I learned that Levy was the main inspiration during the creation of *The Sopranos* TV series. He was a real life Tony Soprano. Our new best friend had ripped off dozens of American rock acts, dating back to the mid-1950s – and The Hollies escaped unscathed.

Morris had co-founded the world-famous Birdland jazz club. When I told him that I grew up listening to the legendary jazz musicians who had played in his venue, he showered me with free jazz LPs from his Roulette record label. One night when the theatre had closed, he invited us to the Roundtable club. Belly dancers were performing and the booze was flowing. Before long, an amusing sideshow began as a sozzled guy in a business suit tried to ingratiate himself with the gyrating buxom belly dancer. She was shaking her booty right under his nose, and he was skidding around, spilling his bourbon and Coke, hypnotised by her snake-like movements. It was hilarious, and as far as we were concerned, he was the star of the show. Sadly, the management didn't share our opinion. The bouncers moved in and the poor chap was dragged across the floor. 'Heavy hand upon my collar throws me in the street...' comes from our 1966 hit, the Clarke, Hicks and Nash composition 'Stop Stop Stop'. 'She's the girl with cymbals on her fingers entering through the door'. Check out the lyrics and there you have it – a masterful illustration of the evening's events at the Roundtable by The Hollies front line of songwriters.

During that first American trip, we appeared on NBC's TV rock show *Hullabaloo* at the Rockefeller Plaza. The Paramount kindly allowed us time off so that we could perform on the show, which was recorded on Friday, April 23. The Mindbenders were also appearing and Ric Rothwell let me use his drums. Between rehearsals there was a lot of hanging around, and we'd sit and chat with other artists on the show. The Hollies had recorded 'You Must Believe Me', which was written by Curtis Mayfield, and now here we were, hanging out with the man himself and his band, The Impressions. Seated nearby were The Ronettes. What a way to pass the time chatting to the gorgeous threesome Estelle, Ronnie and Nedra, who were the major girl band in the sixties.

An animated George Hamilton proclaimed: 'Here they are for the first time on *Hullabaloo*, The Hollies.' We lip-sync'd our way through 'Yes I Will', flanked by a pair of frenzied go-go dancers housed in cages.

While we were in the States, Levy made Bell Sound recording studios available to us so that we could make demo discs of three new songs that Graham, Allan and Tony had written. I'd always wanted to record in America and now, thanks to Morris, we had a trio of tracks as a memento. It was in this studio that Buddy Holly had recorded 'Rave On'. I used a battered old drum set that appeared to be a studio fixture; it looked as if it had lived there forever. I felt elated as I drummed away on a piece of musical history.

The day before we were due to fly home, Rod and I took the subway to the World's Fair. Ford Motor's Magic Skyway, the Turnpike of Tomorrow, was impressive. You could take your pick. I selected a mint Mustang that was slowly gliding along, nose to tail, amid the full range of 1965 Fords. Our tour manager Rod Shields filmed the occasion on his trusty 8 mm movie camera.

As we were saying our goodbyes to the acts and staff at the theatre, Morris asked if he could get us a farewell gift. We'd seen walkie-talkies in the shops round Times Square and thought we could have fun with them back home – but it was late and the stores were closed. No problem. Morris was on the phone and our walkie-talkies magically appeared.

The following day we flew home on a Qantas 707. Sadly, my case of cymbals had been lost, but that was the only thing that had gone astray. We had no complaints – just fond memories of our first visit to the Big Apple.

Krupa's Last Stand

They called us Limey weirdos as we dropped in from the skies
We landed 'mongst the straight cropped Yanks in their suits and ties
They pointed and they goaded; they couldn't believe their eyes
Then flower power struck in '67 and they all looked like Jesus Christ.

My hero Little Richard – to me there's no one greater
Cop's gun sticking in his neck in the Paramount elevator
'Those little white girls they love me,' he struggled and he cried,
And this was New York City, back in '65

Richard left the show with Hendrix talented and mighty
An Animal took Jimi under his wing and flew him back to Blighty
A bed of nails awaited, I first witnessed it with Bill
An air-breaking experience that gave the chattering class a thrill

Now the winds of change were blowing and a strong Westerly took hold
The Canadian blonde got Willy and led him from the fold
She served up both sides now over crumpet, tea and toast
He liked her capotasto and they headed for the Coast

We came, we saw, we partied; but most of all we played
And ended up preaching brotherly love to the land that freed the slaves
We hit them with our three-way, the front line was all smiles
Then a long cool woman shook her ass, and they were dancing in the aisles.

I'M ALIVE

Words and Music by CLINT BALLARD JR.

THE HOLLIES

Recording on PARLOPHONE R 5287

3/-

SHAPIRO, BERNSTEIN & CO. LTD

Warwick House, 38, Soho Square, London W.1.

Sole Selling Agents:- SOUTHERN MUSIC PUBLISHING CO. LTD. 8, Denmark St. London W.C.2.

CHAPTER EIGHT:

Bloodied Bouquets

After our trip to the States, we recorded our next single, 'I'm Alive'. It was released a couple of weeks after we recorded it in late May, and within a short time it was our first official number one.

It was fantastic, of course it was. We were happy and proud, as were our families. But the pace of our lives was such that there was barely time to stop and blink. We were on a non-stop merry-go-round of TV and radio shows, magazine photo shoots and live appearances.

We were playing one-nighters in Stockholm and Copenhagen then dashing back to London for ITV's *Ready Steady Go!* Then off to Bristol to appear on *Discs-A-Gogo* followed by the Light Programme's *Easy Beat*, a photo session for *Fab Magazine* or BBC radio's *Saturday Club*. A late night out down at the Scotch of St James might precede the next day's appearance on *Pop Inn* – a BBC lunchtime radio show live from the Paris Theatre on Lower Regent Street – before a dash north to Manchester to record yet another *Top Of The Pops*. On Thursday, November 25, 1965, we appeared on the 100th edition of *Top Of The Pops*, miming to 'I'm Alive'. The show was still being produced in the old church building on Dickenson Road in Manchester, and later the same day we were onstage in Blackpool's Winter Gardens.

I now had all I ever wanted, and I managed to keep my feet on the ground and enjoy it all. The stabilising ingredients were going home to Maureen, being close to my parents and the ability to rock on without going completely off the rails. I wasn't interested in drugs, though I could drink with the best of 'em. I was in the band because it meant I could spend my life following my drumming dream with people that I loved. My work was appreciated, and I was being rewarded both financially and spiritually. In my previous life, I'd experienced how the other half really lived, in the most dramatic, dangerous and graphic circumstances. I couldn't have been any further down the ladder, at the bottom of a coal mine, handling dangerous limb-breaking machinery 1,600 feet underground.

Looking through my 1960s diaries, I'm amazed at the number of times that we travelled by sleeper train, mainly from Marylebone to Manchester Piccadilly, but also from Glasgow to Manchester Victoria. We'd get aboard, go to sleep, and be woken by the attendant with a brew and a digestive biscuit. Happy days.

The Manchester Pullman used to operate out of the Central station. Today, the huge wrought iron single-span arched roof houses a convention complex. In the mid-1960s, diesel-hauled trains would run to St Pancras station in London, passing through the stunning scenery of the Derbyshire Dales, gliding beside gushing rivers, through ravines and tunnels, leaving me to marvel at the great engineering feats of our forefathers. Nowadays, the most beautiful stretches of track are enjoyed by walkers and cyclists. The tunnels have been boarded up to protect the public, who can only wonder at how exhilarating it must have felt roller-coasting in comfort while taking tea at 60 mph.

In the final days of 1965 we flew to Glasgow to perform on Scottish TV's short-lived rock programme, *Stramash!* After the show we caught the sleeper back to Manchester, where we performed on *Top Of The Pops*. On New Year's Eve we played at the New Century Hall, where roadie and van driver, Johnny 'Muck and Bullets' Mac, performed his final drunken act of throwing the van keys on the floor and handing in his notice.

Mac was replaced by Derek 'Dek' Whyment. A new era had begun. Dek was to become a sound buddy and soon proved to be a talented technician, able to fix anything.

On the night of January 4, Allan, Graham and Tony were adding their vocals to the French version of our new single, 'Look Through Any Window', at Abbey Road. Our record company thought it might help us break into the French market. We didn't have an official translation, but Clarkey said

111

that his brother-in-law spoke French. Fine. The guys sang the lyrics with convincing Gallic gusto, but as none of us *parlez vous'd* the lingo, the finished recording was sent across the Channel and that's the last we heard of it. I must admit, one of the lines *sur la pissoire* did sound a little salty though. Ah well. It was a number four hit for us, but the French version disappeared without trace, although you can find it on a 1988 album compilation called *Rarities*.

A day later we were travelling to Great Yarmouth with Rod Shields, attired in his blue insulated car coat, seated at the wheel of our Ford Zephyr. As the miles passed, a knocking sound could be heard coming from under the car. It was getting louder. Was it that naughty Eric teasing our loyal driver? Bang. No, the nearside back wheel had fallen off. 'Never trust a fella in a foamback,' cried Eric, helpfully. We were passing through the village of Saxmundham at the time, and we all slid slowly to one side of the car. Taxi for The Hollies!

On January 7 Cathy McGowan interviewed me live on *Ready Steady Go!*, after which I did a rundown of the current charts. I think that one of my lines was: '"My Ship is Coming In" by The Walker Brothers has finally run aground at number three.' Thanks, Bob, we'll let you know.

After the show, we dashed to Heathrow and caught a flight to Amsterdam, where we stayed at the Grand Krasnapolsky. The following day we had photos taken and did a couple of gigs near Rotterdam, and played The Hague and Eindhoven. On Monday we flew back to London, played to another wild crowd down in Chatham, and then caught the sleeper from Marylebone to Manchester Piccadilly where my dad picked me up and drove me home. I took every chance to go back home, even if it was only for only one night. The next day it was a Sheffield University gig, after which Graham drove me down to our London base at the Carlisle House Hotel. A couple of days later we recorded the Chip Taylor/Al Gorgoni song 'I Can't Let Go'. In case anyone is interested, Chip was actor Jon Voight's brother, so that made him Angelina Jolie's uncle.

Even though I was very much a home bird, I loved hanging out at the Scotch of St James. I'd discovered Mateus Rosé and was happy carousing with a variety of clubland regulars, including Allan, Keith Moon and Jimmy Tarbuck. The Cromwellian was another favourite haunt. The club had begun life as a gambling establishment, but a tightening of gambling laws meant it became a venue where I saw Patti LaBelle, Stevie Wonder, and Ike and Tina Turner play in the basement. Amazingly, these wonderful artists were struggling to find the prestigious work that they deserved. The British Invasion had hit hard in the States and things were not much better for them over here.

Our new roadie Derek Whyment, now christened Dek Duck, would accompany me, and we'd loll against the bar chatting to Jimmy Page while being entertained by the diminutive barman, Harry Hart. He drank Campari: 'Mine's a Camp, babe,' he would trill, when customers offered him a drink, and he would slosh a generous measure of his favourite tipple into a large, long-stemmed goldfish bowl. By midnight it would be full to overflowing with the red liquid, fruit and cucumber as Harry paraded up and down, delivering innuendos to the assembled loafers with vaudevillian aplomb. At first, I presumed that he was of average height, as he glided to and fro dispensing drinks, but when he stepped out from behind the bar, he shrank by about six inches. A specially constructed wooden walkway, his personal stage, enabled him to strut up and down with an impressive air of authority. His cry of: 'Drink up my babes, drink up my queens,' signalled the end of Harry-time and we'd move on to the Speakeasy.

It was a cold day at the end of January when we boarded the old American-built Icelandair Douglas DC-6 airliner at Glasgow airport. It was a prop-driven plane powered by four Pratt & Whitney piston engines. As I sat comfortably in my leather seat, I looked out from the aeroplane's large window at the engine's propellers. For a fleeting moment, my thoughts flashed back to my childhood adventure high up on the Pennine moors, frantically sawing away at the alloy propeller blades with my chums to earn a few bob from the scrap dealers. These engines were identical to the ones that powered the crashed B-24 Liberator bomber we used to visit all those years ago. Some of these DC-6 rivet-rattlers dated back to the end of World War II.

The plane positioned at the end of the runway, the pilot revved the engines up to full power. At maximum vibration, he released the brakes, we lumbered down the runway and lifted off to head north to Iceland. In those days, Reykjavík's airport was located below the surrounding mountains and it was a tricky approach. The pilot had to dive in at a steep angle, pull back on the stick, and drop the plane on the runway. It was scary, and to make matters worse, we were buffeted by severe turbulence and wind shear. There was great relief as we landed; my stomach had been seriously churned. That was probably the scariest landing I ever experienced.

We played a couple of shows in the city's modern theatre, and in-between I sat in on drums in a nearby jazz club.

Back home we played Stockton Fiesta to packed audiences for a full week, and in the afternoons we rehearsed a beautiful Clarke, Nash and Hicks song called 'Oriental Sadness', which became a track on our album *Would You Believe?*

On February 18 I was invited to Johnny Kidd's wedding party at his home in north London where artists and musicians mingled and chatted. Earlier that day Johnny had married Jean Complin at Caxton Hall. In the evening there was a friendly, informal vibe. There were various instruments lying around and Tom Jones got up to sing and invited me to play the drums for him. I don't recall what songs Tom performed, but I do remember what followed. Johnny (real name Fred Heath), flanked by his two small sons from his first marriage, sang 'I'll Never Get Over You'. It was an honour for me to play drums behind the guy who, along with his band The Pirates, had been an important influence on me and Tony.

Their sparse instrumentation – just guitar, bass and drums with no rhythm guitar – became the blueprint for our early Hollies instrumental sound.

It had all been going so well. Then the peace was broken when some guy began shouting at Tom Jones. It seems one of the guests had been caught in a clinch with the Welsh Sex Bomb. Her boyfriend was obviously not happy and there was a bit of a scuffle, nothing serious, but I bade farewell to the newlyweds and headed back to Carlisle House.

Tragically, Johnny was killed in a car crash just eight months later. He was still only thirty and it was a huge shock to all of us. Johnny Kidd was an original talent and a gifted musician. He had penned 'Shakin' All Over', a song that was not just a hit for him, but that was covered literally hundreds of times. It had been number one in the British charts for nineteen weeks. Thanks to Freddie Heath – or 'Heef' as Pirates drummer Clem Cattini called him – this record, engineered by Peter Bown (who later worked with The Hollies), marked the beginning of serious British rock. Even today 'Shakin' All Over' reverberates throughout the land from pubs and venues, as young bands try to emulate what was created sixty years ago.

Top Of The Pops had moved from Manchester to the BBC's Lime Grove studios in Shepherd's Bush. When we performed our latest single 'I Can't Let Go', which was on its way up the charts, I couldn't help feeling that *TOTP* had lost something in the move south.

Photographer Harry Goodwin was still part of the team and would travel down from Chorlton-cum-Hardy every week to badger all the appearing artists until he had a suitable image of them for the show's Top 20 rundown. Harry now had a sidekick, Ron Howard, who lived nearby. He had helped Harry keep his job by allowing him access to his photographic darkroom. Meanwhile, Mr Goodwin realised that he could boost his income by knocking off a few extra rolls of colour film for the thriving teenage magazine market. It was hilarious to hear his patter. Ron played the straight man, while our cheeky lensman would try every trick in the book to get what he called his 'winner' or 'Rembrandt' – the perfect picture.

Days later we headed off on our first visit to Poland. We were to be one of the first Western groups to perform behind what was known as the Iron Curtain – a post-war division of Europe into Western- and Soviet-controlled areas. The Russians and their satellite countries (including Poland) wanted to minimise influence and contact with the outside world and stop their citizens escaping to the West. The Berlin Wall, built in 1961 to divide East and West Berlin, was another device of division. There was little contact between the folk of the East and the West, and there was a growing restlessness in the countries stuck behind the heavily policed border. By inviting a Western pop group to perform in Poland, the authorities were attempting to keep the natives happy. It would be 1989 before the Cold War ended and the Berlin Wall was torn down, but I like to think we did our bit to help.

We flew to Warsaw on a BEA Comet and checked into the Hotel Bristol. Lulu and her Luvvers were going to be our supporting act. She was the young Scottish singer who'd had a hit with her first single, 'Shout', the previous year. The Luvvers were her backing group and they seemed a nice bunch of guys, although Lulu went solo shortly after she returned home from Poland.

Tony had met Lulu previously. She had visited our hotel with her friend Fiona. I don't know what went on between Hicks and Lulu, but some time later, when I saw Maureen, she told me that Lulu had been phoning the family home in Nelson and asking for Tony. A week or so later, she called again. I heard Mo's mum saying on the phone: 'No he doesn't live here any more… he's moved to London.' A few days later, after a hard day at the garage, Tony's dad, Alan, was about to sit down and tuck into his well-earned dinner when the phone rang. Slamming down his knife and fork in annoyance, he walked over and picked up the Bakelite handset. After a pause, Hicks senior delivered his withering riposte: 'No, we've told you before, he doesn't live here any more.' And with that, he hung up. 'Who was that?' enquired Peggy from the kitchen. 'It's that bloody Lulu again,' came the reply. From then on, the feisty songstress became affectionately known as 'Bloody Lulu'.

As we sat down to dinner on our first night in Warsaw, a telegram was delivered to our table and Clarkey read it out: 'Congratulations "I Can't Let Go" number one in the *NME*.' Champagne all round! A great way to start a tour.

The hotel was the finest in town, but the rooms had a distinctly Eastern Bloc feel – they were old-fashioned and spartan. I was, as usual, sharing with Eric, and we vigilantly checked our room for bugs (listening devices). At the end of each corridor, a surly woman attendant was seated, presumably to keep an eagle eye on any untrustworthy Westerners who were staying in the hotel. The following morning I drew back the curtains and peered out of the window. I couldn't believe my eyes. A huge Nazi swastika flag was billowing in the breeze. The street was swarming with Germans. Nazi troops and military vehicles were everywhere.

It turned out that Anatole Litvak was filming *The Night Of The Generals*. We got dressed and were soon outside, excitedly clocking the proceedings. Eventually the action was halted; the filming ended and we set off to explore the city. But we were being followed. A German officer, dressed in trademark jackboots and full military regalia, was stalking us. We stopped and confronted him. It turned out he was carrying a fully loaded script: it was the charming English actor John Gregson.

We played two shows in the Congress Hall, a 3,000-seat theatre, built for Communist Party meetings, in what was known as the Palace of Culture, Stalin's gift to the citizens of Warsaw. Afterwards, we were ushered to the station where we stood waiting on the deserted platform. Eventually, a massive black and red steam locomotive gushed and clanked to a halt and we climbed aboard the solidly constructed sleeper coaches. Our destination was the city of Gdańsk and a sense of adventure prevailed. We were four to a cabin, and I was sharing with Eric and a couple of Lulu's Luvvers.

All the guys were mingling and chattering excitedly as the train powered out of the station. I'd seen railway coaches like this in war films, and my imagination was running wild. An elderly attendant was housed in a cosy cabin at the end of the rake of coaches. His quarters sported a roasting hot coal-fired stove. Our new-found friend kept us supplied with reasonably priced refreshments. The bunks were comfy and the compartment was warm. The Polish bottled beer flowed freely as we took turns to buy the rounds. The thrill of rushing through the darkness in the mysterious Polish countryside, hauled along by a pre-war monster of a steam locomotive, was exhilarating. The Glaswegian Luvvers nattered and joked well into the night until, exhausted and inebriated, everyone took to their beds. At 7 a.m. we were woken by our purveyor of ale, the cabin attendant, and discharged onto the station platform. I had a terrible hangover, and it was snowing. We checked into our hotel in Gdańsk, at which point I began to feel very sick. Thankfully, I managed to grab some sleep before playing two shows that night, then two more the following night. More snow began to fall as we clambered aboard another sleeper train, this time headed for Kraków.

At the time I wrote in my diary: *Depressing atmosphere – crowds great!* That about summed up Poland for me. It was a bleak place, but the crowds of kids were excited and happy.

For them the chance to see Western bands was so rare that they lapped it all up.

Before we left for Poland, it had been agreed that I would share The Luvvers' drum kit, leaving my gear back home. Unfortunately, in a fit of enthusiastic drumming, I broke the skin on the snare drum. They didn't have any spare drum heads, so I attempted to glue the damaged one. After that, drumming was a chore because the pressure was on not to break it again. That fitted with the generally gloomy atmosphere. We witnessed the desperate poverty everywhere as we travelled by bus through the snow-covered countryside.

Back in Warsaw we played two more shows in the Congress Hall, and the following day we were invited to the British Embassy for lunch. The staff formed a small English community holed up in the middle of an austere communist regime. Each of the embassy staff would be followed home every night after work. 'See that guy standing by the lamp post? He's my tail and shadows my every move,' said one member of staff as we peered from the window of the British outpost. Poland in those days was a frightening country. Even the friendly kids who talked to us in the street were constantly glancing around to see if the secret police were lurking and listening.

After another gloomy six-hour bus journey, we arrived in Wrocław in western Poland. During our performance that night, we worked the excited crowd, as usual. And as usual, heavily armed police were very visibly in attendance. So far during our shows they had simply watched the crowd, but this time some girls approached the stage holding bunches of flowers. As the first girl reached up to place the bouquets on the front of the stage, a policeman rushed forward and started clubbing her arms with his baton. There was blood everywhere. We stopped playing and walked off in protest, disgusted and shocked by what we had just witnessed. Mayhem followed. The audience was booing and shouting at the police, who followed us backstage. Their leader demanded that we return and complete our set, which we did after making our feelings known. There's only so much you can do when confronted by armed militia.

For our labours in Poland, we were paid half in British pounds and half in złotys. We didn't realise until we got there that the złoty could only be spent in Poland and was worthless back home in England. What was there to spend it on? Not much apart from knick-knacks and wooden musical boxes. I bought a Russian camera that I never used and, as it was almost home time, I showered a street beggar with złoty banknotes. At least he was happy.

LOOK THROUGH ANY WINDOW

Written and composed by GRAHAM GOULDMAN & CHARLES SILVERMAN

RECORDED BY
The Hollies
ON PARLOPHONE

2/6

B. FELDMAN & CO. LTD
64. DEAN STREET
LONDON, W.1

CHAPTER NINE:

Blood Brothers

B urt Bacharach invited us over to his house for a meeting, and we jumped at the chance. Then in his late thirties, he was a brilliant composer. Already hugely successful when we met him – he had discovered Dionne Warwick and written several huge hits, including 'Anyone Who Had A Heart', which gave Cilla Black a number one in 1964 – he would go on to win six Grammies and three Oscars, and his songs were recorded by over a thousand artists.

We were interested to know why he wanted to meet us. Graham, Allan, Tony and I arrived at his mews house in London without Eric, who didn't show up. This was happening increasingly frequently, and we weren't happy. Burt surprised us with his friendliness, his good manners and what he knew about The Hollies. It turned out that he wanted us to sing the title song for the next Peter Sellers film, *After The Fox*, which would also be starring Victor Mature (lured out of retirement to parody himself) and Sellers' wife, Britt Ekland. We said we'd be delighted to do it, and Burt was knocked out and told us we were his first choice. Our only disappointment was that Burt's wife, film actress Angie Dickinson, who we all fancied, didn't make an appearance while we were there.

The day after we met Burt, we headed for the States again. It was the end of March, and we were due to stay until mid-May, touring for a series of appearances and concerts. We started at Murray the K's World, a former aircraft hangar at Roosevelt Field on Long Island. Aviator Charles Lindbergh had made the first transatlantic solo flight from there in 1927. The Hollies played three nights there after it had been transformed into the world's first multimedia discotheque.

After that we had a couple of days off, which gave me a chance to hang out back at the Village Vanguard, where I sat drinking beer within touching distance of legendary jazz trumpeter Miles Davis as he performed with Tony Williams on drums. I also saw Chuck Berry and The Four Tops on the same bill at Carnegie Hall.

We headed out for our first gigs in the Midwest – Cedar Rapids in Iowa, Sioux Falls in South Dakota and on to Milwaukee in Wisconsin. It was here that we realised our agents, Premier Talent, had not cleared some of our planned performances with the immigration authorities. The local sheriff arrived at our Holiday Inn and began checking the hotel register. We'd all signed in and were on our best behaviour. If the Yankee plod wasn't happy then we could all be thrown out of the country. The cop studied our signatures and then said: 'When you hear your name, identify yourself. Which one of you is Clarence Marold?' After some deliberation we realised it was Allan. He'd hastily penned his real name (he was born Harold Clark) surname first, as the receptionist had directed: Clarke, Harold. We chuckled and the sheriff eventually saw the funny side. The tension eased and we signed a Hollies photo for his kids. I scribbled 'Best Wishes' followed by my moniker. 'Ah, so you're Bert Withers!' exclaimed the uniformed Mr Magoo, in yet another memorable gem.

As we walked across the car park to our rooms, grateful to get back to a bit of peace and sanity, the surreal rumbled into view in the shape of a giant mobile sausage. The weinermobile came to a halt and some little people dropped to earth. I rubbed my eyes. Had my coffee been spiked? On closer inspection it turned out to be Oscar Mayer's promotional vehicle; a giant sausage on four wheels, manned by a family of dwarfs.

Hey man – that was some trip.

By mid-April we arrived in Chicago and checked into the Sheraton hotel. As we had the rest of the day off, Eric and I ventured out to explore the Windy City. We soon realised that we were not alone; two girls were tailing us. We would stop to look in a shop window and so would our followers, who quietly emitted strange phrases like 'Barclays Bank' and other suggestive equivalents of English rhyming slang. At the time I had no idea what they wanted, but later, when we met again, I realised that it was Cynthia Albritton and her sidekick

Pest, who were soon to be internationally known as the 'Plaster Casters of Chicago'. Young Cynthia discovered her vocation when she was given an assignment to make a plaster cast of 'something hard' by her art teacher.

Later Cynthia and Pest turned up at our hotel carrying a doctor's bag containing moulds, a cocktail shaker and casting paraphernalia. Hollies tour manager Rod Shields had the pair thrown out. That was a close shave. But for dear Rod, a casting of my tackle could now be standing to attention in some seedy American rock 'n' roll, British Invasion peep show. Over the ensuing years, Cynthia mastered the art of stand-up, amassing thirty-six castings of celebrity penises, Jimi Hendrix's being paramount in her legendary collection of rock-world pricks.

Cynthia, whose path has crossed mine a few times and who describes herself as a 'recovering groupie', recently told me: 'You and Eric were the first musicians my friend and I talked with about plaster casting. At that point I didn't quite know how to do it.' Quite.

WLS was one of the most listened to radio stations in the Chicago area, and we were invited on for an interview with DJ Ron Riley. We liked Ron and he seemed to like us. He asked us to take turns manning the phones so that kids could call in and ask questions or chat to us. Good fun and a first for us.

A couple of days later we performed at McCormick Place, the largest convention centre in the US. As our Lincoln sedan approached, the security gates opened and our limo glided underground to the backstage area. The perfect way to arrive. After a good show we went to a club where I made the innocent mistake of getting up on the drums and jamming with the resident band. The following day I had a phone call from the head of Premier Talent in New York. I don't know how he knew, but he was angry. He told me in no uncertain terms that if the authorities found out what I had done, they would 'pull the whole Hollies tour'. British musicians could not perform with US artists, not even for an informal jam session in a club, without a special permit.

It took a day on the phone to various immigration departments before we were cleared to go to Los Angeles. Not because of my sitting in with local musicians, which no one dared breathe a word about, but because each different state had to give approval for artists to perform. When we finally got the OK, we flew from O'Hare to Los Angeles and had our first sighting of the Grand Canyon. It was a jaw-dropping sight. Geography on a scale that none of us had ever seen before.

We booked into the old Knickerbocker Hotel where Elvis had stayed in the 1950s. Stars had actually lived at the Knickerbocker: Sinatra, Lana Turner, Mae West, Laurel and Hardy, Cecil B. DeMille, the list goes on. We loved it there. One morning I pressed the elevator button and when the doors opened out walked veterans of movie slapstick Larry, Moe and Curly, the Three Stooges! I couldn't believe it.

Our label, Imperial Records, threw a welcome reception for us. Burt Bacharach was back in the States and he and singer/songwriter Jackie DeShannon came along. The following day we did interviews for the West Coast media and photographer

Henry Diltz took pictures of us by the hotel pool, and then we went to a Mamas & The Papas recording session, where I met legendary session drummer Hal Blaine. This was around the time when Graham met Mama Cass Elliot, who later introduced him to David Crosby and Stephen Stills.

I spent a couple of nights hanging out with a young Rodney 'what's happening' Bingenheimer, who went on to be a hugely successful DJ. He knew everyone in Hollywood and, after some heavy carousing in the Whisky a Go Go, he drove me on a personal sightseeing tour up Laurel Canyon and on to Bel Air, while pointing out film stars' mansions. The one that I recognised instantly was the Beverly Hillbillies' house. Those imposing gates were used for the external shots in the TV series. I was impressed, but feeling queasy after the wallowing car travel, I got out and was sick on the flowering shrubs by Jed Clampett's iron gates in true boozy-Brit-abroad-style.

We went on to Tucson, Arizona where we enjoyed watching a cowboy shootout staged specially for tourists. The heat was intense, and we passed enormous cacti in the desert just like we'd seen in the old western movies. Driving in from the airport, I'd noticed a scrapyard full of old aircraft. The following morning we had a very early call in order to fly on to Phoenix. The sun was rising and there wasn't a soul in sight as Rod inched our hired station wagon through the half-open rickety wire gates. Once inside the aeroplane graveyard I persuaded the band to clamber onto a black sad-looking B-26 bomber, and we posed as Rod took photos.

The flight to Phoenix was memorable because the hot air currents buffeted the plane as we flew over the mountains. A businessman seated across the aisle from me had just been served coffee. Wind shear. The plane dropped suddenly. I watched as a string of the dark liquid was momentarily suspended above his cup, before cascading into his lap.

After Phoenix, where I bought my first authentic western shirt, we flew to Los Angeles where we had photos taken by the great Earl Leaf, an interesting character. Better known as 'Loose Leaf', he had been the first US journalist to photograph Chinese leader Mao Zedong in 1939. He went on to photograph many Hollywood and music legends, including Humphrey Bogart and Lauren Bacall, James Dean, Marilyn Monroe and Frank Sinatra. He was a cool character who seemed to live off coffee and cigarettes. He also wrote stories and magazine columns.

Buffalo Springfield were appearing at the Whisky. We met the band between sets, and drummer Dewey Martin's girlfriend invited me to sit by her when the band took to the stage. We got on well, and she offered to drive me along Sunset. As our sightseeing progressed, she stopped the car, gave me the keys and I took the wheel of her brand new Chevy Corvette. That was some drive. Up and down the Hollywood hills, round Bel Air, followed by some hot passion in the Stingray (not an easy manoeuvre, I can assure you). I thought I had found the Promised Land until the cops shone a torch through the rear window. I quickly regained my English stiff upper lip, rolled back into the driver's seat, kicked the big V8 motor into life and cruised off into the hills of paradise.

Back in London in mid-May we joined Burt Bacharach in Studio Two at Abbey Road to record the title track for *After The Fox*. Once again Eric didn't turn up. Fortunately, Ron had bass player Jack Bruce's phone number. He arrived and the session was saved. Jack was a fine musician, and I found him a joy to work with. A few months later he joined up with Ginger Baker and Eric Clapton and the band Cream was born.

Burt played a harpsichord that had been hired especially for the session, but something was lacking. An upright Challen piano that lived in the studio supplied the perfect sound for the track. This particular model is known as a 'jangle box' or 'tack' piano, due to the optional tone controlled by a third foot pedal. The piano was fitted with brass-tipped felt strips, which could be moved between the hammers and strings, and when the key-operated hammer hit the brass against the string, a hard percussive edge to the note resulted.

After the third take, Tony, Jack and I thought we had the track nailed. So did Ron who was up in the control room. But we soon realised that Burt was not easily satisfied, as he always wanted to go again. After several more performances, Ron had to lay down the law and insist that we move on to record The Hollies' vocal tracks.

Allan, Graham and Tony sang and the Hollies' work was done. Next, ex-Goon Peter Sellers arrived, escorted by his producer George Martin. Now it was Peter's job to overdub his 'humorous' scripted asides. 'I am zee fox' etc. As we were all huge Sellers fans, we eagerly hung around, hoping to hear some humorous banter. Sadly, the only sign of his comic genius was a pretend animated karate-chop aimed at the Steinway piano. It was now George Martin's turn to climb the wooden staircase to the control room. Peter and George had worked together some years earlier and the album, *Songs For Swingin' Sellers*, and single, 'Goodness Gracious Me' with Sophia Loren, were both hits.

Peter recorded his comic comments and the finished track then had to be mixed. George had The Hollies' three-way harmony too low in relation to Sellers' voice. Credit to our Ron, he fought our corner and eventually a mix was created that was acceptable to both parties. The single was released under the United Artists banner and not our trademark Parlophone label, so legally we weren't allowed to promote it.

We were getting increasingly fed up with Eric who, as the 'After The Fox' recording demonstrated, would simply not turn up if he didn't feel like it. He missed a few major dates, including an appearance at the London Palladium. He had recently married his girlfriend, Pamela, and he just did what he wanted. Interestingly, Pam later divorced him and married Peter Clowes, a man who became the symbol of eighties greed, with his and hers Lear jets and a chateau in France. He was later jailed for stealing from investors in his company.

Eric was a fine bass player, but that was no use to us if he wasn't there. He wasn't exactly fired, he more or less just fizzled out. He emerged a few weeks later fronting his own band, Haydock's Rockhouse.

I was sorry to see him go. He and I had been one of the best rhythm sections in the land. How would we find a player of Haydock's quality? Our ex-bandmate, Dolphin Bernie Calvert, was the obvious choice. He was still working at Burco in Burnley and playing piano in a blues band by night. Maureen rang his workplace, and he was brought to the factory phone. 'Hi Bernie, it's Maureen. Tony says would you like to join The Hollies?'

Needless to say, he was delighted to join us and he fitted in well. He was a nice guy, a solid bass player and keyboardist – and he was reliable. He stayed with us for the next fifteen years until he retired from the band in 1981.

Months later, in December 1966, we flew to Berlin for our first concert there. Someone suggested that we board an open-topped sightseeing bus to see the infamous Berlin Wall. It was still the height of the Cold War and from the top of our icy conveyance we were able to peer over the twelve-foot high wall at the desolate scene beyond. Tenement block gable ends and windows bricked up to deter the locals from getting ideas about escaping.

The bus stopped right next to one of the many watchtowers, which was manned by a heavily armed, stern-faced Eastern Bloc guard. It was tense. He was outnumbered and within touching distance of five wisecracking sons of Tommy. To break the ice, Allan opened up with a burst of

Frankie Vaughan's 'Give Me The Moonlight'. The soldier hit us with a withering glare as he hitched his AK-47 higher onto his shoulder. We recoiled, laughing nervously. We just wanted to make friends with him, but he wasn't happy. Had this confrontation happened a year later, when flower power reached its height, Graham might have stuck a rose of peace down the muzzle of his gun.

Fortunately, we moved on unscathed. That soldier and his colleagues had shot dead dozens of innocent men, women and children for trying to escape over the wall and through the barbed wire to rejoin their families, or to make a new life in the West. The wall was a monstrosity that caused endless heartache, and we celebrated with the rest of the world when it came down in 1989, and East and West Germany were united once more.

After that we played Copenhagen, Stockholm, Gothenburg, Malmö, Helsinki and Oslo. On Christmas Day we flew to Kennedy Airport for another tour of the States. Our aircraft was unable to land because of snow on the runway, and we had to circle New York for three hours until we finally touched down at 11 p.m. The following day we joined Herman's Hermits on their private plane at LaGuardia airport. 'Mrs Brown You've Got A Lovely Daughter' had been number one in the States. The Hermits had enjoyed several big hits over there, and Herman had become a household name.

Our equipment was stacked inside the aircraft and held in place by large nets as we took off to perform in a snowbound

Green Bay, Wisconsin. The next day came Fort Worth, after which we flew on to El Paso overnight, arriving about 4 a.m.

Future Led Zeppelin guitarist Jimmy Page had alerted us to the bargain basement source of guitars-to-kill-for. He had implored Tony and Graham to explore the cities of America and, in particular, to check out the downtown pawn shops. Following Page's tip, we found ourselves in Milwaukee, peering through the security mesh at instrument cases stacked on shelves, gathering dust and abandoned. If you were lucky, $50 would buy you a 1950s Fender Stratocaster or an early Gibson Les Paul. At that time, Americans wanted shiny, new instruments like The Beatles played. They didn't realise that almost every city had hidden treasures stashed away, unloved and unwanted, and destined to be worth a fortune.

A CBS TV crew had been following Herman around, and the director was looking for some points of interest. Although the film crew had been assigned to make a documentary on the Hermits, they had been impressed by The Hollies' stage performance and persona, so the camera began focusing on us. We got on well with the TV guys, who were intrigued by our guitar-hunting adventures, and asked if they could tag along. In one pawn shop they filmed Tony haggling over the price of a Gibson Les Paul. He was only willing to pay $70 for it, and the pawnbroker wouldn't take less than $90. Tony was ready to walk away until the disappointed director whispered that he would like to see the deal go through and reached into his pocket to provide the necessary funds. The sequence was then shot, complete with happy ending for our Tony who was then filmed leaving the store, carrying the guitar and looking very pleased with himself.

The tour ended in Chicago and the CBS producer threw a lavish party for The Hollies and the Hermits in the Astor Tower.

The following evening we flew back to New York. Throughout the tour I'd spent time socialising with our two pilots, so towards the end of our journey, they invited me to sit between them on the jump seat of the Convair 440 for our low-level approach along the East River to LaGuardia Airport. A cold, frosty night enhanced the twinkling lights of Manhattan. The buildings were on the same level as our plane, and I witnessed a stunning 3D reach-out-and-touch panorama. What a way to end a tour. I'll never forget that wonderful sight.

In January 1967 we were in another documentary. The recording of our new single, 'On A Carousel', was filmed by Granada TV for a *World In Action* programme about the music industry. The black and white footage was shot in Abbey Road's Studio Three while the session was in progress. At the time we weren't thrilled because the red light was on. We were all primed and ready to go for a take when the door opened and in walked George Martin, trailed by a gaggle of technicians who proceeded to set up their gear, throwing our concentration. It was annoying, but we ignored their clutter and completed the track, and the resulting footage is one of the best examples of The Hollies at work in a recording studio.

Thank you Sir George for having the foresight to gatecrash the red light. It set the whole thing up.

That same month The Hollies recorded two tracks in Italian. We had, a little bizarrely, agreed to take part in the Sanremo Music Festival. The organisers had sent over a guy to make sure the front line would deliver the lyrics with convincing Italian flair. Maybe they'd heard our French version of 'Look Through Any Window'! We were instructed to address our tutor as 'Maestro', and the likeable old cove perched on his stool and patiently coached Allan, Graham and Tony in the art of singing like the Italians. We recorded 'Non Prego Per Me' and 'Di Aver Fiducia In Me' and then headed to Sanremo where we partied on the yacht that singer Gene Pitney, of 'Twenty Four Hours From Tulsa' fame, had hired for his wedding to his childhood sweetheart, Lynne. That was the first time we met Robin Britten. At the time Robbo was Gene's publicist, but he would soon become The Hollies' manager.

Our songs were not good enough to get us through to the finals of the festival, but we didn't mind – by then we were eager to get home after all the hanging around. Tragically, after hearing that his song 'Ciao Amore, Ciao' had been eliminated, and that he would not be in the finals either, twenty-eight-year-old singer Luigi Tenco went to his hotel room and blasted a bullet into his left temple. By his side was a note denouncing the jury and the public's choice of winner. He and his singing partner Dalida, who found his body, had recently announced the date of their forthcoming wedding.

She went on to have a stunningly successful singing career, recording in ten languages, before also committing suicide twenty years later. Tenco become an Italian icon of love and despair, and each year since then an award has been given in his name at the festival.

On February 8 we recorded *Top Of The Pops* then flew to Frankfurt on a BOAC VC10. We stayed at the Intercontinental hotel and the following day performed live on German TV. 'On A Carousel' was released on the tenth, and we played Brunswick and then Herford.

By March 11 I had developed agonising stomach pains. I had no idea what the cause was and presumed it was food poisoning. I was lying on the dressing room floor in the Jaguar-Club, and people were coming in and looking at me, but I was too ill to care. A doctor arrived and he made a joke – something about indigestion – laughed and gave me a pill, which made me throw up. Somehow I managed to play the full Hollies set. Carola Frauli, the club manager, later said that I was 'a hero' and gave 'a towering performance, completing the full show before collapsing'. What else could I do? Although I didn't know it at the time, my whole body had become infected, and I was fighting for my life. Pride and passion carried me, and I managed to keep going until Valentine's Day. In a break from rehearsing for another TV show, this time in Hamburg, the guys were listening to The Beatles' latest single. I faded out to the strains of 'Strawberry Fields Forever'. I vaguely remember a stretcher... ambulance... a haze of German spiel, then the welcome white sheets of Hamburg hospital. I later wrote in my diary: *'In a private ward, injections, etc. No one seems to know what's wrong with me.'* None of the doctors or nurses spoke English.

The remainder of our German tour was cancelled and the band went home. I am eternally grateful to Graham and Rod Shields, who kept an eye on me until my parents arrived from England. Before leaving, Rod thoughtfully left me a Schaub-Lorenz radio (I still have it), so that I could listen to the BBC, and a brown paper package, which was placed next to my bed. It turned out to be a jigsaw puzzle – the lid of which sported a graphic action picture and in big letters proclaimed: The Dam Busters! Yikes. Panic. I quickly hid the box under the blankets. I didn't want the sight of a Lancaster bomber, which had helped to pulverise the city of Hamburg just over twenty years earlier, to jeopardise my recovery.

When Mum arrived, the first thing she did was to ask if she could make a cup of tea for me: 'The way Robert likes it.' That brew lifted my spirits.

Acute peritonitis was diagnosed. My appendix had burst, and all my blood had been poisoned. More injections were administered, and I was coupled up to various tubes. I was being sick and still in pain. The plan was to treat the infection, get the swelling down, and in a couple of months, operate to remove the problem area once I was back home in England. I had a complete change of blood courtesy of the good donors of Hamburg.

On February 23 I wrote: *'Slept well. Improvement. Thanks to my German blood brothers and sisters.'*

My English-speaking nurse, brought in specially from another department to help, kindly showed my parents around Hamburg while off-duty. RAF Bomber Command had destroyed the massive dockland area and other parts of the city, and Mum and Dad were shocked to see many women going about their daily lives dressed in black, still mourning those they had lost in a conflict that had ended twenty-two years earlier.

Bob and Edna's Deutschmarks were running out. Harold Wilson's government had decreed that Brits would only be allowed to take a meagre £50 out of Britain when travelling abroad. In order to preserve their precious funds, my parents had to move out of their comfortable hotel and into cheap lodgings.

On March 1 I thanked the doctors and nurses at the Hamburg hospital and said my farewells. 'On A Carousel' was topping the charts back home as I boarded the propeller-driven British European Airways Vickers Vanguard. My parents and I headed west to Manchester Airport. Back in my own bed in Rose Cottage, I was weak and tired. Recovery was slow. Tony came to visit me. The Hollies tour was due to start on March 11 and there was no way I could be part of it. The rest of The Hollies were going through hell, he told me, trying to find someone who could do my job. Different drummers were tried out, but the guys were unhappy.

'It just doesn't work,' Graham had said in an interview. 'Bobby's the best drummer in the country, and we're inseparable. The other drummers were given hell because we got so bad-tempered – it wasn't fair on them.'

Eventually they agreed to replace me with Tony Mansfield, who had been the drummer in the Manchester group The Dakotas. Against doctor's orders, I played with the guys for the two nights at the ABC in Blackpool, on March 25 and 26. The shows went well, but I was too weak, and the tour carried on without me. I finally had the operation in Burnley General Hospital on May 16, and the poisoned appendix was removed three months after my collapse in the Hamburg TV studios.

I CAN'T LET GO

By Chip Taylor and Al Gorgoni

RECORDED BY **THE HOLLIES** ON PARLOPHONE

MARIBUS MUSIC LIMITED 3'-

CHAPTER TEN:

Lack of Cash and Marrakesh

Before he left the band, Eric Haydock had warned us a few times that Michael Cohen was ripping us off. In the early days, Eric used to travel with Johnny MacDonald in the van, and Mac told him how he'd noticed Michael being dodgy around money. At the time, we didn't listen. We didn't care much about money. The fact that Michael shoved receipts into an old drawer, and doled out dosh to us or to wives and girlfriends from his cash register, never really meant a lot to us. We just assumed that everything was OK, as Mike was a 'businessman'. But we were beginning to realise that something was very wrong.

We were staying at the Holiday Inn on West 57th Street in New York, and record producer Ron had just arrived in town. He phoned, saying that he urgently needed to see us and came round to our hotel, where we assembled in one of the bedrooms. Ron got straight to the point: 'You owe the taxman

£250,000.' That was one hell of a lot of money. It seemed the UK taxman had made contact with John Burgess about several years' worth of unpaid taxes. We knew John well. He would often drop into a Hollies recording session to see what we were up to and chat with his fellow EMI Abbey Road producer Ron Richards. He was a likeable A&R man who had worked with many artists, including Manfred Mann, John Barry and Matt Monro. His expertise during this stressful period would prove to be invaluable.

We all sat in silence for some time trying to get our heads around the enormity of the demand. Just when we thought the worst was over, we were being hit with a bill for a quarter of a million pounds.

What could we do? Pack it in?

Michael Cohen's name was spat out a few times, but as we recovered from the shock of the news, Graham rallied the troops and the jokes and wisecracks began to flow. As long as people still wanted to hear our music, we'd keep earning and we'd pay it all off. And so we did. Thanks to 'Carrie Anne' we carried on. The strength of the Clarke, Nash and Hicks songwriting team made sure that the hit records kept coming and the tax bill was paid.

In early January 1968, I had a meeting with Burgess. John was now part of the newly formed AIR London. Four of Britain's top record producers – our own Ron Richards, George Martin, Peter Sullivan and Burgess – had got together to form their own breakaway company. As staff producers, they had been paid moderate salaries; scant reward for clocking up huge record sales and launching the careers of the likes of The Beatles and Tom Jones – not to mention helping to amass huge profits for the big conglomerates, EMI and Decca. Under Ron's persuasive leadership they had taken the plunge and broken away from the major labels, forming a prestigious independent production company. Now they were free to offer their individual services under the AIR London umbrella, for which they would each be amply rewarded.

I went to see John because, in addition to being a record producer, he was an able accountant. Our company finances were beginning to recover after the taxman had come knocking. Thanks to our new CBS/Epic record deal, there was money in the kitty, but The Hollies and I needed help. Ron had told John of our problem, and he had kindly offered to give us professional advice and hopefully steady the ship.

Michael Cohen had been an expert suit maker. As tailor to the stars, he had taken the inside leg measurements of The Beatles and Tom Jones, but he was unskilled in the art of managing a modern rock band or, it seems, handling the finances. As a result of our success, new Toggery boutiques had sprung up in the north and he had indulged in some extravagant ventures. Michael had opened Rails, a short-lived Manchester discotheque and, before that, a trendy boutique in Back Pool Fold that went by the name of Pygmalia. Tony and Graham were installed as the store's figureheads and consequently became Cohen's business partners. The opening day press launch involved footballers and celebrities, and *Ready Steady Go!*'s Cathy McGowan travelled up from London to declare the shop open for business, posing for photographers with a Hollies gold record. Unfortunately, as the champagne corks popped and the press cameras flashed, the gold record slipped from Cathy's grip and crashed to the ground. Not a good omen. As it lay in pieces on the floor, Cathy burst into tears and Pygmalia was born.

Sadly, but predictably, both Rails and Pygmalia were short-lived ventures. A spare pair of Hollies Vox column speakers had been commandeered to provide Pygmalia with the musical ambience. These were later abandoned, hanging concealed in the shop's ceiling, and are possibly still there today. Rose, Graham's wife, was especially down in the mouth when it closed. As the sometimes manageress of the trendy clothes shop, she would take whatever garment she fancied from the display racks before enjoying an evening out in Manchester's trendy Phonograph club. The following day, after a night of rubbing shoulders with the likes of footballer George Best and various *Coronation Street* actors, the dresses, sometimes sporting the odd blemish, would be back on display in the shop.

John Burgess met me in AIR's offices. As he scrutinised Cohen's account book, his opening line was: 'Bob, you have some catching up to do. I see that Allan, Graham and Tony have all bought houses, but you've had very little in the way of funds.' John suggested that I take a small amount of money out

(Clockwise) Graham Nash, Allan Clarke, me, Tony Hicks and Eric Haydock. The Hollies, 1963.

My favourite Hollies snap – after the gig in Wallington, south London, 1963.

The local paper advert for our gig at the Nelson Imperial, 1963.

Square collar suits, *Ready Steady Go!*, 1963.

An after-show interview for British Forces Radio in Peterborough, 1964.

Marianne Faithfull and me. Relaxing after a good lunch – she chose the wine. The Castle Hotel, Taunton, September, 1964.

The Hollies down the original Liverpool Cavern Club, 1964.

Premier Tops The 1965 Beat Instrumental Drummers' Poll

1st: Bobby Elliott - The Hollies | 3rd: Keith Moon - The Who

Beat Instrumental magazine readers voted, 1965.

The Hollies in Calais, 1965.

Here I am discussing the Top 20 with Cathy McGowan on ITV's *Ready Steady Go!*, 1966.

Greenwich Village, NYC, 1966. HENRY DILTZ

Niagara Falls, 1966. ROD SHIELDS

Me, 1966. HENRY DILTZ

And thereby hangs a tail, 1967. HENRY DILTZ

Our Swedish tour manager, Jay (Yumping Yiminy) Elwing, steals the show on our 1966 Folk Parks tour. ROD SHIELDS

Me on the diving board at the Knickerbocker Hotel, Hollywood, 1966. HENRY DILTZ

Flower Power, 1967.

Standing room only – The Hollies and pilot aboard a Britten Norman Islander, 1970. We flew from Belgium to Leeds.

Maureen and me, by Lake Ullswater, 1975.

The Hollies' manager, Robin Britten, 1977.

of the company. 'It's only fair,' he said. I gratefully accepted. Cohen's accounting, it seems, had been almost non-existent. Among other things, there were no detailed records of the cash that he had generously doled out.

We needed the mess sorting out and decided to employ the services of solicitor Bernard Sheridan of Red Lion Square in London. His future clients would be, among others, Pink Floyd and Kate Bush. We'd been slow to heed the warning signs. As early as 1964, Michael had traded in his old Austin Cambridge four door saloon for a brand new primrose yellow E-type Jaguar.

My first royalty cheque had been for just under £1,000 for co-writing 'Keep Off That Friend Of Mine', the B-side of our chart-topping 'Just One Look'. In those days that sort of bread would have bought a brand new MGB sports car, with change to spare. Michael had advised me to open an account at the Stockport branch of Williams Deacon's Bank as it was conveniently located near to The Hollies' HQ, The Toggery. A few years later, when I contacted the bank to withdraw some money, I was informed that there was only £10 left. They showed me a document signed '*Bobby Elliot*'. That was not how I signed or spelled my name. My signature had been forged and my precious savings plundered.

Things were about to get worse. I remembered the five Standard Life insurance policies taken out for all the Hollies, Allan, Graham, Tony, Eric and me. We checked. Our signatures had been forged and our policies cashed in.

The day before we were due to depart for one of our tours of the USA, Rod Shields had arrived in Abbey Road's Studio Two where we were recording. He had a bunch of official-looking papers under his arm. 'Michael said that you must all sign these before you go,' he said. Fortunately, producer Ron Richards was listening. Annoyed that the session had been interrupted, he grabbed the top sheet, took a look at the first page and was visibly shocked.

'Power of Attorney!' he exclaimed. 'You'll be signing your lives away. Do not sign those forms!'

Had we signed, Cohen would have owned the five of us, lock, stock and barrel. Our desperate manager was now clutching at straws. How could we work with this guy? Michael Cohen had now become The Hollies' ex-manager. He tried pleading poverty. We heard that his father had disowned him and considered taking him to court. But we knew that he had a wife and kids to take care of. Through his solicitor he admitted his wrongdoings, citing unpaid commission, of which we had no knowledge as he had been in a position to pay himself out of Hollies Ltd when he felt it necessary. Now the well was dry and the money was gone. He offered to pay us back at the rate of £10 a month. If we'd let our solicitor Sheridan have his way, our one-time friend would have ended up in prison, but we had no intention of jailing the poor guy. He'd been out of his depth, naïve and incompetent.

Thankfully, we got off lightly, and we were wiser in the knowledge that we had the ability, passion and talent to recover. We moved on. But the northern innocence had been knocked out of us, and we had come to realise that the music business was not just about making music. And the fallout wasn't over yet.

We'd had an expensive lesson in how not to run a company business. From then on, we agreed The Hollies' financial affairs would be taken care of by London accountancy firm Citroen Wells. At the end of January 1968 we met with CEO Eric Charles at their offices off Regent Street, and to this day Citroen Wells handles Hollies Ltd's financial affairs under the watchful eye of Jonathan Prevezer and Alistair Thomas.

The financial crisis in remission, we needed a new manager. Step forward Robin 'Robbo' Britten. He was respected within the industry and had guided not only Gene Pitney but several other American artists with his PR prowess. We decided unanimously that he would make a good manager.

Robbo accompanied us on our next tour of the States. We stayed at the Beverly Comstock (today it's known as the Beverly Hills Plaza) at 10300 Wilshire Boulevard. Through the reception area, you could look into the central garden and see the welcoming sight of the swimming pool, surrounded by palms and leafy apartments. It was a scene reminiscent of old Hollywood, with familiar looking actors wandering about. New manager, Robin, was in his element. He instantly took to the hotel owner and his wife and soon had the run of the restaurant and bar. He'd mix cocktails, exchange tales and chain smoke into the wee small hours with his new-found friends.

My Premier drum kit endorsement deal had expired, and I'd arranged with the Ludwig Drum Company for them to fly a new blue sparkle Super Classic drum set direct from the factory in Chicago to my hotel room at the Comstock. I was like a kid at Christmas, opening the cardboard boxes and lifting out the gleaming drums. I'll never forget the smell of the new wood. It reminded me of my visits to 'H. Elliott Furniture Manufacturer' and my dad's workshop.

We were booked to perform on a couple of top TV shows: ABC TV's *The Hollywood Palace*, where we mimed to 'Jennifer Eccles', and *The Dating Game*. Producer Chuck Barris had requested that we perform 'Bus Stop' and we duly obliged after which, against his better judgement, Tony reluctantly agreed to be the guest eligible bachelor on the show. He had to pick from three contestants who were concealed behind a partition. After a series of questions, he had to choose one of the bachelorettes (such a great name).

Recently, I asked Tony what the lovely couple had won all those years ago. He replied: 'An 8-track cartridge player and a trip to a tropical island with the winning contestant. I'm still waiting for both.'

We were due for a couple of days off in Hollywood and Graham's friend Mama Cass Elliot suggested that we play a showcase gig at the Whisky a Go Go in front of a specially invited celebrity audience. We agreed. We only had a few days to get the word out, so manager Robin sprang into action directing record company PR people to let everyone know that The Hollies were in town.

There was a problem. Our trusty Swedish Ackuset PA system had been air freighted to LA ahead of the band. By sheer chance, record producer Mickie Most, who had flown into town on an earlier flight, had seen cargo cases similar to ours crash onto the tarmac at Los Angeles Airport. There were no tough flight cases back in the 1960s. He contacted Graham and the information proved to be correct. Our trusty tech Dek Whyment went to collect the damaged equipment from LAX and trucked it to the Whisky. When he got it back to the club, he cut the metal bands that the airline had put around the boxes and they fell apart like broken eggshells. He spent hours piecing wires and valves together on the floor of the club, working his magic, and the Ackuset was up and running in time for the Whisky gig. That night we stormed the assembled assortment of musicians, celebrities and performers. One of the West Coast music papers said:

'*On Valentine's day, The Hollies opened their only Los Angeles live appearance EVER at the Whisky a Go Go and EVERYONE in Hollywood was there – all the Monkees (Mickey introduced The Hollies), David Crosby, The Byrds, Buffalo Springfield, Jackie DeShannon, Mama Cass, Wolfman Jack – actually EVERYONE. I don't know how many people the Whisky holds, but I'll bet they went over the limit. If the Fire Department had seen...*'

Robbo was chuffed: 'It was so packed that little Davy Jones of The Monkees was bouncing excitedly around on Mama Cass's knee.'

'*Everyone was convinced that we were the best group in the world,*' I wrote from Gainesville, Florida to Mum and Dad, a couple of days later.

It turned out that the event had been a showcase not only for The Hollies, but for Graham, who was already planning his exodus from our ranks. During our performance he'd been able to demonstrate his harmony prowess to his future colleagues Crosby and Stills, and they were rightly impressed. Graham was the best high-end singer of our era. No Beach Boy thin falsetto, Willy could hit those stratospheric highs with natural ease. He was pitch perfect, giving The Hollies' three-way harmony its unique timbre.

Since Graham's marriage had come to an end in 1966, he'd found a new family of friends on America's West Coast. We knew he was spending more time with them, and was becoming disenchanted. But we didn't yet know that he was on the brink of upping sticks to start a completely new life, leaving behind the two things he'd fallen out of love with – Rose Eccles and The Hollies.

On Friday, March 1 we were aboard the mighty aircraft carrier USS *Independence*. We had arrived in Virginia Beach to play a concert at the Dome that night, and the Navy heard that we were in town and asked if we'd play a free show for the crew in their enormous hangar below decks that afternoon.

We were happy to oblige, and I was quite excited at the thought of looking round the ship. I was able to sit on the captain's high chair up on the bridge, where the view of the landing decks was incredible. The captain proudly pointed out the catapult device used for launching the planes into the air. He went on to sing the praises of the branch-off deck that enabled aeroplanes to take off and land freely without interfering with planes parked at the end of the main runway. I gently reminded him that both the steam catapult and the angled deck were British inventions. He smiled knowingly and agreed that we Limeys were talented in other fields as well as music.

Showtime was in front of an assemble crowd of sailors and crew, with just one female.

Postcard home:
Holiday Inn, New York City
Sunday night, March 3

Dear Mum and Dad
Just arrived here tonight. We played Chattanooga last
night. While we were in Virginia Beach, we played on
the aircraft carrier USS Independence. *We did it for*
the US Navy and sailors as a free show in the afternoon.
There were about 3,000 personnel there below deck in
the massive hangar. We looked around the ship and had
a meal on board. After our performance, the admiral of
the fleet came onstage and presented each of us with a

Zippo cigarette lighter. It has the ship's crest on the side. Very Yankee Doodle Dandy except that on the bottom is stamped: 'Made in Japan'.

I'm ready to come home, though we have another two weeks to work yet! As things are, the last show is in Toronto, Canada on 17 March. We are booked on a flight to Manchester from Toronto on Monday night. Should arrive Tuesday at 9.35 a.m. If there's any change I'll let you know.

Love Rob

Ten days later we met with our label Epic Records in their New York offices. They were not impressed with our latest album, *Butterfly*. I remember a dapper little guy, wearing shiny black shoes and a sharp suit, delivering his car-salesman-style patter, ending with the line: 'We need you to be more like The Association.'

They were an easy-listening, middle-of-the-road American band. My heart sank. His attitude was cold and dismissive, and he did little to elaborate or offer any specific ideas on the band's way forward. It was a brief meeting, and we left feeling confused and depressed.

We were at the end of our tour of the States and needed cheering up. Thankfully, the good people north of the border in Canada obliged. Rousing audiences in packed concert halls in Ottawa, Winnipeg and Toronto lifted our spirits and we ended our North American tour on a high.

On returning to the hotel after our evening performance in Ottawa on March 15, 1968 we could hear voices further along the corridor. Graham Nash and I went to investigate. It was some record company guys having fun. We entered the room to check out the action. Seated just inside I couldn't help but notice a blonde wearing a pink mini dress. Graham whispered that it was Joni Mitchell. At that point we hadn't been introduced so I carried on chatting to the assembled carousers. After a while I made my way back to my room, leaving Nash in full flow. The following morning we were leaving for our next gig in Winnipeg. Where's Graham? On seeing his bedroom door ajar I wandered in to find him sat up in bed drinking tea. He wasn't alone. 'Hey Bobby meet Joni, Joni play Bobby that song'. She dragged the big acoustic guitar onto the bed and began strumming the uniquely tuned instrument singing: 'Rows and flows and angel hair...' It was an early version of 'Both Sides Now'.

We'd been away for almost six weeks. It was time to go home to recharge and regroup. And there were decisions to be made.

Graham had been on holiday to Morocco, and a train journey had planted the seed of a song in his mind. He'd serenaded the rest of us with 'Marrakesh Express', but for some reason, Ron didn't seem impressed. Allan, who had not been involved in writing the song, also seemed detached.

Tony thought the exercise a bit pointless. I liked the song – I'm an old trainspotter. I enthused and we began laying a basic track, but it was hard work. We weren't fully motivated and the session simply ran out of steam. Sadly, rusting in The Hollies' tape shed is a half-hearted, half-finished tribute to Willy's North African adventure. The song would surface again after Graham left when he recorded it with Crosby and Stills. Released by them in 1969, it was a modest hit but has remained memorable ever since.

As we prepared to visit Japan, we had to suffer the ordeal of compulsory vaccinations. The side effects could be unpleasant: tiredness, lethargy, queasiness and the runs. We had to deal with all that while racing to gigs in Germany and Stockholm, doing TV in Holland, filming in Brussels, back for *TOTP* and then Simon Dee's *Dee Time* TV show. 'Jennifer Eccles' was high in the charts, and we were in demand, but the future was uncertain.

CHAPTER ELEVEN:

Willy Heads West

On Friday, April 19 we left Heathrow bound for Japan. It would be a journey of twenty-six hours, with stopovers at Frankfurt, Rome, Cairo, Karachi, Calcutta, Bangkok and Hong Kong. We arrived and were greeted by the promoter and taken to our hotel in downtown Tokyo. The following morning I drew back my bedroom curtains. Directly across the street was a tall office block. On each floor, from top to bottom, every single person was in the process of performing synchronised exercises, hands high in the air, jumping and bending. They were all at it. The image of programmed and passionate hamsters-on-a-treadmill has stayed with me to this day. But I shouldn't scoff. Maybe if our corporations, councils and big businesses had followed the Japanese antics that I witnessed over fifty years ago, we'd be fitter and healthier, and our overburdened National Health Service would breathe a sigh of relief.

The Japanese consider it an insult if the person they have arranged to meet arrives even a minute late. Time is valuable as we are only allotted so much of the precious stuff in a lifetime. Unfortunately, a couple of our guys were a few minutes late coming down to rendezvous with the record company people in the reception of our hotel. This indiscretion resulted in our whole entourage being given stern but polite advice on the importance of arriving promptly at the stipulated time while we were guests of the Japanese.

During the ten days we were there, we performed on TV, gave interviews and played a few live concerts. The girls who hung around for autographs were very polite, even bordering on the subservient. We referred to them affectionately as the Mice.

For me, the highlight of our time in Japan was riding to Kyoto on the Tokaido Shinkansen bullet train on the high-speed line that had opened in 1964. The streamlined, aerodynamic appearance of the rolling stock all those years ago was very similar to the High Speed Train and Eurostar designs that eventually appeared in the UK a lifetime later.

The train was fast and impressive, and our route provided a stunning view of snow-capped Mount Fuji. In Kyoto we walked to the old town, where the pink cherry blossom trees, in full bloom, provided a picture-postcard backdrop to the ancient temples. As we wandered around, a long shed-like building looked mysteriously inviting. At one end the entrance channelled us along a dark, narrow walkway parallel

162

to hundreds of evil-looking statues of grimacing old warriors. By the time I was halfway along the creepy corridor, I could feel bad vibes emanating from these lifelike figures, and I had to make a speedy exit. Thankfully, I was soon outside in the fresh air, taking deep breaths and heading briskly back to the station.

Our hotel was near the Ginza district of Tokyo, where Dek and Allan could usually be found in a dodgy bar consuming beer with the friendly locals. Graham, on the other hand, was inspired to write the line: 'Twixt the Hilton and the go-go girls', a reference to a calm, peaceful oasis that lay close to our hotel.

We heard that our latest single, 'Jennifer Eccles', was number five in the British charts as we appeared on a Fuji TV show, attired in Japanese traditional costume, singing the famous Japanese spring song 'Sakura'. All part of a day's work in Hollieland.

The Mice were there to bid us farewell as we emerged from our hotel on May 1. They tearfully presented us with handwritten messages as we climbed into the waiting cars. We thanked them and waved goodbye before boarding a Japan Airlines DC-8 and flying via Anchorage, Alaska, over the North Pole and back home to England.

As always, I headed straight for home. I was still living at my parents' cottage in Roughlee, just over the hill from Nelson. That evening I jumped into my racing green MGB and went to see Maureen at her folks' place in Nelson, and we whizzed over to one of my favourite pubs, the Rib, or Ribblesdale Arms, in the Yorkshire village of Gisburn. In those days the small hamlet was full of character and characters. Only a hundred or so souls lived there, but the place had four pubs. Situated on the busy east to west A59 trunk road, Gisburn had been a stopover for stagecoaches and horses travelling from Yorkshire to the west side of the country. Later, passenger coaches and commercial traffic used those same hostelries to stop for refreshment before continuing on to the holiday towns of Blackpool and Southport or the ports of Fleetwood and Liverpool.

What none of us knew, as Maureen and I sipped our drinks in the Rib back in the late-sixties, was that the M62 motorway would arrive a few years later, and it would wipe out the old traditions at a stroke. The motorway was finished in 1976 and as a result the village withered. Today the old Rib has been converted into apartments and sadly there is only one surviving pub.

The Rib was the place where fiery Labour MP Barbara Castle would arrive in her chauffeur-driven car, dressed in designer clothes. She would go up to her room and reappear, minutes later, decked out in well-worn working class garb, before being whisked away to address her Blackburn constituents up the road.

Occasionally, a resident judge provided our evening's entertainment. Seated at the end of the bar the old boy would hold court, slurring out advice to the local butcher and assembled farmers. After he'd satisfied his thirst, he would attempt to climb the stairs and head to his bedroom. This usually ended with him crawling up the final few steps and, more often than not, he would lose his balance and roll all the way back down to the bar area. We were so used to this performance that everyone would just carry on carousing as the old boy lay in a crumpled heap at the bottom of the stairs.

When the landlord wanted the – mainly young – crowd to leave, at his idea of closing time, he would yell out: 'Come along you monkeys, get down Coal Pit Lane.' This was a cart track on the edge of the village frequented by amorous couples.

The Rolls-Royce Aerospace factory and research centre was in nearby Barnoldswick. Quite a few young guys were employed there as engineers or apprentices and items could be made to order if you knew the right people. As a result, many of the local lads' cars were fitted with specially constructed titanium exhausts courtesy of Rolls-Royce.

One warm summer's evening George Poole, the local village bobby, and his chief constable were comfortably seated on a bench outside the Rib. They were enjoying a leisurely chat when there was a sudden ear-splitting roar. It was my friend Mike Holden firing up his high performance Alfa Romeo Spider, which had been fitted with a large-bore titanium exhaust specially designed by local blacksmith Harry Driver. Mike was leaving the pub car park in a hurry. The tyres squealed, the wheels spun, and Holden shot off down the main street to his next watering hole.

The chief constable sat bolt-upright and shouted: 'What the hell was that? Get after him, George. Get after him!' At which point the genial sergeant staggered to his feet and replied: 'What? In a Morris Minor, sir?'

The Hollies, meanwhile, had a silver-grey Mark 10 Jaguar based up north. Driven by the ever reliable Rod Shields, the car's main purpose was to transport Bernie and me to and from London – the idea being that we could make an appearance in London and still get home for a day or two of normal life before the next show. That summer we headlined a brave new venture, a tour with Paul Jones, formerly of Manfred Mann, Scaffold and the Mike Vickers Orchestra.

The tour over, Maureen and I set off from Nelson to Cornwall in my MGB in convoy with two good friends, John Bradley and Andrew Winchester, who were driving a brand new MGC with a Fletcher speedboat in tow. We stayed in a small cottage near Prussia Cove and spent idyllic days on Praa Sands. It was mid-July, the weather was perfect, and the MG was the ideal vehicle for chugging around the Cornish lanes with the top down. But the rocky track to our cottage proved too much for it. MGs are very low-slung, and the exhaust was damaged, resulting in a tractor-like roar every time I started up. I had to drive to Redruth to get it fixed. Then it was back to the beach across from St Michael's Mount where John and Andrew were trying to launch the speedboat. The plan was for all of us to power round the promontory. There was a fair swell, the sea was crashing onto the sand,

and the bow of the boat pointed skyward as we pushed it into the surf. It didn't want to go and seemed intent on looping the loop. This boat was designed for use on smooth surfaces like Lake Windermere, where it had spent most of its sailing hours. Eventually, we all piled aboard. As we got further out to sea, the ocean swell appeared higher than the boat. It was scary, and I started to picture the headline: 'Hollies Drummer Missing At Sea'. Thankfully, as water spilled into the fibreglass hull at an alarming rate, Bradley carefully powered us back to the safety of the shore.

A couple of weeks later, Maureen phoned to say that Andrew had been killed in his MGC while driving back from the Lakes. In those days, we could cover the journey from Windermere to Nelson in an hour. It seemed that another friend had wagered a bet that his blue MGB, fitted with overdrive, was quicker than the new red six cylinder MGC. The race was on. The two cars set off for home. Along their route, near the village of Ingleton on the A65, was a disused railway bridge. The steel span had been removed and the remaining stone sides of the structure were at an angle to the straight road, forming a sort of chicane. If you aimed the car correctly, and there was nothing coming in the opposite direction, you could drive an almost straight line. But at this point the two cars were racing flat out side by side. Poor Andrew had nowhere to go. He hit the side of the stone bridge at very high speed and was killed instantly. His girlfriend, in the passenger seat, died shortly afterwards. The news of this tragedy shook me. When I got home, I paid a visit to Andrew's parents, who lived in Burnley. It was a sad time and, frustratingly, Hollies commitments prevented me from attending his funeral. We were scheduled to perform a string of concerts in the Swedish Folkparks.

Days later, sitting with Allan, Tony and Graham in the Foresta Hotel in Stockholm, I felt it my duty to kick-start the three guys into songwriting action. After venting my thoughts, I almost manhandled them into the bedroom across from the lounge where we had been sitting. As I closed the door, I told them to get writing and not to come out until they had a song. It worked. About an hour later they emerged and played 'She's so empty inside, she lies to herself and her public...'

'What's the title?' I asked.

'We don't have one,' came the reply.

'Right. "Survival Of The Fittest",' I said.

Although those words don't appear anywhere in the song, the phrase was intended to be a veiled challenge to each of us as our lives and careers moved forward. And although we didn't know it at the time, that turned out to be the last of a long line of songs from the songwriting team of Graham Nash, Allan Clarke and Tony Hicks.

In early August we flew to Yugoslavia, to the part that is now Croatia. The International Festival of Pop Music was being held in the city of Split, and we were there to top the bill. As we drove round the harbour to get to our hotel, we

168

were greeted by a pungent nautical smell. Manager Robin seemed please and exclaimed: 'Excellent. The lobsters here should be terrific!'

Back home, we began a week at Yorkshire's famous Batley Variety Club. It had opened in 1967 with jazz legend Louis Armstrong headlining. If it was good enough for Satchmo, it was good enough for The Hollies. Tina Turner, The Everly Brothers, Tom Jones, Roy Orbison, Dusty Springfield, the Bee Gees and Johnny Mathis would all perform there.

For us, times were changing and we all felt it. Things came to a head as the week of our Yorkshire residency was drawing to a close. Backstage in Batley, a dramatic duel was about to take place. Tony, Allan and I were donning our white suits in readiness to perform, and the smoke from Robin's endless cigarettes added to the stifling pre-show tension. The temperature was rising, in more ways than one. Graham sat on the arm of a dressing room easy chair with his feet resting on the cushioned seat. He was still in his civvies and probably frustrated by the thought that in twenty minutes he'd have to be a chirpy Hollie before another packed house for seventy-five minutes. He launched a verbal broadside at Robin. He was incensed about the calibre of work that we were being offered. He said we shouldn't be playing the likes of Batley because it conveyed the wrong image for the band. He was right. But performing was The Hollies' *raison d'être*. Graham and Allan had been performing since they were children, as had a ten-year-old Hicks, who had appeared on a certain ITV

169

talent show playing guitar in Les Skifflettes. Besides which, these gigs paid the bills. A sold out week at Batley was a well-paid stroll in the park for us.

Robbo was shocked although he later downplayed Nash's tantrum, describing him as being 'a little stampy-footy'. But the truth was that Graham already had a foot out of the door. He was, perhaps, feeling torn. Drawn by his new-found friends in the States, and the promise of fresh musical adventures, he still valued The Hollies. The band had been his life for a long time and walking away would be hard.

But Graham didn't like where The Hollies seemed to be heading. In the late 1960s the music business was in transition. Robin moved in establishment circles and his chums in the business were mainly of the old guard. The Hollies had arrived at a crossroads, and Robin opted to turn into the cul-de-sac of cabaret. It was an easy route to riches, but it wounded our image. The northern theatre club scene was frowned upon by the southern-based right-on music press. With one phone call to our new agent Jimmy Smith, Robbo could fill the date sheet with well-paid weeks of work up and down the country and draw his commission in the time it took him to finish his Benson & Hedges.

Graham had pleaded with us to let him lead the group along a new musical path, but when he didn't elaborate on the route he had in mind, we thought it was a pipe dream – in more ways than one. Robin went as far as to dismiss our Willy as a 'hophead'.

Batley and California were two separate planets and perhaps, even as he was yelling at Robin, Willy was mentally preparing to pack his bags and become a Yank. His unease may have been what led him to write one of his last recordings with us, 'Man With No Expression'. Penned with Terry Reid, the song is one of the finest tracks we ever laid down. We recorded it in Abbey Road three or four months before Graham left the band. This parting shot seemed to extol the virtues of taking acid, and invited the listener, or maybe Allan, Tony and I, into his new-found world of 'riding horses through a rainstorm' or 'leading a lion through a busy street bazaar'.

Psychologist Timothy Leary was famous at the time for advocating the therapeutic potential of psychedelic drugs. His catchphrases, such as 'turn off your mind, relax, float downstream', formed an illusionary fairy tale backdrop to the tail end of the late-sixties flower power period. But producer Ron poured cold water on Graham's progressive leap and showed little interest in 'Man With No Expression', one of my favourite Hollies tracks. In fact, it never saw the light of day until Tim Chacksfield and I rescued it thirty years later and included it on the CD *The Hollies At Abbey Road 1966–1970*, which was released in 1998.

On August 28, 1968, with Nicky Hopkins on piano, we crafted another Hollies hit, 'Listen To Me', penned by Tony Hazzard. It was released on September 27 and was Graham's final recording with the band. Although our album *Hollies'*

Greatest had been sitting at number one in the album charts for four weeks, life for us was tinged with apprehension and uncertainty as Graham travelled back and forth to the States, loath to leave us but drawn to new opportunities. From my retreat up north, I never quite knew what Willy was up to or which country he was in. Although still officially a Hollie, he was often over in LA hanging out with Crosby, Stills and an assortment of backslapping dudes. None of us knew which way things would go until the crunch came.

'Listen To Me' was climbing the British charts. Colour TV had recently arrived in Britain, and we were invited to appear on BBC2's late night show, forerunner to *The Old Grey Whistle Test*, *Colour Me Pop*. Sadly, all the taped episodes were later deleted. I believe the culprit was the same guy who wiped all the recordings of *Top Of The Pops* from 1964 to 1969. Performances by us, Hendrix, The Beatles, The Rolling Stones… the list is endless. A *Who's Who* of pop and rock music gone forever. I often wonder where the person is who pressed the delete button on that valuable musical treasure trove. Maybe he was promoted to some prestigious position in the corporation, like director general.

Top Of The Pops producer Johnnie Stewart phoned our manager Robin. Great news – they wanted us to appear on Thursday, October 24. Johnny said that if we were to appear, our record would probably make the Top 5. As usual, I was excited at the thought of performing on the show, after which Dek and I could hang out in the BBC Club followed by a few drinks in the Cromwellian. But it wasn't to be; Graham was in Los Angeles and couldn't get back in time for the Wednesday recording. As a result, 'Listen To Me' ran out of steam, peaking at number eleven, and we ran out of patience. The will-he-won't-he guessing game came to an abrupt end. We didn't want him to leave, but it was now make-your-mind-up-time. Nash was given the long-awaited hard word, and he agreed to leave The Hollies.

The Save Rave!, a charity event, was due to be held at the London Palladium on December 8, and it was agreed that this would be Graham's final gig with us. It happened to be my twenty-seventh birthday too. We performed well. Everyone gave their best, knowing we had reached the end of an era. We'd had so many good times together. But GW Nash had to follow his dreams. I was happy for him, and I felt privileged to have shared his humour and to have watched his creative talent blossom.

We had to plan ahead. The Hollies were contracted to supply our record company with an agreed number of tracks per year. We urgently needed new songs, and the Dylan songbook looked like an attractive project. 'Blowin' In The Wind', with Graham, was already in the can. One down, eleven to go. As Tony pointed out: 'Bob Dylan wrote some great songs, but they sounded unfinished.' We treated his recordings as demos and arranged them in our own distinctive way. Even though Willy Nash was still officially a Hollie at the time, we had begun recording the backing tracks for our album *Hollies*

Sing Dylan without involving him. We had full access to Abbey Road's facilities, and the atmosphere was relaxed and confident. Engineer Peter Bown and producer Ron Richards were happily aboard, and the tracks just fell into place. Each song had been chosen and arranged by Tony, Allan and me, so as to create the perfect vehicle for The Hollies' three-way harmony. The orchestral arrangement for 'Blowin' In The Wind' was my idea. King Curtis, our Paramount Theatre buddy, had given me a 45 rpm disc of his instrumental version of the song. I borrowed the riff from Curtis and la-la'd it to arranger Mike Vickers, but his finished work sounded more like the Northern Dance Orchestra. The cool, understated effect I'd envisaged didn't happen. It was Ron Richards' idea for us to employ arranger Lou Warburton for the remaining tracks. His charts were more of a representation of what I'd had in mind.

At the end of November *Hollies' Greatest* had been number one in the British album charts for ten weeks. We were filmed on a freezing cold day in the grounds of the Park Hotel, Bremen. This was Graham's last TV appearance with us.

In Sweden the previous July, Graham had played me the tapes of his recordings with Crosby and Stills as we sat on the floor of my hotel room in Stockholm. It was The Hollies' three-way harmonies but with Graham and two strangers. I had quite liked what I heard and wished him well with the project.

Here's an excerpt from the liner notes that I wrote for The Hollies' 2015 five-CD set, *Changin' Times*:

Elucidating Observations

A cape-wearing David Crosby was strutting down the cramped and funky backstage corridors of the London Palladium – a sight to behold. He'd come to rescue his new friend Graham Nash from the clutches of this backward-looking, beer swilling, bubblegum band, and whisk him to La La Land where they could associate with like-thinking, drug-addled 'free thinkers'. I heard David Crosby say: 'Is it cool?' He clearly intended coming into our dressing room but was quickly ushered away by our loyal tour manager Rod Shields. Allan Clarke was livid at Crosby's insensitivity. Harold (Allan) and Willy (Graham) had been childhood chums and were like brothers. Al was losing his best mate. He simmered with rage at the audacity of Crosby even showing his face on Hollies' territory and had to be persuaded not to give the American a good thumping, or worse.

We all felt sad, very sad, at the loss of Graham. Did we think it was the end of The Hollies though? Not for a minute. We all felt, as we always had, that the band was bigger than any single member. We'd find someone else, but we all knew that to replace Graham's unique voice would be damn near impossible.

CHAPTER TWELVE:

A Tailor-Made Transition

A month later we had found Graham's replacement. Terry Sylvester hails from Merseyside and is a fanatical supporter of Liverpool Football Club. Although he was only twenty-two when he joined us in January 1969, he was already a seasoned musician, having first been in The Escorts and later The Swinging Blue Jeans. The Escorts had supported us in 1965 when we played Munich, after which Terry used to come to our gigs and we'd hang out. He was a good rhythm guitarist and he came close to replicating Willy Nash's high harmony. He was also a reasonable songwriter and blended favourably with Allan and Tony – a good writing style.

By the time he came aboard, we had completed all the backing tracks for *Hollies Sing Dylan*. Once again, we had the three voices to provide that front line vocal blast. We announced Terry as the new Hollie to the press on Thursday, January 16, 1969, in the Westbury Hotel in London's Bond Street. Robin was in his element; chain smoking and drinking copious quantities of cognac and ginger while ushering us around like a mother hen. In those days our tipple was cognac and Coke or champagne, interspersed with the odd brandy sour, usually at Robin's insistence. 'Here Bob, you'll need this,' he would say, putting a glass into my hand and pushing me forward into a gaggle of press guys.

Tony had found our next hit, 'Sorry Suzanne'. He could really sniff 'em out in those days. A dull demo by Tony Macaulay and Geoff Stephens was transformed by our arranging skills into another Hollies chart-topper. And Terry fitted in pretty seamlessly, singing the top line on the single with Allan and Tony alongside. On January 28 we completed the recording of 'Sorry Suzanne' and the B-side 'Not That Way At All' at Abbey Road. A month later the record was in the shops.

Terry's first live gigs with the band were in Cardiff and Swansea on February 12 and 13, a couple of low profile dates to bed him in. We were satisfied with the new boy's performance, and the following week he, Allan and Tony completed vocals on all the Dylan tracks. After that we met with arranger Alan Tew and talked him through what we had in mind for the orchestral overdubs. On Tuesday, March 4 *Hollies Sing Dylan* was finished and ready to go. Everything was fitting into place perfectly and Ron was ecstatic. Recording over, we celebrated in The Carpenters Arms on Seymour Place, just a short walk from Ron's London home. He would usually round off the night with a pint of bitter followed by a whisky chaser.

Now even I had a London base: a flat in Thurloe Square, Kensington, which Terry shared with me. He was great company and we would carouse together down at the Speakeasy or the Cromwellian Club.

After seeing Ron home that night, we walked to our favourite Indian restaurant, the Diwan-i-Am on George Street, for supper. Then it was club time. In the Speakeasy Dek and I were at the bar, deep in conversation, when a stoned Brian Jones barged up beside me and exclaimed: 'It's great to be amongst real people again.'

'Fuck off,' Derek snapped.

Jones took the hint and staggered on, looking for someone else to talk at.

Later, while walking along Oxford Street, we spotted a dishevelled figure lying in the gutter; not an unusual sight in London at that time in the morning. As we got nearer, I recognised him.

'Hey Dek, it's Viv Prince, the drummer from The Pretty Things,' I exclaimed.

'Ignore him,' Dek advised. 'He's just showing off.' And with that, we continued on our way.

We performed 'Sorry Suzanne' on *Dee Time* and *TOTP*. We had probably been on the latter more times than any other band. Unfortunately, there is no way of checking, thanks to the BBC's phantom tape wiper. We appeared wearing our famous white suits. Graham's abandoned togs fitted Terry perfectly, so we didn't even need to get him a new suit.

Our appearance, with Terry, Allan and Tony on the front line, was well-received by fans and critics alike.

Tour manager Rod Shields had proved his worth with a camera when he filmed us clowning around New York in the early years. His stunning footage of NYC's Times Square in 1965 can be seen on various TV documentaries, notably *The Hollies: Look Through Any Window* by the Reelin' in the Years production team. Back in 1969 we agreed to give him his head. One of ITN's studios in central London was hired, and Rod became director for a day and produced a promotional video of us performing 'Sorry Suzanne'.

In early March we made one of our many day trips to Hilversum, Holland, to appear on Dutch TV. We would catch a morning flight out of either Heathrow, or Manchester if I was up at my folks' place, to Schiphol airport. I could be home in time for the last pint at my local pub.

Days later we took a two and a half hour British European Airways flight from Heathrow to Berlin, where we checked into the Hilton hotel. We were in town to take part in a TV spectacular: *Gala-Abend der Schallplatte 1969 (Evening Gala of Discs 1969)*. Rehearsals were spread over a couple of days, and it turned out to be a real home from home. The after-hours social scene was very healthy. We hung out with some of the gorgeous dancers from the Young Generation and an old friend, Lesley Duncan, who was one of Dusty Springfield's backing singers.

There were about twenty acts on the bill, including Dusty, Sylvie Vartan, Los Paraguayos, Mantovani, The Sandpipers,

Nina & Frederik, Miriam Makeba, Ray Conniff and French songstress Mireille Mathieu, who closed the show. The Hollies were scheduled to perform two songs. First, our new record 'Sorry Suzanne', after which we were joined by the massive assembled orchestra and stormed the proceedings with a powerhouse version of 'Blowin' In The Wind'. A lavish beer-fest was laid on after the show. The Germans really knew how to make us welcome.

Back in England we had discussions with EMI on what the *Dylan* album cover should look like. Bob Richards' photo of us wearing the white suits was chosen, and the *Hollies Sing Dylan* package was complete.

With 'Sorry Suzanne' at number three in the charts, The Hollies were in demand. We had become regulars at Television Centre where *Top Of The Pops* was filmed. We even knew the names of floor managers and camera crews and, more importantly, the names of the commissaries and barmen up in the BBC Club. After a trip over to Bremen for another *Beat Club* TV performance, we recorded *Hollies In Concert* at the Golders Green Theatre, complete with orchestra, on Sunday, March 30.

Ace snapper Wolfgang Heilemann had organised a photo session for Germany's *Bravo* magazine. 'Bubi', as he was known, snapped the five of us sitting on a plank supported by trestles, dressed in space suits, complete with silver-sprayed wellies – you can still see the picture on his website. At a later date, the clever artists in the *Bravo* design studio transformed the wooden plank into a thrusting projectile. Anyone who bought a copy of the magazine could see the happy Hollies zooming through space, straddling what looked like a V-2 rocket.

We recorded a backing track for Tom Jones's TV show at Elstree studios. On the night, the front line would sing live to the pre-recorded track, and we instrumentalists would appear to be playing in a convincing manner. Miming is a skilled form of deception and TV producers loved it. It made their jobs easier. It was something I quite enjoyed. As long as I remembered every drum fill and flourish then the viewer at home would be none the wiser. Sadly though, the person in charge of mixing the sound usually had the live vocals too loud and the pre-recorded track too low. This was the case on Tom's show and it still happens today.

Stevie Wonder was also on the show. He's a fine drummer and needed a drum kit so that he could play on his own backing tracks. He asked if he could borrow my blue Ludwig set. I'm proud to be able to say that Stevie can be heard playing my drums with the Jack Parnell Orchestra on the episode of *This Is Tom Jones* that aired in April 1969.

It was the great Ronnie Verrell who drummed week in, week out with the Parnell Orchestra. He brought out the best in our boy from the valleys. Tom loved Ronnie's playing, so much so that he asked him to be his permanent drummer, but Ronnie turned down the generous offer. Having been on the road for years with the Ted Heath band, Ronnie now wanted to spend time with his family and get back to his own bed each night.

Hollies Sing Dylan was released on April 2. The following day most of the band travelled by hovercraft from Southsea to the Isle of Wight, where Robin had invited us to stay at his family home. The family's fine detached red brick house, St Denis, had been built in 1903 in the village of Bembridge. There was a croquet lawn, and the grounds were edged by woodland complete with red squirrels. Not only that, but the Britten family had invested in the latest model of colour TV just in time for us house guests to watch the recently recorded *Hollies In Concert*.

Robbo's brother, John, had worked at the De Havilland aircraft factory, and in the wood there was a shed crammed with bits of early jet aeroplanes. John, along with his friend Desmond Norman, had designed and built the Britten-Norman Islander, a high-winged twin-engine utility aircraft. The new plane was destined to be an international bestseller and production was about to begin nearby at Bembridge Airport.

Robin took great pride in being chief cook at these get-togethers. With the ever-constant Benson & Hedges dangling from his lips, he would peer into his dish of the day, prodding the ingredients, as he laced them with red wine or brandy. After dinner the drinks continued to flow. Robin's mother, Zoe, a tweedy Margaret Rutherford type, could often be seen riding through the village in her pony and trap. Her favourite tipple was Bosun's Blood, a concoction that I believe consisted of brandy and Dubonnet. Robin called it liquid dynamite. After a couple of glasses, a fired-up mother Britten was ready to play games. She liked everyone to conceal themselves around the house, upstairs and downstairs. Robin would then count down to zero, after which Ma would launch herself excitedly into the hunt. Chuckling and giggling, the old girl would totter from room to room searching out each guest, then gleefully pick them off. It was a game of hide and seek, although the Brittens had a more exotic name for the shenanigans which eludes me.

Hollies Sing Dylan made number three in the album charts. It was a vindication of our choice to go with Dylan and proof that we could make the transition, fairly seamlessly, from Graham to Terry. Meanwhile Graham and his new band were busy with their own album, *Crosby, Stills & Nash*, which also did well. 'Marrakesh Express' was issued as a single and made number twenty-eight in the charts. We had all moved on and, as far as I was concerned, there were no hard feelings.

In 1969 Tony had taken a liking to visiting music publishers' offices. He would search out songs, especially if The Hollies' writing team was going through a lean spell. Over the years we'd got to know an assortment of colourful characters and song pluggers in London's Tin Pan Alley. I think our Tony enjoyed the chirpy banter as they tried to persuade him that they had the very tune The Hollies were looking for. One day he popped into the offices of Cyril Shane Music. Cyril liked to play foreign language ballads to his customers while murmuring the English translation into their ears. Just as Tony was extricating himself from another Cyril performance, he spotted a demo disc he hadn't heard.

'What's that one?' Hicks enquired.

'I don't think that it's suitable for The Hollies, but you might as well have a listen,' replied Cyril as he placed the stylus onto the black shiny acetate that was now spinning on the record player.

Tony loved the song. 'I think that we can do something with this, Cyril. Can I let Ron and the boys have a listen?'

It was a song written by Americans Bobby Scott and Bob Russell. Ron approved of Hicks' discovery and Allan and I loved it, but we needed a pianist. Hollies music publisher Dick James had signed a guy called Reg Dwight who we'd heard was a fine piano player. He was booked for the session and arrived in the control room of Studio Two, eager to get to work. Not much was said as Reg, Bernie and I made our way down the wooden stairs to the parquet floor of the famous old studio. I set my drums by the grand piano at which Reg, who told us he was changing his name to Elton John, was seated. Bernie plugged his Fender bass into an amp and sat on a spare piano stool. We were set to go. The red studio light lit up and Reg/Elton counted: 'One, two, three...' Playing alongside the lad was a breeze. His rhythmic piano style would later be overlaid by Allan's haunting harmonica introduction. We nailed the track first or second take, with Al on a high stool singing a rough guide vocal. I remember saying to our producer Ron after he played the track back to us: 'I made a mistake.' To which he replied: 'Don't worry, Bob, it's nothing. You won't hear it when we get the strings on.'

There are no guitars on 'He Ain't Heavy'. Tony was happy to watch as the Elton John trio breezed through the recording session. On live performances of the song Tony would play bass and Bernie moved onto the piano, impressing everyone with his keyboard technique. I mention the word keyboard. There was no such thing at the end of the 1960s and we would tour extra musicians to supply the strings and extra orchestration on our live concerts. Although the Moog synthesizer made its debut around this time, no way could this pile of wires and boxes be described as portable, and it was horrendously expensive. As we moved into the 1970s we became a six-piece band. Pianist Pete Wingfield had been recruited. Around this time the first affordable synths had come on the market. 'Wingy' would balance his little ARP synth keyboard on top of the grand piano and attempt to reproduce the orchestral arrangement of 'Heavy' – and later 'The Air That I Breathe'; no real substitute for the real thing but quite effective onstage.

Allan seemed a little apprehensive as he took up his position within kissing distance of the iconic Neumann U47 microphone. He was concerned that his voice was not at its best. He needn't have worried. A touch of laryngitis was not going to hinder him as he gave a classic Clarkey performance of what was to become The Hollies' finest anthem. A few weeks later John Scott added his beautifully sympathetic orchestral overdub and the Mike Sammes Singers added a final choral blast to round off a superb production: Ron Richards at his best. 'He Ain't Heavy, He's My Brother' was complete.

That recording elevated us to a whole new level. The listening public was moved by the song's message and today, as we perform what has become the Hollies anthem, looking down from my drum riser, I can often see tears of emotion on the audience's faces seated along the front rows. Over half a century since the track was committed to tape the effect of the message has snowballed. It's become part of people's lives. Today, onstage, as I count the song in, I have to totally immerse myself in the mood of brotherly love to enable me to get inside the track and perform with complete conviction.

In 1969 we had been held at number two in the charts by a cartoon band – The Archies and their chart topper 'Sugar, Sugar' – but 'He Ain't Heavy' became number one for us when it was released again in 1988. Later it was even recorded by Granada TV's *Coronation Street* cast. But the use of 'Heavy', sung by various celebrities of the day, to raise funds for the families of 96 Liverpool football fans who lost their lives in the Hillsborough disaster is the most satisfying outcome of all.

Not many people know that Bernie made a whole album with Elton John, recorded around the time of the 'Heavy' session. The Bread And Beer Band featured Reg/Elton on keyboards, along with guitarist Caleb Quaye and The Hollies' bass player. It was never officially released, although bootleg versions seem to have escaped. Bernie tells me that he receives royalties from Japan for a track that he played on titled 'Breakdown Blues', created during a session in Abbey Road when the recording equipment failed. The assembled musicians jammed while they waited for the repairmen, so it's quite an apt title. I can picture those white-coated EMI technicians coming in to take away the broken-down piece of machinery.

RECORDED BY THE HOLLIES
ON IMPERIAL RECORDS **ON A**
CAROUSEL
WORDS AND MUSIC BY GRAHAM NASH, TONY HICKS & ALLAN CLARKE

KEYS
04958

MARIBUS MUSIC, INC.

75¢

CHAPTER THIRTEEN:

Man Overboard

The person who had suffered most when Graham left was Allan. The break-up, not just of the band, but of his oldest, closest friendship left him devastated. The Hollies continued, and in many ways went from strength to strength, but Allan had changed. He felt left behind by Graham, and he became restless. A couple of years after Graham left he jumped ship too.

To be fair, his hand was slightly forced. He announced that he planned to make a solo album, and Tony and I weren't happy. Tony said to him: 'Fine, make your album, but you must choose between being loyal to The Hollies or going solo. You can't do both.' To stick with the nautical nuances, the lad was made to walk the plank, and we were now, so to speak, rudderless (stop it Bob). Who knows how things might have panned out had we just swallowed our pride? If he had worked on his solo project while remaining in the band, it would surely have diluted our musical output.

Was this our Beatles moment? A year earlier in 1970, the Fab Four had split when John Lennon left to go his own way with Yoko Ono. The group couldn't survive his departure. He and McCartney were the creative dynamite behind hit after hit, and there was no replacing him.

We were different – at least we hoped we were. Losing Allan shook us, as losing Graham had. Both of them were brilliant and inspirational musicians. But there were still four of us left, and we didn't want to stop. Tony was an extraordinary guitarist and a songwriter too. I had reached the top of my game and in Bernie and Terry we had two excellent band members. We would go on. It might be a bumpy ride for a bit, but we could take it.

The search was on for a replacement for Allan. Days after his departure, on Wednesday, December 29, 1971, high above the bustling crossroads of London's Oxford Circus, blond-haired Nordic musician Mikael Rickfors ambled out of the recording studio and into the AIR London control room. Ron Richards had just coaxed a vocal performance out of the singer from Stockholm, with the rest of us sitting round the mixing console watching and listening. It was a make-or-break recording session. Mikael had just laid his vocal track down on what was possibly The Hollies' next single, a Chip Taylor composition called 'The Baby'.

It had been Tony's idea to insert an unknown, unproven wildcard between himself and Sylvester on The Hollies' vocal front line. A few years earlier when The Hollies were performing in Sweden, Tony had drawn my attention to our support band, Bamboo. Mikael had been the lead vocalist. He was good, and when Allan left, Tony remembered him. Now, sitting in the control room, none of us were quite sure if our Swedish import would be the man for the job. Although he was a fine singer, he struggled with the English language and he never seemed comfortable being away from his beloved homeland. But as he entered the control room, Ron got up from his chair at the mixing desk, shook him by the hand and said: 'Congratulations, Mikael, you are now The Hollies' lead singer.'

The rest of us looked bemused and slightly stunned. There had been no discussion. He'd given the guy the job without talking over the pros and cons with the very people who would have to honour his casual commitment and make the re-jigged Hollies into a working band. It felt as though we had been left, literally, holding the baby. Ron, apparently oblivious to our dazed faces, made small talk as he donned his raincoat and invited everyone round to the pub.

How on earth was this going to work, I thought, as I followed him out of the door. Rickfors didn't really fit The Hollies mould. He was a musician, yes, but that's about the only thing we had in common. Fronting The Hollies was going to be a whole different ball game to Bamboo, a group that had lasted two years and released two singles before breaking up.

Rickfors' voice wasn't the same as Allan's either. Allan had a strident, distinctive throat-driven voice and was the arrowhead of The Hollies' three-way harmony. Tony and

Graham, and later Terry, became familiar with the way Allan breathed and tailored their harmonies accordingly. Rickfors had a deeper voice, he sang in a lower register. A Clarkey clone had been impossible to find. But was this guy the only option? Ron had told him he was in, and now the deed was done we had to make it work.

On January 10, 1972, the orchestral embellishments, arranged by Richard Hewson, were added to 'The Baby' and the track was mixed. The following day I took Mikael round various boutiques to let him check out the London fashion scene. Later top photographer Duffy shot the band in his north London studio, and the new boy was launched on Friday, January 21. Mother hen Robin had arranged for a Rolls-Royce to deliver us five Hollies to the Westbury Hotel off Bond Street. It was the point of entry to Hollieland for new vocal recruits. Again, old Robbo was in his element as he schmoozed the music press and journalists, generously splashing the champagne here and there to one and all. Later in the day we had a photo session for the German pop magazine, *Bravo*, with our old snapper chum Bubi Heilemann. News of The Hollies' Swedish import made the *Daily Mail* and the *Daily Express* and pop picker DJ Alan Freeman actually played 'The Baby' twice on his BBC Radio 1 programme. All right. Not 'arf.

We were now signed to Polydor Records, and they were intent on getting their first Hollies single into the charts. That was the good news. The not so good news was that our old

194

record label, EMI, were smarting over the fact that we had left them for Polydor's more lucrative deal. They had followed the Americans' lead and lifted 'Long Cool Woman (In A Black Dress)' off our LP *Distant Light* and they proceeded to promote it as The Hollies' latest platter. What timing! We now had two singles out on two different labels. We couldn't put our weight behind both, and we were committed to Polydor, so we had to go with 'The Baby'. Had we focussed on 'LCW' – with Allan still in harness – we would have had a chart-topper on both sides of the Atlantic. As it was, both singles suffered. 'The Baby' made number twenty-six and 'LCW' made number thirty-two.

Robin and our new people at Polydor had worked hard to kill off 'the opposition', even though it was a Hollies track. Now the beaming Hollies manager puffed on his fag, wiped his brow and, quaffing a large brandy, declared: 'Job done.' This must have hurt Allan as he set out to pursue his solo career. He had co-written the song, and it was his voice on the recording, but it had The Hollies' name on the disc.

However, in the States we hadn't changed record companies. We were still with CBS/Epic and it was a different story. 'The Baby' went nowhere, but 'Long Cool Woman' made number one. It also made number one in Canada and did well around the world. It was one of the best songs we ever recorded. To this day, every time I pass through Oxford Circus, I look up to the top floor windows, high above the Nike store, and doff my cap. Old Ron didn't sniff that American number one out; he wasn't even there at her birth. AIR London engineer John Punter twiddled the knobs, pushed faders and encouraged us to lay it down with pride.

Back then, in 1970, not only did we have a clash on our hands, but the recording of *Top Of The Pops* in which we were due to sing 'The Baby' was cancelled because of a power blackout. The miner's strike was in full flow (it lasted from January 9 to the end of February), and blackouts were occurring up and down the country.

Under the terms of our new recording contract, we were committed to giving Polydor a brand new album: *Romany*. Ron had fixed it for the band to go into the countryside and, as the cool dudes of the time would drawl: 'Get it together.' He suggested a bijou village hall in the village of Cholesbury, not far from his home in Chesham. Set in the Chiltern Hills, it became our haven for a few days in April as we rehearsed and went through our routines. After that, it was back to Abbey Road to record 'Delaware Taggett And The Outlaw Boys'. The following day my favourite Mikael song, 'Touch', was committed to tape. Then we returned to our retreat to rehearse the next lot of tracks.

We shuttled between rehearsals and recording, but after a decade of red-light-rush, we felt we'd earned the right to chill, and we took our time with some more laid-back numbers. The trouble was Ron, our producer and father figure for so long, was from the era of the Tin Pan Alley hit factory. Nothing wrong with that, but he liked to work quickly and churn out the toe-tappers then move on to the next track. When we didn't fall into line, he decided that he didn't want to be involved in the album and went off to tend to his vegetables and potter round his garden on his new ride-on mower. Like Allan, Ron would soon be back, but for the moment we were on our own. We carried on recording at Abbey Road, aided by legendary EMI engineer Peter Bown. He was the guy who had mic'd my drums up on my very first session with The Hollies in 1963. Pete knew how we worked, and he helped us enjoy our time recording with Mikael – it led to the emergence of The Hollies' in-house production.

The country hideaway location was too far out of town, but fortunately George Martin suggested a Boy Scout hall round the corner from Abbey Road Studios. Perfect. Talk about 'Be Prepared'. In just a few minutes we could be out of the Scout hall, across the road, through a secret shortcut between private properties, then nip through the back door of Abbey Road Studios, through the old squash court (echo chamber) and into Studio Two by way of the emergency exit.

By Sunday, May 21 the album was mixed and in the can. Relief all round. *Romany* was to be the follow-up album to *Distant Light*. Storm Thorgerson, at design firm Hipgnosis, had come up with the double-gate sleeve for that one, and it seemed like a natural progression for the same team to create the *Romany* artwork. Between us, we chose a similar scene set in wintertime. Maybe this was a nod to the colder Swedish climate.

Tony's girlfriend, Roedean-educated *Vogue* model Jane
Lumb, made dinner for the band at the Hicks residence on
Loudoun Road in St John's Wood. Jane was good fun. She
was from Mytholmroyd, a few miles from where Tony and
I were born, and she became one of the faces of the sixties,
alongside Twiggy and a couple of others. She was best
known for being in the first Pirelli calendar and for an ad for
Fry's Turkish Delight. She and Tony had been together for
a few years by this time. They both went on to marry other
people, but for a long time they were very happy together.
Anyway, that evening is recorded for posterity – we can be
seen on the inside of the *Romany* record sleeve, carousing
round the dining table while the Hipgnosis guy snapped
us glugging fine wines. He captured yours truly operating a
blurred ventriloquist's dummy and trying to recite 'Baubles,
bangles and bright shining beads'. Try saying that without
moving your lips.

The following day I was driven north in our van by Dek
Whyment. To call Dek a roadie would be unfair; he was a
talented Mancunian tech and a loyal friend. Back in 1968
when we were looking for something a little different to add
to our 'Jennifer Eccles' track, I had suggested that we try a
steel or Hawaiian guitar. But where could we find someone to
fit the bill? Dek had chirped up: 'When I was a TV repairman,
I worked with a guy called Rod King. He's a good pedal steel
player.' The next day Mr King had arrived at Chappell's studio
on Bond Street and entertained us with his cheeky steel wolf

whistles, culminating in a perfect steel guitar solo, nicely enhancing our forthcoming hit. Opening line: 'White chalk written on red brick' – memories of a Salford playground.

America wanted The Hollies and an autumn tour in the States had been lined up. As usual, I suffered from the after-effects of the smallpox jab and during the re-recording of 'Magic Woman Touch' on October 6, my arm became inflamed and painful as I was playing conga drums. I travelled back north for a couple of days to recuperate at the family cottage and to catch up with my parents and Maureen.

Dad, as usual, ran me to Manchester where I boarded the London train. I stayed overnight at Tony's, and the following day the pair of us were picked up by our favourite driver, Daimler Hire's Johnny Catton. He always made us chuckle. When asked how he'd been, he would reply: 'I've been up and down, up and down.' He never disappointed.

There was no business class in 1972; the choice was simple – economy or first class. The champagne flowed as we sat up front in a BOAC 747 jumbo and headed out over south Wales. A few hours later limos picked us up from Kennedy Airport and delivered us to our hotel, the Essex House on Central Park. And as usual, Tony and I went straight round to Manny's Music to see what was new on the equipment front and to say hello to the guys there.

In those days, we took amps, drums and even airfreighted our Swedish Ackuset PA system to the States. In the cities the five of us, along with Rod and Robin, would travel in a couple of black Cadillacs and when Dek the tech had loaded the gear into a U-Haul truck, off we would go. Out in the country Rod would usually drive us all in a big station wagon.

We made our way through Durham, North Carolina; Baltimore; Albany; Buffalo; Keene State College, New Hampshire; and Portland, Maine before we flew down to Palm Beach for a few days' break. We attempted to play golf on a perfect sun-baked course, pausing to knock coconuts out of the trees and quench our thirst while we watched pelicans diving for fish in the clear blue ocean.

Back on the trail we started with State College, North Carolina. Diary entry: '*Good crowd. They were shouting for more. Our PA system is sounding great. Dek had stayed up near Boston to fix the fault on our sound system, which made the vocalists very happy.*'

After that we headed over the Blue Ridge Mountains of Virginia to Charlotte, North Carolina, before going back to New York for a show at the Lincoln Center. We were thirty-five floors up in the Essex House, and the view over Central Park was amazing. We could see people ice skating down below, looking like L. S. Lowry's matchstick people.

Frontman Mikael liked to take a nap before a show. The problem was that he took a while to fully awaken in time for the major event of the day. Rod Shields told me that he often had to call Rickfors several times before a performance to wake him from his slumber. As a result, he started off a little on the dopey side, and as we progressed through the set list, he would gradually come to life. Sometimes, in the early numbers, I felt like getting off my drum stool and shaking him. By the end of the show when we were back in the dressing room, he would proclaim: 'Now I feel as though I could sing all night!'

The day after the Lincoln Center performance, we met the press then lunched with the CBS/Epic Records people who presented us with gold records celebrating the chart-topping success of 'Long Cool Woman'. Unfortunately, they had spelled my name incorrectly on the disc. Shame, but it didn't tarnish the day; we were very chuffed with the new discs to add to our collection. I felt saddened that Allan, the guy who wrote and sang the song, wasn't there alongside us to enjoy the occasion.

The following day, Tuesday, November 7, was election day in the US. Nixon v McGovern for president. Nixon won by a landslide. We had the day off, so we jetted to Atlanta and stayed at the Marriott.

We were in Augusta, Georgia when we heard that our new single, 'Long Dark Road', composed by Tony, had entered the US Top 50. That evening we went onstage later than scheduled and ran over the finish time, resulting in the cops turning on all the house lights and cutting the power supply. We were guillotined in full flow. Not a nice feeling.

Louisville, Kentucky came next, followed by the Auditorium in Chicago. I wrote: 'Great theatre. We played here last time. I drove the band along and played good. Feeling *tired but rising to the occasion.'* No surprise that I was tired, we were doing a huge amount of travelling between non-stop gigs. And it wasn't over yet. We were due to travel to Seattle. First, though, I needed to pay homage to the Ludwig factory on North Damen Avenue. I'd first visited the red brick building in 1967, but this time I was invited into the office of William Ludwig II, or 'Bill Two' as he was affectionately known. There I picked up a new Super Sensitive 402 snare drum along with some spare parts. Bill gave me a quick tour of a new department where he proudly announced that they were developing effects for guitars. Guitars! They were supposed to be a drum company. Dear Bill had no idea what these guitar gadgets were for. Worse still, a new modern Ludwig badge in blue and olive had replaced the revered Keystone emblem that had been attached to every Ludwig drum shell throughout the 1960s. What a mistake. Would Mercedes scrap their famous three pointed star badge and replace it with a bland sticker? No way. That move heralded the start of the Ludwig company's demise. The brand had become the byword for drums, thanks to bands like us and The Beatles who had displayed the famous logo script on the front of our bass drums. Since then, the factory had been churning out drum kits day and night to satisfy global demand. As a result, the Ludwig family was awash with cash, but sadly, they squandered their fortune on the wrong things – like bits for guitars and new badges. The young generation in the form of Bill Three, or William Ludwig III, was coming, and the end was in sight; the Japanese were on the horizon, in the guise of Pearl, Yamaha and Tama.

Clutching my precious snare drum, I said goodbye to the kindly Mr Ludwig, jumped into a taxi and dashed to O'Hare Airport to meet up with the lads and catch our flight to the West Coast. I needn't have rushed. Our plane, a McDonnell Douglas DC-10, powered by three engines, had a problem. The cargo door wouldn't close and the flight was delayed. This was a design fault. A few months earlier, a similar aircraft had taken off from Detroit Metro Airport and at 11,000 feet, the door blew off, causing an explosive decompression. Fortunately, that didn't happen to our plane. They got the door shut, and we eventually landed in Seattle.

We checked into the Edgewater Inn, a hotel built out over the harbour. Guests could buy fishing equipment and bait from the hotel gift shop, go to their rooms, slide back the windows and cast their lines down into Elliott Bay. Yes, it seems my ancestors had got here first. Correct spelling too. The Beatles had stayed at the Edgewater in 1964 and had posed for photographs while fishing from a bedroom window. By 1969, rock gods were not so benign. Members of Led Zeppelin, while in residence, dangled their tackle out of the hotel windows and landed several large mud sharks which then flip-flopped around the bedroom carpet. Apparently, John Bonham and the boys threw the dead creatures around the hotel then tucked the slippery bodies into unsuspecting guests' beds.

The following morning I woke at 8.45 a.m., drew back my bedroom curtains and looked out at the sun rising through the mist. A ghostly ferryboat was creeping along and ocean-going freighters were appearing one by one, sounding their horns, while edging their way into port. I watched a small diving seabird submerge for ages, and when it resurfaced a horde of bullying gulls snatched its hard-earned fish. The phone rang, interrupting my reverie. It was Robin, who said: 'Tonight's show is cancelled.' I didn't ask why and hung up. In the afternoon we played nine holes of golf. I hated it, but it passed the time. Afterwards we ate oysters and drank all evening.

Feeling depressed, I phoned Maureen. I needed to hear her voice. It was just after midnight for us, and in England they were eight hours ahead. Maureen was having breakfast at our bass player's house; she and Bernie's wife, Shirley, were friends. Maureen said that she'd had a bad night's sleep due to a banging noise in the next bedroom.

It always cheered me up talking to Mo. I had almost lost her once, and I didn't plan to let it happen again. Back in the mid-sixties we had drifted apart. She began going out with Willie Morgan, one of the players from Burnley Football Club, known as the Clarets. Willie later went on to play for Scotland and Manchester United. Years later, when Mo and I were back together, I met Willie when I was out drinking with some Burnley footballers in Angels night club. He told me sadly: 'I wish I'd married that girl.' That made me sit up and think. Maureen and I had been together since 1960, and I had taken her for granted. I promised myself I would let her know, more often, how much she meant to me. She was very special.

In Los Angeles we stayed at the Beverly Comstock. That night Dek, Tony, Terry and I headed for the Whisky a Go Go, where I shared a table with Who drummer Keith Moon, who, bizarrely, was dressed in full fox-hunting regalia, including a riding hat strapped firmly to his head. He said he'd been taking part in some sort of street parade. On the table was a bottle of Courvoisier, from which Moon would occasionally swig while rolling his eyes in classic Robert-Newton-*Treasure-Island*-movie fashion. He was like a supercharged kid. In between jumping up and down and heckling the resident band he demonstrated how fast he could drum on the table top with his hands.

Over the next couple of days I began writing a song. As no one seemed to be in composing mode, I thought I'd shake things up by writing one myself. I called it 'Transatlantic Westbound Jet'. I hoped it might kick-start some sort of front line writing revival. I had the lyrics, but Tony didn't seem interested in helping with a tune, so I asked Terry to strum a few chords. We got the structure of the song together before our gig at the Santa Monica Auditorium on November 22.

After that it was time to go home. The London boys flew direct to Heathrow from LA, while the northern contingent of Dek, Bernie, Rod and I had to fly, first class of course, the 3,000 miles to JFK. We changed planes and continued on a BOAC Vickers Super VC10, powered by four Rolls-

Royce Conway jet engines mounted at the rear beneath the T-shaped tail. This aircraft had the ability to cross the pond faster than any other commercial jet, until Concorde came along. I think our flight from the US to the UK took just over five hours. Our first stop was Prestwick, where Scottish passengers were able to disembark. The rest of us had yet to clear immigration and we were now under surveillance by Her Majesty's Customs and Excise. A uniformed official had boarded the jet and sat up at the front on a rear-facing seat, solemnly looking down the length of the aircraft as if guarding a load of convicts. Maybe he was there to see if any of us weary travellers had been passed Scottish contraband while the plane was on the tarmac. Welcome to England.

On the first day of December, *Romany*, our first release on the Polydor label, was issued. The new company hadn't sent me a copy, so I bought one from Boots in Burnley.

A week later on my birthday, Friday, December 8, Bernie picked me up and drove me to Manchester Airport for a flight to Schiphol. We did our usual round trip, recorded a Dutch television show – in this instance, we lip-sync'd to 'Magic Woman Touch' and 'Won't We Feel Good' – and then dashed back to Schiphol and home. I was aiming to be back in my local pub in time for last orders, only this time our Aer Lingus flight was delayed. To make things even more stressful, on arrival at Manchester Airport, a sullen, uniformed customs man blocked my escape and ordered me to open my bag and empty my pockets. I had nothing to declare. I'd only been out of old Blighty for a few hours. All I had was my duty-free allowance of Grand Marnier liqueur for Mum and 200 cigarettes for Dad. I guess I ruined his day.

CARRIE – ANNE

Words & Music by ALLAN CLARKE, GRAHAM NASH & TONY HICKS

Recorded by **THE HOLLIES** on Parlophone

GRALTO MUSIC LIMITED

3/-

CHAPTER FOURTEEN:

All is Forgiven

The first page in my diary for 1973 is blank. 'Nuff said. New Year's Eve must have been a rocking affair down at the Bay Horse in Roughlee.

The following day, January 2, I was back in Abbey Road with the boys, recording Mikael's song 'Don't Leave The Child Alone'. A day later we set up in a circle, facing one another, just as we did on our early 1960s sessions, and recorded 'They Don't Realise I'm Down'. It felt good. As usual, after a long day in the studio, Dek and I rewarded ourselves, along with Bernie and Rod, with curry at Diwan-i-Am on our way to our Speakeasy hangout on Margaret Street. By the end of the week the two tracks were mixed and Rod drove Bernie and me back north.

At the end of January after an eleven-hour TWA flight over the volcanic eruptions of Iceland, we landed at Los Angeles International Airport. The following day, after a cooked breakfast in Robin's room at the Beverly Comstock, we recorded *In Concert* at Santa Monica Auditorium. The audience was great, and we were on form, but it was jinxed. The monitor system was feeding back, the front line couldn't hear their own voices and I broke a drum skin. Wally Heider's mobile studio was recording the show, and fortunately we were able to go into his studio a couple of days later to repair the damage. Some of the vocals were re-recorded and we oversaw the final mix. Once we were happy, we went off to the Whisky on Sunset Strip to have some fun. Some of the strippers from the nearby clubs befriended us – they liked British bands. They'd join our table and pass on the latest gossip. This time one of the girls said she had just returned from Bob Hope's house in Bel Air. She was dressed as an old-fashioned, glamorous movie star, and she looked like a very fetching Marilyn Monroe. She had been entertaining the old rascal.

The following day Tony flew up the coast to see Graham in San Francisco. He had dinner with Willy and David Crosby and stayed overnight. When he came back, he said there was a stream running through the house. Very Timothy Leary.

After recording a TV show for NBC's Burbank Studios, we boarded a Western Airlines flight to Minneapolis and then flew on to Fargo. After the warmth of California, we were plunged into freezing temperatures and travelled on roads lined with walls of snow. Quite an adjustment!

We played to a sold out Fargo Auditorium and afterwards Robin told us there had been 2,000 people outside who couldn't get in. Sioux Falls followed, with an audience of 4,000. Next came Minneapolis, and then we flew home via Chicago. I slept until teatime the following day then went over to Causey Foot in Nelson, the home of Alan and Peggy Hicks – and my Maureen.

On March 29 The Hollies' second album with Mikael Rickfors as our lead singer, *Out On The Road*, was finished and mixed. Then it was straight to Heathrow and on to Australia, via Los Angeles. The Australians had tried to book the band throughout the 1960s, but what with my illness and other work commitments, we were latecomers to the Oz circuit and our first Aussie tour had not been until January 1970.

We loved going to Oz. Still do. The thought of escaping the damp chill of the English winter and soaking up the warmth of the Australian sun draws us Down Under, though I'm still not quite sure if the water spins down the gurgler clockwise or the other way when the bath plug is pulled.

On that 1973 trip I was seated right in the nose of the jumbo jet. Visibility was perfect as we headed north. As we reached cruising height, I unbuckled my seat belt, intent on viewing our green and pleasant land from 36,000 feet. From the left-hand window I spied the gleaming Mersey estuary and Liverpool, and there was Manchester down below. Moving across to the right-hand window, my eyes zoomed in on the town where I was born: Burnley. I recognised the locally famous mile-long stretch of the Leeds to Liverpool canal, gleaming like a straight, silver thread. Nearby, there was Turf

Moor football ground, home of the Clarets. I even spotted Hanson Parker's farm, highlighted by the bright sunshine in Roughlee, and Mum and Dad's favourite bird watching area, Stocks Reservoir, shimmering in the Forest of Bowland.

The TWA cabin crews were the wackiest and most entertaining. On one transatlantic trip, the guys and I were sipping our welcome aboard champers when the aircraft began to push back in readiness for take-off. The flirty stewardess apologised as she confiscated our unfinished drinks and disappeared to the service area. A few seconds later her head popped through the curtain, and she exclaimed: 'Don't worry, after take-off we're gonna party all the way.' Then, holding her index finger to her lips and with a saucy giggle added: 'But shhh, don't tell the captain!' and the curtain closed.

Rod Shields checked us into the Beverly Comstock for an unexpected overnight stopover in LA. We had missed our connection, so the following evening we caught a jumbo to Honolulu. There, our entourage boarded a Boeing 707 and flew for a further ten and a half hours before touching down in Sydney. Because of the international dateline, we lost May Day 1973 forever, or at least it seemed that way. Maybe we sampled too much complimentary vino with our fellow passengers, Alan Whicker and his charming partner Valerie. It was the middle of the night, mid-Pacific time, and our plane had stopped in Fiji to refuel. We were led to a comfortable lounge for refreshments. While chatting to Whicker, I explored the treats on offer. New Zealand wines were a rarity back then, especially the red variety. World-traveller Alan drew my attention to a bottle of Kiwi Pinot Noir. It turned out to be a gorgeous light red that had been slightly chilled. The remainder of the journey to Sydney was heaven. I was tucked up under a blanket enjoying sweet dreams at 40,000 feet.

We landed at Kingsford Smith Airport, Sydney, tired and unshaven, to find that the press, TV and radio were there in force. Thankfully, a press reception was arranged for 5 p.m. at the hotel, giving us a chance to check into our rooms and recharge, ready to be 'on parade', as Robin liked to say, at teatime.

After we'd done with the media, we were off to the legendary Doyles fish restaurant at Watsons Bay. Back then it was just a cabin on the beach. The staff served the freshest produce but no alcohol. No problem. We resorted to Bring Your Own, or B-Y-O, three letters that were part of the Aussie lexicon. Thirsty Robin would scurry off to the nearby off-licence, or 'selling out shop' as they're known in Burnley. He'd return with two heavy plastic bags, one in each hand, clanking and puffing like an old steam locomotive, to unload his welcome selection of wines. We were never without a full glass with old Robbo around. Afterwards, suitably lubricated, Tony and Terry appeared on some late night TV chat show.

Our first gig was at the Festival Hall up in Brisbane, followed the next day by the Hordern Pavilion in Sydney. The PA was awful, we couldn't hear our instruments and vocals, and after the show I was depressed. Back at the hotel I watched the FA Cup final live on TV. That perked me up.

After concerts in Melbourne and Adelaide, I wrote: '*Show not so good, singer not making it. We obviously made an error in Mikael.*' We were all giving our best, but it was never quite the same with the Swedish songster.

Rain in Perth, Western Australia, on May 12 meant our scheduled concert in Beatty Park had to be moved indoors to the new Concert Hall for a sold out midnight gig. It was our final night of the tour in Australia and thankfully it was a good show. Then it was all the way across Oz, changing planes in Sydney and flying via Nadi, Fiji to Honolulu, where we boarded a Continental Airlines flight to Los Angeles. The following day we flew out of LA via Denver to play in Casper, Wyoming. Cowboy country. Five flights in three days. Seemingly endless hours in the air had become a way of life.

In Casper we went to check out the venue. Two truckloads of gear had been provided; we had a special lighting gantry above the stage and the luxury of several microphones on my drums. Advancements in technology and demand from audiences and performers for better sound amplification was spawning a plethora of independent contractors producing enhanced audio systems. Stage lighting also improved dramatically. When The Hollies started out, we were five guys sporting two Vox amps and a drum kit. We had to thrash and strain to be heard. Now, thanks to bigger, more elaborate PA systems, we could relax, safe in the knowledge that the highs and lows, the light and shade of our performance, would be heard and seen throughout the venue. But all this came at a cost. Bigger trucks were now needed to transport the lighting rigs and speaker systems, coupled with the need for technicians and crew to operate the increasingly sophisticated consoles onstage and front of house.

The gig was sold out. So was the next day's in Billings, Montana, up on the edge of the Rockies. It was windy and dusty. We had planned to drive the 228 miles from Billings to Butte, but Rod booked flights instead. We had two twenty-minute hops over and through the mountains in a big jet via Great Falls. The pilot of our powerful Boeing 737 gave us an exhilarating ride, jockeying the big jet through the ravines and canyons like a boy racer, after which he landed us gently in the city of Butte, 6,000 feet above sea level.

Bismark, North Dakota was next, then Grand Forks and Minot. The Holiday Inns were identical. Thankfully our performances were getting better, and I wrote: '*Played well. Good show. After "Long Dark Road" they wanted more. We are really giving the US audiences what they want.*'

Rod had chartered two light aircraft to fly us from Springfield to Kansas, where we would catch a scheduled flight on to our final show of the tour in Evansville. I was in the first plane with Rod, Bernie, Terry and Mikael. The remaining three, Robin, Tony and Dek, were going to follow on in a smaller aircraft. About half an hour into our journey, black clouds reared up and we were suddenly in the middle of a storm. It was scary, but we eventually landed safely at Kansas City International Airport. But the small plane didn't arrive. I felt sick with worry. Had it gone down *à la* Buddy Holly? Our twin-engine planes were similar to the one that rock legends the Big Bopper (Jiles Perry Richardson), Ritchie Valens and Buddy were travelling in when it crashed in February 1959, killing all three and the pilot. But thankfully there was no tragedy for us – the second plane had turned back. The Big Boozer (Robin Colville Britten), Tony and Dek met up with us the following day, and all was well. The Evansville gig was supposed to be an afternoon outdoor affair, but at that point there was a tornado warning. Happily, the weather held and we got onstage after Rare Earth and Canned Heat.

I was ready to go home. The next day we flew from Springfield to Newark. There was heavy fog, so we couldn't use the helicopter link to JFK, but we got there by road. The bad weather had disrupted all flights, but we made it eventually. Bernie's wife, Shirley, met us at Manchester Airport.

It was time to pause and take stock. The Hollies had supplied two albums to Polydor, and under the terms of our agreement we needed to keep 'em coming. But Tony and I were aware that we didn't want to go on with the band as it was. Dynamic live performances were The Hollies' lifeblood, and they just weren't happening. Mikael was a fine artist, but some of our tour performances had been, to be honest, pretty mediocre in the grand scheme of all things Hollies. We were missing the cut and thrust of our trademark energy-driven hit-'em-between-the-eyes live show delivery.

One morning while the two of us were drinking tea and mulling things over in the sitting room of Tony's house at 132 Loudoun Road, St John's Wood (which in the mid-1990s became the home of Liam Gallagher), Hicks declared: 'I think I'll give Clarkey a call.' It was what we'd both been thinking. Time to swallow our pride. Tony picked up the phone and dialled. It was a case of 'come home, Allan, all is forgiven'. But had our frontman forgiven the two of us for stubbornly sticking to our principles? Was he bitter? The Hollies wanted Allan, but did Allan want us?

Cut to a scene a few days later in Tramp, the much-famed private member's club on Jermyn Street in London. Tony has been an honorary member since Johnny Gold first opened its doors in 1969. Late one hot August night Maureen and I sat alongside Tony and Jane in our favourite spot. Maureen loved coming to town. She enjoyed shopping and would nip along to cult store Biba, then in its heyday.

Tramp was a great place to hang out, and Maureen loved to star-spot. Sitting near us were Roger Moore, Joan Collins, Ryan O'Neal and Michael Caine. Further along the line I could just about make out blonde *Charlie's Angel* Farrah Fawcett. Shadowy celebrities lurked or danced in the dimly lit disco. The four of us were having fun, and I was excited at the thought of meeting up with our prodigal son the following day.

We stayed at Tony's, and the morning after he brought Mo and me mugs of tea in bed. Lunchtime was approaching, and we had an appointment at the Blenheim, a watering hole just a short walk from the Hicks residence. As Tony and I grabbed a drink and a seat, a beaming Allan walked in. It was an as-I-was-saying situation. The conversation flowed as if the three of us had never been apart. Allan told us he had a song that he thought was strong, and we agreed that we should get into Abbey Road ASAP.

The transition was smooth. Mikael knew the fit wasn't right, and he was happy to go back to Sweden, where he was already a star. We parted on good terms, and Allan slipped back into his still-warm lead position.

Once again life had promise; we were all speaking the same musical language, and I felt good. Three days after that pub meeting we recorded 'Mexico Gold' and then, two days later, we nailed Allan's return rocker 'The Day That Curly Billy Shot Down Crazy Sam McGee'. Like the title, the track was overly long, so a couple of weeks later, we chopped thirty seconds from the master tape in readiness for Polydor to press it into a saleable 45 rpm vinyl single. We had the top team at Abbey Road – Hollies headmaster and A&R man Ron Richards was back at the helm, and Alan Parsons who, a few years earlier, had been the young tape operator supplying us with cups of tea, had now become our recording engineer, magically providing special effects and production-enhancing ideas. The slap echo on my snare drum worked well, and

Tony's vari-speed, multitracked guitars added to the Wild West, gun-slinging atmosphere.

Allan lived in Hampstead, in a lovely terrace on Flask Walk, where one of his neighbours was the actor John Hurt. After the recordings, Tony drove me up there in his new Porsche 911 Targa, and we had a pint and a spot of lunch in The Flask pub with Allan, whose house was a short distance away.

The first TV show that we did to plug 'The Day That Curly Billy Shot Down Crazy Sam McGee' was over in Holland. It was all done in a day, as usual. When I joined Maureen at the bar of the Bay Horse Inn in Roughlee for last orders at ten thirty, none of the pub regulars believed I'd done a day's work in Europe. What's more, if my journey home was delayed, the landlord, ex-military man Ted 'Smudger' Smith, would let me in through the back door to join the local drinkers.

On Wednesday, September 26 we were invited to appear, once more, on *Top Of The Pops*. We still loved the process of visiting the Beeb. As usual, Pan's People were doing their stuff in leotards and sequins on what was, by this time, a pretty staid old formula of a chart show. After the recording we sprinted up to my favourite haunt, the rooftop BBC Club. Drinks were cheap, the bar staff were characters, and we could hang out with off-duty dancers, actors, musicians and news presenters. One time the complete cast of *Dad's Army* was on parade. We'd follow our star-studded booze-up with our usual hot curry. Just what the doctor ordered for a peaceful night's sleep.

All seemed well with the world. 'Curly Billy' made number twenty-four in the charts and we were booked to appear on yet another *TOTP*.

Ron Richards and the rest of us sat in the control room of Studio Two and listened to Allan sing and strum his latest offering, 'Don't Let Me Down'. His delivery was passionate and heartfelt, giving us an insight into his life at the time. I, for one, was moved. When he'd finished, we filed down the wooden staircase and onto the studio's parquet floor. Allan sang a guide vocal, Tony and Terry played acoustic guitars, and Bernie and I laid down a bass and drum pattern. The result was good. Some weeks later Chris Gunning added beautifully scored empathic strings, French horns and bowed double basses; a perfect orchestral embellishment to one of Allan's finest compositions.

We were in Studio Two recording 'Falling Calling', a song written by Terry and Allan, when Paul and Linda McCartney, who were working in Studio Three, came in to see what we were up to. After exchanging pleasantries with Ron and the lads, Paul quietly took me aside and said: 'Bobby, do you fancy doing a bit of jammin'?' I replied that I always loved to get up and play drums, no matter what was on the musical menu, and I added: 'As long as it doesn't interfere with Hollies work.' He nodded, smiled and said: 'Right, yeah, I'll see you later then.' And with that, he and Linda went back to Studio Three. I was left none the wiser.

The following evening, with a couple of backing tracks completed, Allan, Tony and Terry were sorting out the vocals and harmonies. It was a slow process, and I was bored. When Hollies tech, Dek, enquired whether the two of us should pop round to the pub for a swift one, his timing was perfect. As we reached the end of the corridor, we saw two green bicycles leant up against the wall in the reception area. They were the McCartneys' mode of transport. A ciggie smoking Paul called out from the doorway of Studio Three: 'Hey Bobby, would you like to come in and have a listen to what we've been doing?' I said I'd love to have a listen, although in truth I was more interested in getting out of the building, clearing my head and quenching my thirst. But it *was* Paul McCartney, and a refusal would have been rude. Maybe Paul hadn't thought much of the Hollies songs he'd heard the previous day and saw this as an opportunity to show me how it was done, Wings style.

Dek followed me into the control room, whispering that we didn't have much time and ought to get round to the pub. As the heavy door closed behind us, a glass was placed in my hand. I remember thinking, this red wine won't mix with my eagerly anticipated pint of beer. Don't mix the grape with the grain.

The spools of tape rolled on the Studer recording machine, and Paul's familiar voice came out of the two big Lockwood speakers. I don't recall the title; I had other things on my mind. After playback, I thanked Paul who then hit me with: 'Bobby, would you like to join my band?' This wasn't about 'jammin''; he was offering me the drumming job with Wings. After a short pause, I told him that I was flattered to be asked adding: 'It's not for me, my gig is with The Hollies.' With Dek tugging discretely at my sleeve, I thanked Linda and Paul for the wine and made my exit through the double doors, down the famous Abbey Road front steps and round the corner to the Heroes of Alma. Dek bought the first round, and after my first mouthful of ale, I looked at him, wiped my beery lips and said: 'Phew – that was a close one. Can you imagine me with Wings!'

Allan told me that Ron Richards' and George Martin's secretaries, Shirley and Carol, had heard a song that would be ideal for The Hollies on a Phil Everly album. Shirley, who had been around since we started working at Abbey Road, had often sat in on our evening recording sessions. She was quite a fun character. She would joke with Ron and offer cheeky suggestive comments to all in the control room. I remember one of her early observations, when she was peering through the large control room window down into Studio Two, watching Tony. 'Look at little Pinocchio, he's singing his heart out!' she grinned.

We listened to the track Shirley and Carol had mentioned and decided they were right. It was a beautiful ballad by Albert Hammond and Mike Hazlewood called 'The Air That I Breathe'. We decided to record it as a possible next single. Days later Tony, Bernie and I laid the basic track. I used my Ludwig drums, along with the deeper, damped Super Sensitive 402 snare drum that Mr Ludwig had given me in Chicago. The following day, vocals were added, followed by my tom-tom overdubs. I'd removed the bottom heads from the two rack toms, and with careful microphone placement and technical wizardry, Alan Parsons made my drums sound like tympani.

Now we needed someone to provide the orchestral finishing touches. Ron phoned Johnny Scott, who had orchestrated 'He Ain't Heavy' in 1969, but he was busy working on his own project. He recommended arranger and composer Chris Gunning, the guy who had written the popular 'Try a taste of Martini' TV ads. Chris went on to write many popular film scores and music for several TV series, including *Agatha Christie's Poirot*.

As was normal practice, the arranger would be given a rough mix of our basic track with bass, drums, guitars and vocals. He would then listen at his leisure, while searching his soul for inspiration. He had to create a sympathetic, symphonic orchestral part that the assembled mass of classical musicians would sight-read and play at the overdub session some weeks later.

The distinctive guitar introduction was all Tony's own work, aided by Parsons who used a Hammond organ's Leslie speaker, giving the first few seconds of the track a haunting quality. Both Christopher Gunning and John Scott told me that when they had worked on 'Air' and 'He Ain't Heavy', my percussive fills influenced the outcome of their arrangements. Listening to the recordings, it sounds as though I was playing along to their scores, but in fact it was the other way round.

The drum phrases, already on the track, dictated what they should write for the orchestral overlay.

We finished the album and approved the sleeve photos. These were black and white Hipgnosis mug shots, back and front, but with the five Hollies' eyes in differing pastel colours. Our latest LP, *Hollies*, was complete.

As a result of conflict in the Middle East, oil exports to various Western countries, including Britain, were restricted. Petrol was rationed, and speed restrictions were imposed on motorways. Travelling by car in 1973 was a slow and uncertain process. Garages would only sell four gallons of fuel at a time and rationing-style coupons had been issued. People were living dangerously, storing what petrol they could get hold of in old tin containers in their homes and vehicles as the price of oil rose steeply.

Christmas was approaching, and as I was in London, it seemed a good time to buy presents. I got Maureen a coat and shoes from Biba and, before heading north, I popped round to Robin's townhouse and office in Bryanston Mews West, where I gave him a bottle of vintage port. He reciprocated by handing me an even older bottle of port with 1958 stamped on the wax seal. I still have it here in my cellar. One day I shall draw the cork and raise a glass to the memory of dear old Robbo.

The year ended with a sumptuous claret-fuelled dinner party at John Bradley's home, about three miles from Roughlee. Brad, as everyone knew him, had ingeniously turned an abandoned farm cottage overlooking the Ribble Valley into a cosy hangout for his chums and their partners. He loved to cook exotic meals, and he managed to work culinary miracles in the small stone-floored kitchen using only an ancient electric oven. Maureen and I had enjoyed countless wild dinner parties in his isolated retreat.

Brad was a loveable rogue whose family had owned cinemas in Burnley. He had been sent away to boarding school as a small child. His parents divorced and his father married a middle-aged ex-dancer. Brad didn't approve and would refer to her as 'the last of the high kickers.'

Bradley later married Cheshire beauty Jocelyn Quick, and soon became involved in property development in London, making all kinds of friends along the way. Charles Delevingne, the father of supermodel Cara, was a regular guest at Bradley's hilltop pad, as was Princes Margaret's one-time walker Ned Ryan. Both of them would sit elbow-to-elbow with Maureen and I as we ate at the rustic dinner table set before a roaring fire. One night, as the port bottle was being passed round, I remember Ned, a proud Irishman, recounting the tale of taking part in a hunting party with the royal family somewhere on the moors. 'We were all carrying guns and standing line abreast,' he said. 'I looked to my right and there was Prince Charles, the Duke of Edinburgh and the Queen. I could have taken the three of 'em out with one bullet,' he joked.

With that, Big Ben struck midnight, heralding a period of petrol rationing, power shortages, the Three-Day Week and miners' strikes. In a bid to save electricity, the Tory government had decreed that all television transmissions would close down at 10.30 p.m.

Welcome to 1974.

KING MIDAS IN REVERSE

WORDS AND MUSIC BY GRAHAM NASH, ALLAN CLARKE AND TONY HICKS

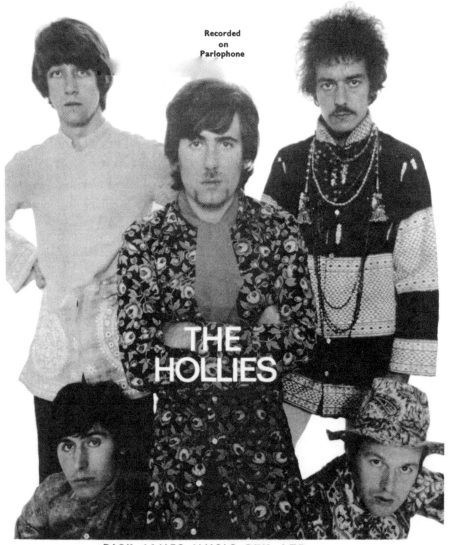

Recorded
on
Parlophone

THE
HOLLIES

DICK JAMES MUSIC PTY. LTD.

Distributors: LEEDS MUSIC PTY. LTD.

UNIVERSAL HOUSE, PELICAN STREET, SYDNEY, N.S.W.

40
CENTS

CHAPTER FIFTEEN:

Stand Up... Fall Down

'The Air That I Breathe' was released as a single on January 25. As with our US hit a couple of years earlier, 'Long Cool Woman', Terry had bagged the B-side, this time for his composition 'No More Riders'.

In the 1960s Robin had been a publicist for several top American artists while they were visiting Britain. Roy Orbison was one of his clients and so was James Brown, the Godfather of Soul. Robin told me that when he was in the presence of James, he was ordered to address him as Mr Brown. When we first met Robin, he was the publicist for American singer Gene Pitney, who was a charming and astute businessman. Gene had advised our Robbo that there was money in music publishing. We'd witnessed the power of the publisher in The Hollies' formative years when Graham, Allan and Tony signed to Dick James and formed GRALTO Music. Now Robin had an 'in' into the trade via Terry, and the pair of them formed Charlotte Music. Robbo's intention was to build 'a music publishing empire'.

The wedge was inserted and the tug of war was about to begin.

Robin had been a good manager. When he was at his buzzing best, he was inspired and talented. But in Allan's absence, he had formed a bond with Terry and when Allan returned, there were tensions from the start. Allan and Terry would argue and bicker, and Robin played to this. He hoped to boost Terry's success with a solo single and to ride the wave.

Robin would coax Terry to assert his position. Terry could be great fun and I enjoyed his company when we hit the bars and clubs. He sang the top harmony almost as well as Nash, but his songwriting abilities fell well short of Graham's talents. Working alongside Clarke and Hicks with their proven track record was a daunting call, and as a new recruit, Terry, light on kudos and musical substance, had to fight his corner. Rod Shields summed up the situation beautifully: 'Robin was always telling Terry to stand up for himself. "Stand up to them," he would say. And that's where he fell down.'

Allan felt that he needed to combat Robbo's devious games. As a result of his solo stint, he now had his own manager who went by the name of David Apps.

Robin was petrified of Allan turning up at the office. He knew that he would be in for a verbal pounding after Allan's lunchtime libations with his drinking pals. In those days the pubs closed at 3 p.m. Later in the afternoon the chatter of the cab's diesel engine was the first alert. The slam of the passenger door was the cue for our pallid manager to pour himself a stiff brandy and ginger. Once inside the mews office, Al would bombard a limp Robbo with questions and demands about the future of the band. He felt, as Tony and I did, that mediocrity was now being embraced as the norm. We'd started out as a rock band, but the excitement that had made The Hollies great was being submerged under a tidal wave of middle-of-the-road-ness. Safe and suited, and with money in the bank, we'd become Robbo's puppets, and our hard-earned integrity and trust had been hijacked. Our bass player Bernard Bamford Calvert, who is also a fine pianist, was now in full recital mode. He had recorded a piano piece, gentle enough to soothe your granny and send our tone-deaf manager into raptures.

Meanwhile, Chris Gunning, who had arranged the additional orchestration for The Hollies' smash 'The Air That I Breathe', was brought in to arrange a Sylvester/Britten venture, 'For The Peace Of All Mankind'. It was written by Albert Hammond, the guy who had penned 'Air'. By copying our winning formula, Robin was convinced that a solo Terry would then top the charts, and the pair would be able to bathe in the glory of a stonking hit. That hit would serve as the foundation stone on which Robin could build his empire. Released in 1974, the expensive venture did not provide the smash hit that the pair had dreamed of and only served to cause more unease within the Hollies camp.

Ted Heath, the Conservative prime minister, resigned on Monday, March 4. 'The Air That I Breathe' was sitting at number three in the charts as Labour leader Harold Wilson took up residence in Downing Street. That Wednesday we recorded another performance of 'Air' for transmission on *TOTP* the following day. Two weeks later we were on the show again. We had moved up a place, just missing out on the number one spot. That programme aired on Thursday, March 21. We didn't bother to watch as we were recording a song written by Terry and Allan, 'Give Me Time', on which Clarkey played the 'gob organ' – his harmonica. The track starts with Al's harp and a hint of a Last Post bugle riff, before handing over to Tony's bottleneck guitar fills and Gibson Jumbo 'music of the mountains' strumming. Al was a great harmonica player, as any Hollies aficionado will know. Right back to our early bluesy busker 'Set Me Free', on which he played a little Echo Vamper, through to 'He Ain't Heavy', where he used a Hohner chromatic, he always came up with the goods.

'The Air That I Breathe' had been a huge hit around the world and we needed a follow-up. And with the current crop of Hollies tunes, surely we had a suitable single in the can? Allan's moving 'Don't Let Me Down' seemed tailor-made, until Chip Taylor (yes, Angelina's uncle), the writer of two of our previous successes, 'The Baby' and 'I Can't Let Go', walked into the studio. He played us a song entitled 'Son Of A Rotten Gambler'. Ron fell for it, and like dopey sheep, so did Tony and I on the basis that: 'If it's good enough for one of the country's best producers...' At the time we had no idea that Ron was going through a bad time and didn't have his sharpest edge to the fore. Foolishly, egged on by our mentor, we recorded Chip's song and it became our new single, but I don't think Allan was convinced it was the right decision. And he was right. 'Son Of A Rotten Gambler' didn't make the UK charts and managed a few desultory Top 100 places elsewhere. Ron, who over the years we had trusted and respected, was sadly losing the plot. His brainchild company AIR London had become highly successful, resulting in buyout bids from Dick James Music and MAM. And the founding partners were divided. George Martin favoured an offer from Chrysalis, while Richards, who was managing director, was opposed to the deal. The stress was affecting Ron's health. Disenchanted with his former friends and colleagues, and with his Midas touch ebbing away, he left the company. It was the end of an era.

A couple of weeks after recording 'Son Of A Rotten Gambler' we began a week's season back at Batley Variety Club. From the late 1960s to 1974 we played to capacity crowds there. The easy-going manager Derek Smith always made us feel welcome with his camp humour and cheeky comments. As previously mentioned, a lot of stars played there and were happy to do so. One of them was US crooner Neil Sedaka. I recently watched Sedaka interviewed on TV. Ensconced in their lavish New York home, he and his wife spoke with disdain about their visits to Batley, for which they had been generously rewarded. Thousands of customers had spent their hard-earned cash while supporting the ungrateful pair. I remember club manager Derek telling me how Sedaka had told him he loved to perform at the venue. He had often expressed his gratitude to the owners, the Corrigans, for employing him at a time when he was almost broke and unemployable in America.

As we were getting changed for our stage appearance, the dressing room door burst open and one of the Bee Gees crashed in. It was an inebriated Maurice, who insisted on regaling us all with long stories, the points of which were hard to ascertain. This was fine, a bit of a novelty, until the same thing happened the following night. It seems that Bee Gee Maurice was in the process of splitting with his then wife, Lulu (yes, the same 'Bloody Lulu' who had once pursued Tony). He was now interested in Yvonne, an attractive girl who ran the late night burger bar in the car park. By midweek Mr Gibb's pre-show entertainment had become something of an irritation. He needed to be given the hard word and Terry was the man for the job. 'Hey lad,' Terry said in his Liverpool lilt, as he pointed to the door, 'on yer way. We need to get changed.'

Derek Smith told me that when Tommy Cooper worked Batley he would remain in his dressing room even as he was being announced onstage. The club's compère would proclaim: 'Ladies and gentlemen, please welcome the great Tommy Cooper.' Comfortably seated, with a glass of whisky in one hand, Tom would then shout into the house microphone held in his other hand: 'Let me out! …How do I get through these curtains?' as one of the stagehands punched and kicked the closed curtains from behind. The audience was in hysterics and the charade continued until Cooper had drained his glass, at which point he would amble nonchalantly from his dressing room to the stage and proceed to entertain his waiting fans. Just like that.

Terry once appeared in the nude on that same stage. We'd performed earlier, and I was front of house with Maureen. It was late and revellers were in the process of drinking up when the curtains went back and our Scouse mischief ran, naked, across the stage. Then the curtains were closed. We all just carried on drinking. It was quite surreal.

On another occasion Shirley Bassey was making her way down the backstage corridor on her way home after the show. As she was passing the resident band room, she saw the door was slightly open and the musicians were viewing a blue movie. Dame Shirley peered into the haze, saw what was going on and exclaimed with a laugh: 'Dirty buggers!'

The house band included a couple of veteran jazz musicians – trumpeter Dickie Hawdon and tenor saxophonist Red Price. They both liked a drink. One night the curtains closed and the band left the stage in readiness for the next solo act. After the introduction, the curtains reopened, revealing a solitary sax player, Red, slumped on his chair fast asleep.

Our Tony was getting married. He had popped the question to his new girlfriend, Jane Dalton. They were married near Henley-on-Thames on Saturday, April 27, 1974. It was a quiet affair, and after the church service the reception took place at his friend Kenny Lynch's house in the village of Nettlebed.

After they came back from honeymoon it was back to work, and we appeared on Les Dawson's popular show *Sez Les* in Yorkshire TV's Leeds studio. It was Sunday lunchtime and Les greeted us with: 'Sounds like you've got another smash on yer 'ands lads.' Followed by: 'Let's pop out t'pub for a quick bevy!' It was to be the one and only plug for our pedestrian new platter 'Son Of A Rotten Gambler'. The following day we played at the Free Trade Hall in Manchester. Our additional backing musicians were from the local Hallé Orchestra. They appeared with us around the country on a tour that ended at the Theatre Royal, Norwich on June 2.

The Chip Taylor single had been a disaster for us, but we were cheered by the good news that 'Air' had entered the US Top 10. On Monday, August 5 we began recording Bruce Springsteen's beautiful ballad '4th Of July, Asbury Park (Sandy)', known thereafter as 'Sandy'. That day I wrote in my diary: *'Played around with "Sandy" to get a good edit in case it ever becomes a single.'* Which it did, the following year.

With Bernie ill and recovering at home, Tony played bass on 'Lucy' and 'Look Out Johnny (There's A Monkey On Your Back)' – one of my favourite Hollies song titles, though sadly not so the song. Our forthcoming album title track, 'Another Night', was completed days later with our engineer, Alan

Parsons, playing a Moog synthesizer we'd borrowed from Paul McCartney.

Ten days later we were on the long and winding road that leads from Naples to Positano. Checking in to the coolest hotel in town, Le Sirenuse, we got our room keys and went straight out onto the terrace, set high above the vertiginous village on Italy's Amalfi Coast. The light from the setting sun created a breathtaking vista of the hillside village and the houses below us. Everyone was in high spirits and soon the light-hearted banter developed into the popular band sport of manager-baiting. Robin usually carried an official-looking briefcase and Terry and Allan's attention soon latched onto this apparently empty and useless accessory.

'Robbo, why do you carry this stupid bag round with you? There's never anything in it,' Terry said. Robin dismissed their antics with a chuckle and a puff of his fag smoke as he continued to admire the dramatic view. Gleefully waving the brown leather bag, Allan and Terry were convinced it was empty. To demonstrate this, one of them held it over the precipitous terrace edge and pulled it open.

Unbeknown to us, Robin had been paid our fee in advance, and cash and banknotes cascaded from the briefcase down onto the steps and passageways below. To top it off, the distant clink, clink of Robin's room key could be heard as it bounced down the ancient stone steps. Almost instantaneously, lights were turned on and shutters opened as the locals' outstretched hands grasped at the paper money as it fluttered by.

I've never seen Sylvester and Clarke move so fast. Out of the front door of the hotel they sprinted, down the road, round the corner and down the steep steps. After an undignified scramble, they managed to retrieve almost all the cash, plus Robin's room key.

The production team had linked up with an Italian film crew, and 'The Air That I Breathe' was shot on the hotel terrace, while 'Long Cool Woman' was filmed down on the beach among an assortment of fishing boats. Allan looked the part in his fetching leather-stitched western outfit as he mimed to our American hit. All in all Positano was a memorable experience.

We began recording our next single, Allan's 'I'm Down', on October 1. Tony Hymas played piano on the track and, on the recommendation of Chris Gunning, later scored the orchestral arrangement. Listening today, I hear a sombre masterpiece. Not a popular theme for Hollies fans and Pop Pickers of the day, and light years away from The Hollies' playground period of 'Jennifer Eccles' and 'Carrie Anne'. The ballad was brilliant in its own way. Maybe those heart-rending songs were a device created by our frontman to try and release the heartache he was experiencing at the time.

Dear Eloise

Words and Music by Allan Clarke, Tony Hicks and Graham Nash

Recorded by THE HOLLIES on Epic Records

05224

MARIBUS MUSIC, INC.

75¢

CHAPTER SIXTEEN:

Kiwi Pop Pickers

In January 1975 we flew to New Zealand. Our records had always done well there, sometimes better than at home in the UK. On arrival at Auckland Airport we were met by an entourage of cars with 'HOLLIES' emblazoned on their sides and whisked to the Intercontinental hotel.

The following day we met the media on board the ferry *Te Kotuku* and cruised round the islands while drinking champagne and chatting to record company executives and journalists. During the boat trip, we were presented with a couple of gold discs. The EMI Kiwis were good at spotting potential Hollies hits. Back in 1970 when they heard our album *Confessions Of The Mind* they spotted the hit potential in Tony's song 'Too Young To Be Married', a musical commentary on life in the 1960s. It was lifted from the LP, released as a single, and topped the charts in both New Zealand and Australia in 1971.

At Western Springs we played an open-air concert for a crowd of 18,000 – one of our largest audiences to date. It was raining as our cars edged their way through the bedraggled bodies attempting to enter the venue. The security guards stopped our lead car, and Robin let forth an instructive English upper class explanation culminating in: 'I'd appreciate it if you also let the following car through as it contains my artistic director and logistical executive.' All he left out was his favourite killer line: 'Have you got the gold records, Rod?'

The next day we flew down to New Plymouth on a twin prop Fokker F27 Friendship. We had a great view of Mount Egmont from our hotel pool. We were surrounded by beautiful countryside and the roads were almost traffic free. There were echoes of my childhood as the occasional motorcar passed by, usually a well-preserved Hillman Minx or maybe a Ford Prefect. Back then, high import duty on new cars meant New Zealanders treasured and preserved what we in the UK now call classic cars.

During our performance at Plymouth Bowl, punters swam in the lake between our stage and the naturally tiered outdoor arena. It was beautiful, although Tony damaged his ankle after tripping over a trailer hitch in the backstage darkness. There had been a lot of rain but the weather stayed fine, although, as I drummed I could see dramatic lightning in the distance.

On our way to South Island, during our stopover at Wellington Airport, there was time for Tony to nip to the local hospital to have his ankle X-rayed. The bone was chipped, so he was hobbling for the next few days. Our next gig was at the Queen Elizabeth II Park in Christchurch. The stadium had been built to accommodate the British Commonwealth Games the previous year. Tonight the weather was against us. It was cold, wet and windy, but thankfully that didn't deter the 15,000 people who were seated on the semi-covered stand across from our rickety stage. We arrived in style with the legendary Australian promoter Jeff Patterson at the wheel of our station wagon. Jeff looked like a cross between Tommy Cooper and the great train robber, Ronnie Biggs. He amused us, unintentionally, by appearing to get smaller as our car journey progressed. He was gradually sliding down in his seat until he was just peering over the steering wheel.

We made a triumphant snail's pace entrance round the running track, with Jeff eventually delivering us to the backstage area. The waiting orchestra were huddled on a platform under a rickety, windswept marquee. This was, apparently, the stage. I climbed aboard, threaded my way through the assembled musicians, sat on my stool, and positioned the drums and swaying cymbal stands. With the guys plugged in, we were off. As I counted in the 'He Ain't Heavy' fanfare, the heavens opened and the deluge hit. We kept going, but as we played on, rainwater built up atop the canvas awning. The roof gradually ballooned downwards, eventually cascading over one side of the stage, and causing a supporting metal pole to fall over, narrowly missing the string section. Unperturbed, the assembled company bravely fiddled on. The torrent of water had not dampened their professionalism, and we ended the show on a high. We ran offstage and jumped into our vehicle. With the illuminated scoreboard spelling out 'HOLLIES', promoter Patterson drove us on a slow lap of honour past the wonderful Christchurch audience, around the athletics track, out of the stadium and back to the hotel for refreshments.

Clearly happy with the night's takings, he regaled us with riveting tales of how he once pulled a gun on the notorious Kray twins, and then miraculously charmed the London gangsters into becoming his business partners. He went on to boast that when he was in the US, he had dined with the Gambino and Gotti crime families. It seemed that Patterson had risen from nothing and had gone on to make, and lose, millions. In his younger days, he had also been a prize fighter, winning the Australian heavyweight boxing championship in 1959. Unfortunately, it was later revealed that the old rogue had rigged the fight so that he could win.

After New Zealand, we went on to play several dates in Australia, the final one being in Perth, where we played two shows at the Concert Hall. Cyclone Tracy had hit Darwin on Christmas Eve, killing seventy-one people and flattening the city. We had seen the devastation on TV, and we were happy to donate our fee for the night to the people struggling with the aftermath up in the Northern Territory. The next day Jeff Patterson waved us off from Perth Airport and a Qantas jumbo jet whisked us back to London, stopping briefly in Bombay to refuel.

Dinner at the Manor Studios with Bernie, Rod, Tony, Alan Parsons, Allan, Dek and Terry, 1976.

'Holliedaze' in the charts and original Hollies are on *Top Of The Pops* again, 1981.

Together again on Abbey Road, 1981.

'What Goes Around' – Graham, me, Tony and Allan at Rudy Records, 1982.

Tony Hicks   Graham Nash   Allan Clarke   Bobby Elliott

THE HOLLIES

Sunset Marquis, North Villa, whilst recording *What Goes Around*, 1982.

A Hollies signing session in Hollywood, 1983.

Album signing in Hollywood with Graham, me, Allan and Tony, 1983.

Elliott and Nash – who's a naughty boy, 1983.

Nash, Clarke and Hicks on the road again, 1983.

Palm Beach, north of Sydney, Australia, 1984.

Graham and Tony backing Buddy Holly for the 1996 tribute album *Not Fade Away*, Abbey Road.

Me and my old boss Shane. He's now Alvin Stardust, 2007.

We got the tunes, 2012.

Me, 2017. ROBERT SHAKESPEARE

The Hollies thank the Birmingham Symphony Hall audience in 2017. (L-R) Tony Hicks, Ian Parker, Peter Howarth, me, Steve Lauri and Ray Stiles. ROB HAYWOOD

My life in The Hollies. ARTWORK BY STEVE LEE VICKERS

The author at work.

Robin's empire, RCB Consultants, was on the up. He had taken on another member of staff, Terry Walker, who joined us on a trip to the Netherlands. Checked in to the Hotel Pulitzer in Amsterdam, I found it impossible to sleep. Throughout the night, the adjacent church clock chimed every fifteen minutes and, just to ensure that sleep was absolutely impossible, the mechanism clanged out a silly tune every time.

The next day, as we drove from our hotel to the Dutch Television Centre in Hilversum, Walker, Allan and Terry recounted tales of their adventures the previous night. They'd been out drinking until 5 a.m., and they were feeling rough – just the look you want for an important TV appearance. Apparently, Walker had got into a fight with a stranger, which wasn't a good way to launch his association with The Hollies. The TV programme we were recording was called *Eddy Go Round*, and ABBA were on it too with their new single 'I Do, I Do, I Do, I Do, I Do'. Frank Ifield and US guitar legend Duane Eddy were also on the show. Later, checking in at Schiphol airport, we saw the ABBA foursome standing at a nearby desk, about to head back to Stockholm. As we said our farewells, pretty Agnetha came over and kissed our Tony. We all stared at him, eyebrows raised, as he smiled sheepishly.

About six weeks later Rod drove Maureen and me to London. We were staying at her brother Tony's place on Loudoun Road. Later that evening a white Rolls-Royce, complete with uniformed chauffeur, drew up outside.

Jeff Patterson was in town, and he had made arrangements for Allan and Jeni, Terry and his wife, Linda, Tony and Jane, plus Mo and me, to be his guests at the Colony Club, a prestigious Mayfair gambling establishment. He greeted us with £100 of free gambling tokens each. I had a spin of this and a throw of that, but eventually, we all came away from the tables empty-handed.

In the course of the evening a row erupted between Jeni Clarke and Terry's wife, Linda. Terry is a lifelong, fanatical supporter of Liverpool Football Club, and he was enthusing passionately about his team to Tony and Jane. Standing a few feet away, chatting to Maureen and me, Jeni overheard Terry's excited soccer talk and, raising her voice, regally exclaimed that no husband of hers would be allowed to go to football matches. On hearing that, Linda hit back in her Scouse lilt: 'Someone's got big ears!'

Allan had become besotted with Bruce Springsteen's track 'Born To Run'. He was in wannabe mode and had learned the song and every nuance of Bruce's vocal delivery. He wanted The Hollies to record it, but to me this seemed misguided. That song was a classic; there was no way it could be improved upon, and I felt we ought to leave it alone. Allan disagreed and became angry. To console him we went about laying a track, but it was a half-hearted affair and we never finished it. What was the point?

We were all fans of Bruce and were delighted when, later in 1975, he came backstage to thank us for recording his song

'4th Of July, Asbury Park (Sandy)', after which he went for a drink with Tony and Allan.

Years later in 2014 we were staying at the Intercontinental hotel in Adelaide during a tour of Oz. After two hours thrashing about onstage, I was hot and sweaty and headed back to my room to change before going to the bar. Coming out of the lift, I spotted the E Street Band's drummer, Max Weinberg, with guitarist Nils Lofgren, which meant Bruce Springsteen was in town and staying in the same hotel. We'd met before, so I invited the two of them to join us for a natter. They did and Max bought me a Grey Goose vodka and ice. Not my usual tipple, but hey, if it's what The Boss's boys drink then I'm happy to be a Grey Goose guy.

The conversation soon switched to music, and Max said: 'Bruce loves you.' I asked if he meant The Hollies and Max said: 'No, he loves you, your playing.' He said that when Bruce and the band were putting together an arrangement at rehearsals, they sometimes got bogged down when it came to finding a way of ending a song. At which point, according to Max, Bruce would call out: 'Do what The Hollies' guy does… do what The Hollies' guy does!' Meaning me. I called Tony over and turned to Max: 'Would you please repeat what you just said.' He did, and I've dined out on: 'Do what The Hollies' guy does' ever since.

Jennifer Eccles

Words and Music by ALLAN CLARKE and GRAHAM NASH

GRALTO MUSIC LIMITED

3/-

CHAPTER SEVENTEEN:

The Wolfman Cometh

Back in LA yet again in early May we arrived at the Comstock to find that it was now in the hands of the liquidators and had changed its name to Derricks. There was no sign of sustenance; the restaurant was gone, although the rooms were still intact. We unpacked our bags and were rescued by Robin, who rose to the occasion and somehow conjured up a stack of bacon and egg sandwiches, which we washed down with a glass or two of champagne. The next day after breakfasting at Ships, we were driven to the CBS TV Studios for our 11 a.m. call for *The Dinah Shore Show*. At the time, singer and actress Dinah Shore was living with Burt Reynolds. We performed 'Another Night' and 'Air' and were finished by 3 p.m., then returned to the hotel in time for a couple of interviews by the pool. Two days later we were live on the daytime *Merv Griffin Show*. Merv struck me as being one of the more affable and informed US TV personalities.

His friendly, relaxed manner made it a joy to be in his company. I was also impressed by the house band, which included three jazz musicians I grew up listening to at Pike Hill all those years earlier: bass player Ray Brown, trombonist Kai Winding and tenor sax star Richie Kamuca.

The next day we arrived at the NBC TV Studios in Burbank to appear on *The Midnight Special*. It was 6.30 p.m. when we were shown to our quarters and we were kept waiting for three and a half hours, during which time we became bored, then a little worse for wear. The monotony was interrupted when the compère of the show, Wolfman Jack, popped into our dressing room and growled: 'Hi guys, I'm Wolfman!' To which our quietly spoken bass player replied in his polite Lancastrian tones: ''Ello Wolfman, I'm Bernie, from The 'ollies.'

On this latest American jaunt, we'd brought in ace pianist Pete Wingfield, who also played synthesizer. With the coming of 'Heavy' and 'Air' we had needed to reproduce the sound of the orchestral backing on the records at our concerts. Now with Wingy and his ARP keyboard and string machine augmenting our sound, we could give both those classics the treatment they deserved – plus the added bonus of his driving piano playing, which elevated our stage performance each night. Pete's keyboard prowess, which he displayed in our extended version of 'Long Cool Woman', was a joyous experience for both the band and the audience.

That summer we began recording 'Love Is The Thing' at Emison Studios on Queensway. To me, it seemed as though we were attempting to ape 'I'm Not In Love', the classic 10cc song. The result was a pointless, pretentious wash.

I'd had enough. That evening Rod drove me from London to Manchester. I rendezvoused with my dad just after midnight, and he ran me home to my secluded northern haven so that I could clear my head.

We had been invited to entertain the staff of CBS/Epic at their annual convention, which took place at the imposing Royal York Hotel in Toronto, Canada. Built in the 1920s by the Canadian Pacific Railway, it was linked to Union Station by underground walkways. The structure is so grand and expansive that it was once described as a city within a city. There was a lot of hanging around and schmoozing, and after our performance we ended up having drinks with the label's top executives, Ron Alexenburg and Steve Popovich. The following evening we were all on the 6.30 p.m. flight out of Toronto, returning to old Blighty. Making the most of what was then 'The World's Favourite Airline', we sampled British Airways' hospitality and drank champagne all the way back to Heathrow.

The first time we recorded on the new 24-track recorder in Abbey Road was on Monday, September 1, 1975. Veteran engineer Peter Bown, who worked with us on 'Stay' and 'Just One Look', was seated at the controls. My diary states: '*First session without Ron Richards.*' In 1963 in this same studio, I'd had a single microphone suspended over my drums. Now I couldn't move for mics – there was one placed on every drum.

With Pete Wingfield on piano, we recorded 'I Won't Move Over' and, the following day, 'Narida'. We had two albums in the pipeline. I'd commissioned a guy that we'd met in the States, Toby Mamis, to write the sleeve notes for our *History Of The Hollies* double album. I read them through, liked his style, and they became the text in the centre spread of our package of *Twenty Four Genuine Top Thirty Hits*.

Sleeve notes:

The first week of May 1975, I'm in the Bottom Line, perhaps the most prestigious place to play in New York besides Carnegie Hall, and The Hollies are onstage. It seems that everyone I know is a zealous Hollies fan, and all of them were at the Bottom Line for the four shows there, or at the Roxy in Hollywood the week before.

The Hollies' career has spanned several distinct periods of productivity. From 1963 through 1972, from 'Ain't That Just Like Me' through 'Long Cool Woman'. It was a journey that took The Hollies a lot farther than just from Manchester to London. It took them into the upper reaches of the charts twenty-four times, and it took them round the world and back again many times on tours of every imaginable nation that buys English pop music, and even a few that don't. Of all the groups that exploded onto the pop music scene in the halcyon and hectic days of the early sixties group explosion that proved to the world that Britons could rock in the same league as Americans, The Hollies are among the few that had distinctive talent. That explains their longevity; where others have long since changed their styles, their names or their occupations.

Good original material was in short supply and, with Polydor wanting non-stop output and fresh albums, we were under pressure. EMI came up with the idea of releasing a 45 rpm single with 'Long Cool Woman' on the A-side and 'Carrie Anne' on the flip. Even though we were no longer officially EMI artists, resident Abbey Roader, Chris Blair, cut the master in a matter of minutes and asked me to have a listen. It sounded great. Chris would sometimes scratch his name in the plastic run-out area, which can sometimes be seen on the old Hollies vinyl where the record grooves end. I remember him as a youngster starting work at the studios, with his cheery disposition and striking red hair. Sadly, he died at quite a young age.

Orchestra was added to 'Write On', 'There's Always Goodbye' and 'I Won't Move Over'. Tony Hymas had scored the string parts and directed the musicians. The morning after, we mixed the final two songs for the album. After lunch Peter Bown and I banded the tracks in Abbey Road's room 14 and separated each song by lengths of white quarter-inch tape, which was inserted between each track in readiness for the cutting of the master. Our album *Write On* was complete. On October 8 the album master was cut at Abbey Road. We all approved the sleeve design and, on the same day, I checked over the *History Of The Hollies* artwork and deemed it ready to go. I was particularly impressed with the centre spread, designed by Steve Newport, with Bill Richmond's photo of some of the items from my personal archive. Liner notes by Toby Mamis rounded off the package beautifully.

The New Year of 1976 brought with it constant rain, snow and floods in some parts of the country. Dustbins were being blown down the back of Rose Cottage and the electricity supply cut out on the evening of January 1. The gales had probably downed the overhead lines. In Roughlee, the high winds overturned mobile homes on Maurice Waine's caravan park.

A few days later I was eating dinner with Dek, Rod and recently moustachioed Bernie Calvert. We'd checked into the Bear Hotel in Woodstock in preparation for our recording session at Richard Branson's Manor recording studios in nearby Shipton-on-Cherwell. The following day, as we were entering the old house, Terry arrived driving a brand new Alfa Romeo Alfetta GT. We spent the day with our new producer, Alan Parsons. I don't recall who suggested it, but we were there to record a song written by Emmylou Harris, 'Boulder To Birmingham'. Pete Wingfield arrived and we laid the basic track. Wingy played a Fender Rhodes electric piano, Bernie was on bass and I played my silver Ludwig drums. Vocals were added, and we trooped off to bed at 1.30 a.m. The following morning after a hearty breakfast in the spacious manor house kitchen, Tony overdubbed some acoustic guitar, and poor Allan had to go home because he'd got gout in his foot. Thankfully our work was done, and the track was mixed.

Another New Zealand and Australian tour began a week later. Landing in distant Dunedin on South Island, the Hollies touring entourage looked pale and weary after a marathon journey from England, by way of Los Angeles and Auckland. It was The Hollies' first visit to the city. I stepped down from the plane and thankfully breathed in the clean, fresh air and walked across the tarmac to the airport terminal. The surrounding mountains, topped with cool mist, reminded me of Scotland. Quite apt, as Dunedin is the Scottish Gaelic name for Edinburgh. We played the Regent Theatre on January 22. Two days later we arrived in Christchurch where we would play for five nights at the recently constructed Town Hall. At a cost of £12,000, every show would be recorded on the country's only 16-track recorder, which had been brought down from Wellington on North Island. Talented engineer Peter Hitchcock was tucked away behind the stage where he operated the Studer multitrack machine and mixing desk. The idea was to use the recording for a future *Live Hits* album.

One night Ivan Owen (the voice of puppet Basil Brush) and *Play In A Day* veteran guitarist Bert Weedon came into our dressing room to say hello. We'd worked with Basil when he was a 'dog', Fred Barker, on ITV's *Five O'Clock Club*. Funny who you meet on the other side of the world.

One of my favourite places in New Zealand is the town of Nelson on South Island. We stayed at the Rutherford Hotel, and there, in each of our rooms, was a bottle of 1964 Piper-Heidsieck, courtesy of EMI. Back in my room after the show I tried to wind down by watching TV. From the floor below, I could hear the voices of Dek and Terry shouting in true Cromwellian Club Harry Hart fashion: 'Drink up my babes!' as they enjoyed their complimentary bottles of fizz.

Two sellout nights at the old Wellington Town Hall followed.

> *After the second, I wrote:*
> 'Show good. Audience marvellous. Standing. Allan took
> a photo of them – they loved it. Feeling knackered. Tea
> and sandwiches back at hotel. Tired. I left Robin drinking
> Bollinger with our promoter, Stewart Macpherson
> and Clarkey ordering a bottle of Southern Comfort. In
> my room, I placed an order for a phone call to Mo in
> England. It came through almost right away – very clear.
> She said that Noel Edmonds had made our LP Write On
> his album of the week.'

Sometimes the non-stop drinking culture was just too much, and I had to escape. The sanity in my life came from thoughts of home and Mo and the peace I found when I returned north. In those pre-iPhone days it was tricky and expensive to call home. Sometimes I had to pre-book a call to Maureen through the hotel reception, and even when I got through, the line could be bad. By the time a tour ended, I was longing to get back home.

After two nights in Auckland Town Hall, we flew back to Wellington to perform an extra show. The last-minute addition had sold out immediately. The New Zealand leg of the tour had been a huge success. Then it was on to Sydney, Australia, and straight into press and radio interviews.

Pete Wingfield, our pianist, was becoming a popular solo artist. His single 'Eighteen With A Bullet' had entered the charts and he was doing the rounds, promoting his hit record.

By the time we got to Brisbane, Allan was ill. We started the show, but he went offstage during 'Star' and was sick into a red sand-filled fire bucket. A doctor was urgently called. Terry took to the centre mic and sang 'Long Cool Woman'. 'Too Young To Be Married', our Down Under number one, was taken care of by the song's composer, Tony. Then during Hicks' guitar solo, a patched-up lead singer entered stage left and completed the song. Allan managed to get through 'He Ain't Heavy, He's My Brother', but during the encore he exited stage right to throw up again. I could see the good doctor – hypodermic needle poised – as Al bent down to jettison his peas and carrots into the waiting bucket. Poor Clarkey was ill, but everyone knew that it was self-inflicted. He was drinking to excess and not taking care of himself.

The trouble was he never knew when to stop partying, and he wouldn't listen to anyone who tried to get him to slow down. We knew he had a problem, but nothing we said made any difference to him. He was a strong character. Eventually, in 1979, he would go into rehab, but for a number of years building up to that, he pushed himself too hard and paid the price.

Looking back, I realise how fortunate I was not to get hooked on alcohol. Being the centre of attention onstage could be addictive, and when the lights went down and the crowds dispersed, the adrenalin was still flowing. You didn't want the elation to end, and when you hit the bar afterwards, the drinks were flowing and usually free. You were elevated back to stage level and it was showtime all over again, with people shaking your hand or patting you on the back. I'm sure that the adulation contributed to our Harold's downfall. The beer flowed endlessly – from the streets of Salford all the way to *Top Of The Pops*.

Sound engineer Simon Hart recalled: 'Allan used to be the life and soul of everything. He was great, really good fun... great to go out with after a show... we'd be in the bar playing snooker, and he'd be walking on bottles across the bar.' Simon was referring to one of Al's party pieces where he would get two empty beer bottles and challenge the assembled circle of revellers to bend down and, with a bottle grasped in each hand, stretch as far as possible parallel to the floor and place one of the bottles as far as possible from one's feet. Then, without touching the floor you had to inch back using the remaining bottle and return to an upright stance.

Down in Melbourne a couple of days later we heard that Emmylou Harris had said how honoured she was that we'd recorded her song, and sent her thanks. But all was not good. Not only was Allan struggling, but our old friend Jeff Patterson was after Robin, saying that our manager owed him money. Robbo went white. You don't mess with those guys.

That night I wrote: *'Very hot in Festival Hall. Onstage, Clarkey cooled us down by snatching some ice creams off a sales boy, and we ate them during 'Sandy'. Knackered – but rallied back at the hotel. We all sat by the pool. Perfect temperature. Took salt tablets and went to bed.'*

In 1976 the selling of alcohol on a Sunday in Western Australia was against the law. It was February 15 and our final show in Oz. The band was staying at the Contacio in Scarborough, up the coast from Perth. Smooth-talking Robin had done a deal with the hotel manager. His old briefcase bulged and we knew that, Sunday or not, we would have our liquid refreshments.

Back in Britain we played to a packed Royal Albert Hall. Our office had booked three suites at the nearby Royal Garden Hotel, and Robin had fixed up a pre-show press schmooze, with Daimler limos laid on to shuttle folk to and from Albert's place, as we called the Royal Albert Hall. During our performance, while pounding away on the big Steinway grand piano, Pete Wingfield kicked the piano stool backwards. The stool teetered on the edge, then fell off the stage. A helpful bloke in the front row kindly placed it back onstage, only for naughty Wingy to kick it off again. This time the stool bounced, hitting another member of the audience. No one was hurt, but it could have been expensive. Thankfully, we were not sued, but some time later we had to pay for a new stool.

LISTEN TO ME

BY TONY HAZZARD

J. ALBERT & SON PTY LTD
MUSIC PUBLISHERS
MELBOURNE SYDNEY WELLINGTON, N.Z.
SYDNEY BRON MUSIC CO. LTD., LONDON
AUTHORISED FOR SALE ONLY IN AUSTRALIA AND NEW ZEALAND

CHAPTER EIGHTEEN:

Going Caracas on Concorde

At the start of 1977, almost a year after the recording had been made in New Zealand, our *Live Hits* album was due for release. We'd had a meeting with people from the advertising agency McCann Erickson before Christmas, and they had come up with an idea on which to base a TV advertising campaign.

On Friday, January 12 a limo collected Bernie and me from the Portman Hotel and delivered us to Twickenham Film Studios, where we met up with Allan, Terry and Tony. Assembled inside were 200 film extras dressed in an assortment of costumes, which I presumed were intended to represent all walks of life. The operation was costing Polydor £150,000. Tony was not happy; it wasn't what he was expecting. He thought the artwork was going to be a representation of the band performing onstage. Instead, the plan was to have a man singing a Hollies song and then dashing down the

261

street pursued by the characters. We should have been told what to expect but we weren't, and Hicks wasn't having it – he could be stubbornly immovable. With the clock ticking and all the actors and crew hanging around, Tony reluctantly agreed to leave the dressing room and take up his position. The sequence was shot, the commercial was aired and the LP reached number four in the charts.

A few days later Maureen ran Bernie and me to Bradford University, where we were booked to perform. After the gig, Mo and I were drinking in the hotel bar and were joined by Allan. As he was leaving for bed, he took off the gold coloured wire bracelet he was wearing and gave it to Mo, saying that Jeni didn't like it. I still have it here in the house somewhere. The next morning Maureen and I ate breakfast, said our farewells and she headed home in her Mini, while the band, along with Wingy and Rod, climbed into the two waiting Daimlers to head north to Edinburgh, by way of Kirkby Lonsdale. As the big cars rolled along the A65, some of us began to feel queasy. Being familiar with the area, I suggested that our driver stop at Devil's Bridge where, from the food trailer, we bought mugs of tea and bacon butties, which we consumed while standing on the old stone bridge that loops over the River Lune. Those dated Daimlers were fine for short, sedate city trips, but on the open road they were draughty and cramped. Eventually, we joined the M6 and arrived at the Caledonian Hotel after lunch. I went to my room and slept and was awakened by a call from Robin. Everyone would meet for brandy sours in the hotel bar at 8 p.m. Our manager was meticulous in his overseeing of the precise mixing of this pre-show delectation and would watch like a hawk as the bartender went about adding the ingredients to the cocktail shaker. The slightest deviation from his tried and tested formula – missing out the whites of fresh hens' eggs for instance – would annoy him so much that he would nip behind the bar and make the concoction himself. On this occasion the mixture received the Britten seal of approval and drinks were served. Suitably fuelled, we climbed into the black Daimlers for the short journey up the road to the Usher Hall, a grand old venue where we had performed with The Rolling Stones in 1965.

Two days later I was opening a magnum of Dom Pérignon in my dressing room at the Royal Albert Hall. After playing to another sellout crowd, I joined Tony, Jane and Kenny Lynch for supper at the Chelsea Rendezvous. The following day there were excellent reviews in the *London Evening Standard* and the *Daily Telegraph*.

Things were going well. *Live Hits* had jumped from thirty-four in the album charts the previous week, to number eight. On Tuesday, March 15 we were handed gold discs in the pressroom at London's Heathrow Airport before we set off on a non-stop tour of Germany. A different venue every night was a tough call, and soon we all began to feel the strain. Buoyed by the news that *Live Hits* was at number five, we pushed on, but after ten days Allan was beginning to lose his voice, and it was affecting his confidence and general well-being. The touring schedule was relentless, and Allan didn't help himself by smoking cigarettes and drinking hard liquor. For the final four nights of the tour we had to cut three songs from the set in an attempt to preserve his voice, as Allan sought comfort of the Southern kind. He was morphing from the Clarkey that I loved into an insecure Mr Angry. The whole band was relieved when the tour ended and we were able to get home again.

Driving round the Burnley and Pendle area one day, I began to think that maybe I should buy a house. A touch of the Chuck Berrys came over me – get a home, settle down and write a book. OK, I'm a bit late with the last item, but I eventually got there. As for the home, I spotted a farmhouse with great views of Pendle Hill to the west and the tip of Ingleborough in the Yorkshire Dales to the north. Ted Smith, landlord of the Bay Horse in Roughlee, once said that when choosing a house, you should consider the distance from the local shops because one day you might not be able to drive a car. It was not too far from civilisation and on the market at the right price. Maureen approved, so I became a homeowner for the first time. Until then, Maureen and I were comfortable living with our parents, like a pair of thirty-odd-year-old teenagers. The farmhouse needed quite a bit of work, but we moved in eventually. We were very happy there, and I've been happy in the old place ever since.

Remember The Dolphins – Tony Hicks, Bernie Calvert and I? We had a singer who went by the name of Ricky Shaw, or to give him his real name, Patrick Belshaw. After Tony and I joined The Hollies, Pat tried his hand, unsuccessfully, at singing with other groups. Then he became a roadie but found that he didn't like being ordered about by spotty wannabes, so he joined the merchant navy and hit the high seas. Eventually, Belsh became a jobbing builder and problem fixer. Fourteen years on from Dolphin days I would sometimes join him for a pint in 'Compost Corner', which was located at the right-hand side of the characterful bar in Ye Olde Sparrow Hawk, or t'Sparrer, as the pub was known locally.

Previous owners of my recently acquired farmhouse had whitewashed the outer walls. The flaking paint had to be removed to show the handsome, locally quarried millstone grit that lay beneath. On mentioning this to Belsh over a beverage, he said that he could do the job cheaper than the quote I'd got from a company of specialist sandblasters. All I had to do was hire the plant, a compressor, headgear, sand, etc., and he would be up his ladder and rid the old place of the nasty whitewash in no time. We shook on it and ordered more beer.

Maureen and I were in the middle of decorating our new home when Robin phoned to say that The Hollies would be going to Venezuela in September. Apparently, the band would be flown over to play two concerts in Caracas, not just on any old jumbo jet but at twice the speed of sound on board an Air France Concorde. We were all buzzing with excitement, so much so that Allan, Terry and Tony knocked together a tribute tune to celebrate our forthcoming adventure. On July 11 we began recording 'Caracas' in Basing Street Studios without

Allan, who was at home in bed suffering from a trapped nerve in his back. Hans Peter Arnesen joined us to lay down some cool piano and basic track, and my old school chum Jimmy Jewell came along with his soprano sax and blew some jazzy embellishments. Tony's driving guitar solo rounded off the picture-postcard production.

After giving us years of loyal service, our trusty tech, Derek 'Dek' Whyment, left the fold. He wanted to start his own car sales business. Simon Hart was now responsible for our logistics and live sound. We first met him on a tour of Germany. Si had been working for our sound company, driving himself around in an old Jaguar with his trusty Labrador, Rocky, riding shotgun in the passenger seat. Simon joined us while we were recording in Basing Street.

By the end of August the album was complete. We had considered calling it *Amnesty*, but *A Crazy Steal* won the day. Gered Mankowitz took photos of a miserable band on a wet day, at the drab, depressing Barbican.

Before Venezuela, we headed off on another whistle-stop tour of Germany. A brand new twin-engine Cessna 404 Titan was waiting for us at Luton Airport and Robin, Rod and new recruit Simon, plus the five of us, took off for Germany. Flying conditions were perfect, and two and a half hours later we landed in Bielefeld where Hamburg-based promoter Karsten Jahnke greeted us. This would be the start of a series of wonderful German concert tours, and our mode of transport would be a Mercedes Jasper bus driven by Franz

Ludwig. Herr Ludwig was an instant hit with us Hollies. He was now 'Frank', and destined to become a treasured member of our deutsches entourage.

Now we had to go through the sound checks every day. Technology was advancing, and audiences were on the receiving end of giant hi-fi sound systems. Every instrument was amplified to a different degree, so fine-tuning the whole system was imperative. This took time, and on a gruelling tour the last thing I needed was to have to expend precious energy banging around on my drums before each show. But needs must.

We started with appearances in Bad Salzuflen, Koblenz and Stuttgart, where we stayed on top of a hill at the wonderful Schloss Solitude, an impressive rococo hunting retreat built in the late 1700s.

Driver Frank had been briefed to find characterful lunch stops as he drove us between gigs. With admirable devotion to duty, he had acquired a good food guide, and he impressed us with his choice of picturesque eateries, including castles and monasteries, located off the beaten track. Dear Franz had been polishing up his English too. During the long journeys I would sometimes sit up front and keep him company. He must have done some research on World War II and would, at times, break into the English Tommy's war chant and sing: 'Vee are hanging out our vashing on the Siegfried line' while glancing at me, clearly expecting me to join in with him. On another occasion the bus was travelling on the autobahn near the French border,

Frank at the wheel and me on the front seat. 'Bobby, see, ze signpost to Paris. We go and drink champagne, then maybe a little hanky-panky?' he offered hopefully.

The Stuttgart area is Porsche country, and the following day we were taken to the Porsche factory to see the assembly line, guided by factory boss Hans Christian Ernst. We ate lunch in their restaurant and had a wonderful few hours nosing around. That night we played in Bad Kissingen. The venue was very echo-prone but, despite that, we performed well. The front row of the stalls was full of record company old boys, and after the show we were invited to the Polydor convention next door, where the suits smiled and applauded as we entered the room.

Australian group Sherbet supported us. We got on well with the lads and their affable manager, Roger Davies, who went on to manage Olivia Newton-John, Tina Turner, Cher, Sade and Pink.

Stuttgart to Bremerhaven is a long way. When we arrived we met record artwork designer Jo Mirowski and photographer Martyn Goddard. The pair had flown over from London. The next day we had photos taken for our forthcoming album cover in the Stadthalle, where we were due to perform that evening. None of us was in the mood for a lengthy shoot. On my way into the venue I had noticed an interesting-looking soft drinks machine and asked if we could use it as a prop. And there it is, whizzing about Dalek-like, on the finished *A Crazy Steal* LP sleeve, with us in pursuit like five Bisto kids.

In Aachen, I wrote:
'Show – I felt good but other guys not happy with sound – seems like we had a row here last time. Allan's voice going a little… Beautiful steak at hotel. I had a talk with Allan – he seems frustrated.'

In Oldenburg:
'Good gig – but lighting gantry too near to me. Hellishly HOT. Tired out by sixth song – sweat pouring off me. Tony's got a cold. Food after at hotel. Pleasant atmosphere. Tired. Robin seems more concerned with laundry than anything else.'

After Flensburg we made it to Hamburg:
'Checked into Hamburg Plaza Hotel. Halle next door. Hot bath – so nice to have sheets and blankets after duvets at every other hotel. Show OK. Polydor party after. Heavy – Terry gassed – I took him back to our hotel in a cab.'

After our final gig in Germany, we flew from Hamburg via Düsseldorf to Paris's Charles de Gaulle Airport:
'Only just made it. Simon had to help load Concorde and three cases were left behind. Stopped off at Santa Maria Island in Azores to refuel. All passengers disembarked and no one bothered me as I wandered around the plane's landing gear. 1,350 mph at 57,000 feet. Dom Pérignon. Food so-so.

Allan asked: Why can't I just be a nice guy flying round the world?
Sylvester replied: It's not in your nature Al.
Clarkey pulled his baseball cap down and slept for the rest of the journey.'

We arrived at our destination at 7 p.m. after a very long flight. From there we were driven to Caracas. It was miles from the airport and nowhere near the 'deep blue sea' as we had envisaged in our song.

We were dropped off at an austere-looking block of apartments, where hot water came out of the cold tap and the single-glazed windows seemed to amplify the noise of the traffic. After a terrible night's sleep we were told that we'd be staying across the racetrack of a road at the Hilton hotel, which was not much better. The Polar beer was good though. That night I took a Mogadon. I needed to sleep. Diary entry: *'The whole Hilton area is surrounded by dual carriageways. Traffic goes like hell. Bad drivers – some don't bother to turn lights on at night. Petrol 20p.'*

Surprisingly, the local technicians gave us a sound onstage that was superior to anything we'd had in Germany, and they were working with inferior equipment. We performed well on both nights, after which everyone was in a good mood. The lengthy tour of Germany directly before these Venezuelan gigs meant that we were looking forward to going home. Then the promoter turned nasty. He insisted that we do a

TV show the following day that was not scheduled in our contract. Foolishly, Robin had parted with our passports, and they refused to return them to us unless we did as we were told. A very heavy meeting followed. As the argument raged, I noticed an expensive handbag on the floor beside one of the promoter's entourage. It was open, and inside was a gun. Fortunately, it remained in the bag. Robin was sweating, but fighting our corner in a tense, high noon scenario: contracts at ten paces. Eventually Robbo won, the injunction was lifted, and we were free to go. Passports in hand, we made a dash to the airport where we boarded a three-engine McDonnell Douglas DC-10. No Concorde for our homeward journey but, at the time, it didn't matter as we were just happy to be leaving the simmering atmosphere of Caracas.

Comfortably seated up front, we were thrust back in our seats as the pilot applied full throttle and the big jet charged down the runway. My heart raced and my head screamed – England here we come. Not so fast, Bobby. Alarm bells and hooters sounded from the cockpit. Abort! Abort! The brakes were applied, the engines were thrown into full-throttle reverse, and we skidded to a halt at the end of the runway. Back in the terminal we were told the number two engine had a fault. From the window of the airport lounge, we could see the DC-10 and a floodlit group of maintenance men looking up at the tail-mounted engine. Time was ticking, and the delay was making us all edgy. The sight of a little man attacking the faulty engine with a big hammer was at first comical, and then quite worrying, as I realised that we would have to fly all the way to London on the bruised monster. It looked as though the engine cowl wouldn't close, so another technician was applying some gentle Latin American persuasion. Three hours later we were airborne and, after nine hours in the air, we landed at Madrid, where we were delayed for a further two hours. At least we were able to make calls to wives and sweethearts to put them, and ourselves, at ease.

When I got home I went to view Belsh's handiwork on the farmhouse walls. He'd sandblasted three of the four walls, and it had taken him almost a month and cost me a fortune. In my absence he'd been going to Maureen for 'a draw'. My spies, located in various watering holes around the area, would tell me that Belshaw had been holding court in t'Sparrer, when he was supposed to be working on my house. Monday was his 'througher' day. Meaning that, in the morning, he would start out drinking at the Liberal Club, then head for the Leeds and Liverpool pub near a certain canal. Next would come 'The Dressers', the Warp Dressers Club, followed by 'The Fast and Slow', official title, Nelson Carters (slow) and Motormen's Club (fast). By the time I went out for the last hour in my local, Ricky Shaw would be rolling drunk, precariously perched on his stool in 'Compost Corner', insulting whoever came into his line of fire.

SORRY SUZANNE

Words and Music by TONY MACAULAY and GEOFF STEPHENS

RECORDED BY

THE HOLLIES

ON PARLOPHONE

WELBECK MUSIC LIMITED/A SCHROEDER MUSIC PUBLISHING CO.LIMITED

Sole selling agents:
WELBECK MUSIC LIMITED, 25 Denmark Street, London W.C.2.

3/-

CHAPTER NINETEEN:

Married In Miami

On September 29 we played the Tivoli in Copenhagen. After the show we went back to the Hotel Plaza and met for drinks in the Library Bar. That has to be one of the best, most atmospheric meeting rooms in the world. And what made it even better was the company. Our supporting band, Sherbet, were there, and I was able to hang out with one of my favourite guitarists, Ritchie Blackmore, and my new-found drummer friend, Cozy Powell from Rainbow. The guys were enjoying a night off and were also staying at the Plaza. The bar was buzzing.

The next day we flew to the Norwegian town of Trondheim. We arrived at the Britannia Hotel and dined in the Palm Court Room to Pete Wingfield's rocking piano accompaniment.

Diary entry:
'Went to gig for sound check. Crew very slow. Monitors needed sorting, short on time. Sherbet's road guys, John

and Howard, really have pulled this Swedish crew out
of the shit. Thanks to them we did a great show. Better
than Caracas and the German gigs. I now have my own
monitor, which is of great assistance.'

A full house in Oslo followed on October 2. Our greeting
on arrival in Bergen was impressive. Two girls, dressed in full
black tie and tails, presented us with a troll. Stavanger followed
then we travelled to Sweden where we played the Concert Hall
in Stockholm. While we were there, Mikael Rickfors called by
to say hello. Allan seemed uncomfortable around him and the
atmosphere became a little awkward. It was a brief meeting.

Back home I visited the farmhouse to see the results of
Belshaw's handiwork. The building was free of white paint
but it was now surrounded by white sand. I was reminded
of the dunes at St Anne's-on-the-Sea. Maureen told me that
Pat had gone through eleven tons of the stuff. Today, as I
stand and look at my home, my eyes are drawn to dear Belsh's
strap pointed handiwork that holds the locally quarried stone
together, and Peter Croasdale's artful cementation along the
north facing rear wall. They were two local characters I was
proud to stand shoulder to shoulder with while raising a glass
in 'Compost Corner'.

Days later we were off to Vancouver and Allan's wife, Jeni,
joined The Hollies' travelling party at Heathrow. Until then
there had been a long-standing tacit agreement that wives and
girlfriends didn't come along. If everyone in the band brought

along loved ones, the extra expense could put a sizeable dent in the end of tour profit. But this was serious. Allan needed Jeni with him and we all understood. I felt for him. He was going through a difficult time, trying to abstain from booze. It was not going to be easy with the likes of cognac-quaffing Robin around, and the rest of us sloshing back the champagne on offer in the Air Canada first class lounge. A rock 'n' roll lifestyle is not for the faint-hearted. It's a tough gig. It's survival of the fittest.

Still very jet-lagged, we played the Queen Elizabeth Theatre in Vancouver. I felt we gave a poor performance but, amazingly, the audience gave us a standing ovation. After that we boarded a DC-8 and hopped over the Rockies to perform in Calgary, then on to Winnipeg where we played two nights at the Centennial Concert Hall. Allan was toughing it out and drinking water, but all was not well.

In Thunder Bay we played a college, then on to Regina where I used Sherbet's drums, as mine wouldn't fit on the plane. Allan told the technicians that it would be his last tour as the doctor arrived to check his throat. In Edmonton we all performed well, but Clarkey had been seen sinking a couple of beers before the show. Next we stormed Saskatoon, and the following morning I opened the paper to see a terrific review of our gig. That bucked me up and compensated for the long flight to Toronto where we played the Massey Hall. The previous year we had played there on exactly the same date, November 14.

Before the show Robin phoned to tell each of us that there was a rumour going round that one of The Hollies was dead. He suggested that we phone home to put our folks' minds at ease. At the venue I counted the band in and counted them out. All present and correct.

I dumped my bags in my room in the Meridian hotel, Montreal, and, as always, went to look out of the window. I pulled back the net curtains to reveal the bebopper-in-chief, Dizzy Gillespie. This giant of modern jazz was being interviewed in the adjacent underground shopping complex. I watched in awe. I had spent my early teens listening to Dizzy and Charlie Parker, two giants of modern jazz.

The Canadian tour ended on a high. Allan had managed to get through the tough schedule thanks, in no small part, to Jeni's presence. Sherbet's manager, Roger Davies, presented Robin with an attaché case as a thank you for his fatherly business advice, and we gave the road crew, John and Howard, a camera each for their invaluable technical assistance and camaraderie.

After a break at home – and yes, the sand was still there – it was on to Hamburg to record a TV show to be transmitted on New Year's Eve. We had two days of rehearsals before the show, and this time Allan had brought his whole family with him – Jeni and their children: Timothy, Toby and Piper.

I'd heard that the Club Amphore in Hamburg was something special and that first evening, Sylvester and I made our way to the secret establishment. As we walked down dimly lit streets, the guy from our record company reeled off a list of famous international celebrities who had hung out at this top-secret bonking bunker. No sign, just a dark entrance accessed through a shady alleyway near the city's waterfront. The place appeared deserted. Our German friend knocked on the door. It opened slowly and an exotically dressed lady beckoned us in and led us to our table. I presumed she was the boss. We sat down and surveyed the scene. Nearby, a man and woman were shagging away on a table. Although somewhat surreal, it seemed the norm. The drinks were flowing and our friend told us that any of the beautiful naked girls strutting round in nothing but a pair of stilettos were happy to perform any sex act at or on the customer's table, or anywhere that took your fancy. The guy who had just been banging away was now swaggering round the club consuming handfuls of peanuts. He was obviously the resident stud and needed to keep his pecker up in readiness for the next performance. From time to time the assembled clientele would spontaneously put on their own little shows, and then they would resume quaffing and chatting as though nothing had happened. Those clever Germans had taken the idea of the *pas de deux* to a whole new level. This was the real hokey-cokey – 1970s lap dancing and beyond.

In the taxi heading back to the hotel Terry and I shook our heads in disbelief. He said: 'Was that real?' I replied: 'Well it's something to tell your grandkids.'

The following day we were back at the hotel bar after completing day one of rehearsals for the TV spectacular.

Amazingly, this was in the same studio where I had collapsed in February 1967 with a burst appendix. I had gone down to the strains of 'Strawberry Fields'.

Kevin Keegan, the ex-Liverpool and England footballer, now playing for Hamburg, joined us in the bar. He and Terry were friends. Robin requested a brandy sour and when the barman admitted he was unsure of the correct ingredients, Robbo was behind the bar before you could say: 'Shaken not stirred'. The whites of egg palaver followed, then the usual stance, Hush Puppies akimbo and a Benson & Hedges gripped firmly between his lips. He shook the precious mixture so vigorously that he broke into a sweat. It tasted bloody good though.

On March 9, 1978, the five of us were sitting in San Frediano, a trendy eatery in South Kensington, lunching with highly rated American record producer John Boylan. He'd been recommended by Steve Popovich, vice president of our US record company CBS/Epic. We'd met on several occasions and been impressed by his drive and enthusiasm. He had told us that John loved The Hollies and would like to work with us. Now Boylan had flown over from the States to meet up and discuss the way forward. He had previously produced records by REO Speedwagon, Linda Ronstadt and Boston. The timing was perfect, and I was beginning to warm to John's ideas and to get excited about recording in America.

Everyone was listening with rapt attention apart from Allan. As our American guest was in full flow, Al would occasionally get up from the table and wander over to the bar and stand there alone. Boylan soldiered on with his pitch, but I sensed that he was wondering what he might be letting himself in for – if this was what happens in a restaurant, how will they behave in a recording studio?

The following morning in Robin's office, the five of us met again. I arrived to see Chrissie, his secretary, had made tea and sandwiches. Not the usual type of refreshment seen in RCB's Bryanston Mews West office, but Robin was shaky and suffering from a hangover. I could sense that something was afoot. To everyone's amazement, Clarkey said that he wanted to call it a day. Was this why he had torpedoed a recording venture that might have raised The Hollies' profile on both sides of the Atlantic? His comment about John Boylan's offer was: 'There's not much in the offing.' He didn't go into detail, and no one asked him to elaborate, although clearly this was not true. Tony looked at me, shrugged and said fine. After working together all these years, we had become used to Allan's behaviour. His unpredictability was becoming all too predictable.

Terry was angry. 'Why didn't you tell us three months ago? Being selfish weren't you?' No answer to that. Allan's decision was a huge disappointment. Was it done out of spite, or was it an act of unintentional professional suicide? Maybe he was just feeling unwell? We knew he had problems with alcohol but unbeknown to us, our Al was in the process of making a solo album in the States. Maybe his people over there would not be happy if he also made an album with The Hollies.

The rest of us felt let down, puzzled and hurt. Allan had, it seemed, killed our golden goose. We never heard from John Boylan again. And, as time proved, Al's new US solo venture proved to be a waste of time and his album bombed.

Meeting over, Tony dropped Bernie and me at Euston Station. We caught the 1.55 p.m. to Manchester and were picked up by Bernie's wife, Shirley, in her Range Rover. Now I could get down to sorting out the farmhouse and spending more time with Maureen and friends in the real world up north.

In early June I was at the Inn on the Park hotel for EMI's launch of The Hollies' *20 Golden Greats*. A lavish dinner had been laid on for record stores and dealers from all over Britain. A glossy video presentation followed, with Alan Freeman's voice-over linking together a score of Hollies hits. First, we'd had champagne in Bernie's room, followed by a little schmoozing with some of the assembled diners, after which I ended up in Tramp with Tony and Jane.

The album went on to be a bestseller, although, like me, Friends of the Earth might have been horrified by the front of the LP. It featured a picture of a polluting power station with the sun setting behind it. The caption read: '20 great sounds that grew out of the North'. But in spite of the *Quatermass*-style cover, and the designer's vision of the area north of Watford, *20 Golden Greats* stuck at number two in the album charts for weeks on end and sold by the barrowload.

Allan was absent when The Hollies were number one in the American singles chart with a song he co-wrote. Sadly, he'd gone AWOL when we were at number two on his home turf, with an album on which he was a major player.

Word had got round that we were, yet again, looking for a new singer. A few came to Robin's office, where they were vetted and then politely shown the door.

On October 3 Chrissie, Robin's secretary, phoned to tell me that Clarkey was now asking if he could come back into the band. I said that it was fine by me and went back to clearing out my barn.

A couple of weeks later we all met at Robbo's. A smiling Allan appeared to be his old charming self, and we chatted as though nothing had happened. It was also a nice surprise to see Ron Richards again as he joined in the discussions. Ron had a bunch of songs, several of which had been written by Jack Bruce and Tony Hymas, two former Hollies associates, and our old mentor was eager to get back in Abbey Road with us. Four days later we were in Studio Three where we recorded two tracks written by Murray Head, 'Say It Ain't So, Joe' and 'When I'm Yours'. By December 16 we had enough tracks for our album *Five Three One – Double Seven 0 Four*. 5317704. Enter that number into a 1970s calculator, turn it upside down and it reads 'hollies'. At the time we thought it was pretty cool. To drive the point home, the front of the album showed two monolithic adding machines docking together like a couple of mating space stations. There was only one in-house composition on the album, the haunting 'Satellite Three', co-written by Allan and Gary Benson. 'Boys In The Band', with

Terry on lead vocals, eased the tedium of Ron Richards' last piece of work for The Hollies. At one stage of the recording process, Ron arrived accompanied by a scruffy geezer who was wearing a pair of carpet slippers. It turned out that he was the landlord of our producer's local pub. Ron played him a couple of our unfinished tracks and asked the old boy for his opinion. It was a jaw-dropping interlude. Sadly, that incident illustrated the demise of a once great A&R man, and with the completion of *Five Three One – Double Seven 0 Four*, it was time to finally say goodbye to dear Ron.

The massive consoles at Abbey Road were now computerised, and engineer Mike Jarratt had a 16- and a 24-track machine linked together. Very impressive, but advancing technology, ironically, meant that it was now taking much longer to mix a Hollies track.

Early in January 1979, I set my drums up in Studio Two in readiness for the orchestral session that was booked to begin at 10 a.m. the following morning. We planned to record a song written by David Pomeranz, 'It's In Every One of Us'. Tony Hymas had scored the string arrangement, and he conducted the assembled musicians with Allan singing and me on drums. Musicians' Union rules now dictated that only one title could be recorded in a three-hour session, and instrumental overdubs by members of the orchestra were forbidden, so it was an expensive session for Hollies Ltd. After lunch Allan, Terry and Tony added the harmonies and the track was ready for mixing. By January 18 the album was complete.

In the late 1970s Hollies live concerts in the UK were limited to a week here and a week there. Since the advent of Batley Variety Club, cheap imitations had sprung up all over the country. On March 11 we began a week of concerts at one such place, Wakefield Theatre Club. Robin was happy; the money was good and it was an easy way to fill his date sheet. But this type of work enabled the smug music press to pigeonhole us as a cabaret band. On March 13 my future best man and good friend, John Pratt, was in the audience with his fiancée, Rowena. Allan announced their engagement from the stage and the lovebirds were invited to meet the band afterwards, when we presented them with a bottle of champagne. JP tells me they still have that unopened bottle of Moët & Chandon.

Talking about lovebirds, Maureen and I did finally tie the knot too, although it was some while later. We were taking our annual vacation at the Sonesta Beach Hotel on Key Biscayne, near Miami, when one morning I woke up, drew back the curtains of our room on the fifth floor and surveyed the pool, palms and blue ocean beyond. What a lovely day for getting married I thought. Babe Teeter, our friend and assistant manager at the Sonesta, discretely fixed an appointment at the Marriage License Bureau at 140 W. Flagler Street in downtown Miami.

The following day, as Maureen and I were shopping downtown, I surprised her. 'How would you like to get married?'

'When?' she said.

'Now,' I replied.

'Do you have a ring?' she asked. I hadn't thought of that, but we were just passing a shop called The People's Jewellers. Perfect. I popped in, bought a ring and we proceeded up Flagler to our humble wedding venue. Duty clerk Maria Cruz conducted the ceremony, and we had our photo taken in front of a cheesy backdrop. Back at the hotel Babe and the Sonesta staff sent flowers and a big cake to our room. After all these years we were now Mr and Mrs Elliott. The date was November 30, 1993.

Back in 1979, once the petrol tanker driver's strike was over, there was no shortage of fuel, so after the Wakefield show on Thursday night, Tony, Bernie and I had crossed the Pennines to get home. The following day the snow came down with a vengeance, so we set off early and headed for Todmorden to avoid the deep drifts on the higher moorland route. It was a mistake. The three of us had to turn back because of stranded traffic blocking our way. Had we gone over the Moss, I'm sure the four-wheel drive Range Rover would have made it. Time had run out and we had let the good folk of Yorkshire down. Holed up in the Ram Inn, across the road from my little junior school at Holmes Chapel, we phoned through to give Robin, Allan and Terry the bad news. We tried to make amends on the final Saturday night, although, at the end of the evening, the manager of the place was nowhere to be found, so Robin had to hang around for an extra day to collect our fee.

The following day Terry drove me westward across the M62 in his Jaguar XJ12. The snow on either side of the motorway was deep but our way was clear. We arrived in Southport to be greeted by spring-like sunny weather. That night we played to a packed house in the theatre on the seafront. Robin eventually caught up with us in Oxford. He was a day late, but at least he'd been paid for our Wakefield gig. We had checked into the creaky old Randolph Hotel in the heart of the city, as we would be playing at the New Theatre just around the corner. These characterful old hotels are popular with tourists and poseurs but of no use to musicians and artists, who need to get a peaceful night's sleep and rise at a civilised hour. Sure enough, I was awakened early the next morning by the sound of workmen banging and drilling.

We travelled on to Bristol in a chauffeur-driven Merc and a Volvo. We played the Colston Hall.

Diary entry:
'*The smoke machine blew oil over my drums as I was walking onstage, accompanied by the sound of our new jet-taking-off intro. Creeping through Rod's haze, I found my drums and sat on my stool, but I struggled to play as my feet kept slipping off the hi-hat and bass drum pedals. Eventually, someone chucked sawdust over the wet area. It soaked up the oil, but gummed up my foot operated devices. I soldiered on. Good show – especially for this place. Usually a duff sound, but we played subtly with light and shade.*'

The Carleton in Bournemouth, our next stop, boasted that it was a five star hotel, but my room curtains were too thin – as were the walls. I could hear Terry on one side and Tony on the other. The hotel's saving grace was the ambient downstairs area, as well as the excellent manager and the fab food that was provided for our late supper.

After a day off, Tony was on Radio 1's *Newsbeat*. Allan was also booked but didn't show up. Something wasn't right. During the previous four theatre shows, he'd been fine, but on his arrival at the Albany Hotel in Birmingham, he said that he needed a doctor. He soldiered on, and that night I noted in my diary that it was a good show, even if he was a little tired. The next day, I travelled up to Ipswich in Simon Hart's classic Jaguar, along with Rocky, the Labrador. The show was great, and Allan excelled with his impromptu rock 'n' roll finale, in which he would strap on his Fender Telecaster and hit us with a rock classic, sending the audience into raptures: 'Open up a-honey it's your lover boy me that's a-knocking…'

Clarkey at his best – and the band as one.

Stop! In The Name Of Love

Words and Music by
EDDIE HOLLAND, LAMONT DOZIER and BRIAN HOLLAND
Recorded by THE HOLLIES on ATLANTIC RECORDS

Columbia Pictures Publications

6456SSMX / $2.50

Music Co., Inc.

CHAPTER TWENTY:

'His Welfare Is My Concern'

The cherry blossom was in full bloom and spring was in the air as the limo transported Rod, keyboard player Pete Arnesen, Bernie and me through the London suburbs to Heathrow Airport. There we met the rest of the party and boarded a Lufthansa Airbus bound for Frankfurt. On arrival we were greeted by Herr Jahnke and driver Franz, and we climbed aboard our Jasper bus. We had a sellout tour of Germany ahead of us, and I couldn't wait to play. Everything was nice and pleasant on the way to our first gig at the Rheingoldhalle, by the river in Mainz. Allan had arrived with his manager. We now had a stranger in our midst, a spy in the camp, whose presence served to dampen the usual relaxed banter and camaraderie. But Allan's welfare was paramount, both professionally and as a friend, and we were willing to sacrifice a little of our way of life for our pal's well-being.

Then Al came out with a stunner. Having just arrived, he stated that he wanted to catch the next plane home. Imagine the atmosphere now. I was stressed out before the tour had got under way.

The following day Al appeared fine. We played the Jahrhunderthalle, Frankfurt. Next came Saarbrücken, followed by Bonn, and our old stomping ground at the Beethovenhalle. Here Allan walked offstage after a few songs and left Tony and Terry, who were totally unprepared, to manage the vocals as best they could. In Kassel we had word that our hero must rest for two days. The show went well, with Terry excelling himself at covering that centre spot.

The hotel at Heilbronn was in the prettiest setting of the whole tour, with swallows skimming the adjacent slow-flowing river and ducklings on the doorstep. For a few minutes I was able to mentally escape from the torment of being stuck in a foreign land with a half-cocked band. On we travelled to Hitler's old stomping ground, Nuremberg, where I hoped our frontman might rally, but he was conserving his voice, whispering dramatically that he wanted another night off.

On Saturday, April 28 we were the first rock band to play at Berlin's brand new ICC – Internationales Congress Centrum. Allan performed reasonably well, but we were all racking our brains as to what could be done to rescue him from this downward spiral. Tony suggested that we lower some of the keys of songs in the set, so that it would be easier for him to sing them. In my head, I could hear Paul Robeson singing

'Old Man River'. Three gigs later, while resting in my room in Aachen, Robin phoned to tell me that Allan had suffered a complete nervous breakdown. The doctor had seen him and Clarkey was going home.

Our support act throughout this German tour was an American band called Stumblebunny. As Al was now indisposed, David, their singer, had kindly agreed to help out on vocals. He rehearsed with Terry and Tony and was thrown in at the deep end at the Eurogress in Aachen that very night. Thankfully, the show was well received. As we walked back into the hotel, there standing at the bar in the cocktail lounge was our indisposed lead singer, wearing a white suit and looking radiant. I was tempted to go over and strangle him. He didn't seem to understand what he was putting us through. We were under contract and committed to honouring the agreement with our promoter Karsten Jahnke. The folk of Germany had spent their hard-earned cash supporting us, and we didn't want to let them down. The tour had to be completed, but we would have all preferred to be at home with our loved ones and not stressed out clearing up the mess.

On Thursday, May 3 it was polling day in the UK. Margaret Thatcher became the first British woman prime minister and Allan had flown home. With Clarkey gone, we fought our way through the rest of the tour which, given the circumstances, went surprisingly well. We played Essen, Munich and Augsburg to sellout crowds, and the hole in our midst was barely apparent.

On departing from Augsburg for Mannheim, Robin again performed his party piece of leaving the swag in the hotel safe. Frank had to turn the bus round and return to the Steigenberger Drei Mohren hotel for Robin to retrieve our dosh.

The lovely Mannheim Rosengarten was always a favourite venue of ours.

Diary entry:
'Great audience – killed 'em. Twelve blind young ladies were in the auditorium. After the show they were waiting at the stage door. We chatted to them all. The experience was uplifting – so much so, that we invited them onto the bus, and we all sang Hollies songs as Franz Ludwig drove them back to their home. I felt humbled and privileged to have been in their presence. Tears were flowing as we said goodbye.'

On a beautiful warm day we boarded our Mercedes Jasper bus. As we settled into our regular seats, a waiter from the hotel came down the aisle with a tray of champagne. It was Robin's birthday and promoter Karsten had sprung a pleasant surprise on the old boy.

As we sipped our sparkling fizz, Herr Jahnke regaled us with his latest venture – cutting a deal with the manager of Dire Straits. 'He thought that he had a good deal, but I had the information and had ze better deal – I had him by the short penis hairs,' he said, grinning. After spluttering into our champers, we realised it was his German version of the 'short and curlies'.

After that we went merrily on our way to Cologne and the tour ended in Munster, at Halle Münsterland.

Just ten days later Allan was still in the wilderness, and we returned to Germany. With Paul Bliss making his debut on keyboards, we knocked off a quick version of 'Harlequin' with Terry on lead vocals in the Munich TV studios. The following day, May 22, after flying from Munich to Frankfurt, we travelled in two Mercedes to Baden and checked into the Brenners Park-Hotel. I've stayed in hundreds of hotels around the world but this place is very special. My diary entry reads: *'Beautiful town, surrounding parklands and the best hotel ever. Old and solid. Quite formal with a beautiful outlook from my veranda. Trees and shrubs at their best. Nice scents. I wish Mum and Dad could have seen this.'*

We went to the TV studios for camera rehearsal. The show would be recorded the following day; German production teams like to work at a leisurely pace. Back at the hotel I explored the surrounding parkland and then joined Tony and Paul Bliss, who were playing backgammon, for a fortifying glass of local Baden wine. We weren't allowed in the hotel bar or restaurant without a tie. No problem. The concierge produced a tray of assorted neckties. I lent Terry five hundred Deutschmarks, and he went off to the casino with Robin. With the benefit of hindsight, was it a good idea for The Hollies' manager to be trying his luck at the roulette wheel while being in charge of the band's purse strings?

Robin wasn't seen the next day; he was in bed, ill. The rest of us flew the flag, and Tes sang 'Harlequin' live on the TV show.

Back home I phoned Jeni to see how Allan was. She said that he'd been in rehab for some weeks and was doing as well as could be expected. Tony visited him and told me the poor lad was going through a tough time, but at least he was getting help. He'd been in trouble for a long time, so knowing that he was on the upward path, tough though that must have been for him, was reassuring. I wished him well.

A couple of months later Tony, Robin and I had lunch with Jimmy Smith at Verrey's restaurant on Regent Street. Jim was a booker from London Management, and Robin's new contact enabled him to fill The Hollies' date sheet with an assortment of cabaret-type venues throughout the UK. After lunch, we met at our accountants' office, with David Apps, Allan's manager. He demanded that Tony and I pay Allan money because he was at Wakefield when we had missed a night due to the snowbound roads. We paid up, after which Allan arrived looking better. It was good to see him again.

We began a week of concerts at The Night Out in Birmingham on September 24. Al was still having throat problems but, with Jeni and Apps in attendance, he got through the first night, although the band's stage sound monitors sounded poor, which didn't help. On October 1 we began another week, this time at the Golden Garter near Manchester Airport. On the second night I told Allan that his bad throat was possibly all in his mind. Perhaps not the most sage advice but, in my own way, I was trying to lift him, to boost his confidence, man to man. A singer has nowhere to hide when his vocal cords fail. From my elevated observation point onstage, perched upon my drum throne, I could get away with a dodgy performance, and the average punter would not notice. For a singer it's different. No concealment. No tricks available. No wool to pull. You can't hide behind a metal microphone stand because a couple of pieces of delicate membrane stretched across the larynx have suffered from wear and tear, due to overwork and an unhealthy life on the road.

On the Friday night Maureen and I stayed at The Swan at Bucklow Hill. It was Jeni's birthday and she and Allan, Mo and I had a lovely dinner together.

Tony was now living in Bywater Street, conveniently situated just off the Kings Road in Chelsea. On November 1 Mike Batt collected the pair of us in his Rolls-Royce, and we wombled off to Wedgies Night Club. He played us a song he'd just written, 'Can't Lie No More'. A week or so later we were in Wessex Sound Studios recording Batty's song. For the first time in my life I was playing along to a click track. He had set the tempo too slow, but he was a respected producer, so I went along with it. Later at Lansdowne Studios, Mike recorded our next single, 'Soldier's Song', with the London Symphony Orchestra and also dubbed them onto our 'Lie No More' track.

A week or so later Maureen and I were staying at Tony's, as we were flying out to Miami the next morning. Batty arrived and played us the final mix of 'Soldier's Song'. He told us that we should dump our manager, Robin, as he was out of touch

297

and old-fashioned. It made sense. Times had changed and, sadly, Robbo hadn't changed with them.

The following morning Mo and I boarded a westbound jet at Heathrow and headed off to Miami and our new-found holiday haven, across the Rickenbacker Causeway to Key Biscayne, and the Sonesta Beach Hotel.

CHAPTER TWENTY-ONE:

What Goes Around...

We were met in the foyer of Odyssey Studios near Marble Arch by The Shadows' rhythm guitarist, Bruce Welch. The previous day we had recorded a basic track without him, and he wasn't happy. He went on to say that he didn't like the studio, the engineer, the bass playing or the keyboard player. He planned to book a different studio, along with his choice of bass player and keyboardist.

I don't know how it happened, but Bruce had been recruited to produce our next single, a no-hoper of a song entitled 'I Don't Understand You'. He had successfully produced records for Cliff Richard so, out of respect, and as fans of The Shadows and Cliff, we went along with his demands. But I felt sorry for our bass player, Bernie, a good musician and friend, who had now been cruelly sidelined by Bruce without being given a second chance.

Some weeks later we found ourselves up in Hertfordshire, in Brian Bennett's studio. I'd been a fan of The Shadows' drummer ever since I saw him playing drums with The Wildcats, along with guitarist Jim Sullivan, when they were backing Marty Wilde at the Palace Cinema in Burnley. I was there with an early love of mine, Colne Convent girl Valerie Bellis, who, embarrassingly, insisted on screaming 'Marty' throughout the singer's performance. Later I saw Brian behind his black Trixon drums with Joe Brown's band, The Bruvvers, at the Majestic ballroom in Barnoldswick. He was also one of The Bluegrass Boys on the revolving stage down Nelson Imp, along with Brian 'Licorice' Locking and Jim Sullivan. The trio backed Johnny Duncan of 'Last Train To San Fernando' fame. That was shortly before Brian joined The Shadows. Now I was playing drums in his studio, along with Shads sidekicks, bass player Alan Jones and Cliff Hall on keyboards.

While I was working there, Brian would occasionally invite me to join him for a refreshing glass of champagne and Margaret, his wife, kept our energy levels topped up by furnishing all assembled with a generous supply of tasty toasties. With Allan singing a guide vocal, Tony on guitar and me on drums, supported by Cliff and Alan, the backing track was completed, and we planned to return to add vocals at a later date.

Robin Britten had been The Hollies' manager for fourteen years. On May 19, 1981, we met in his Bryanston Mews West office for an important meeting. We had, after some discussion and soul-searching, decided to let him go. I think he sensed what was coming and, once we told him, his demeanour became more relaxed and a look of relief spread across his face.

He pulled a large handkerchief from his pocket and dabbed his brow, then his moist upper lip. A Benson & Hedges was drawn from his ever-present gold packet of twenty, after which came the familiar clink, plop and fizz as he poured himself a large brandy and ginger.

His health was failing, and now he'd been relieved of his weekly commute from Bembridge on the Isle of Wight to the capital, he looked at ease. He would now be able to enjoy a peaceful life among his friends at the family home across the Solent. We thanked him for all he had done for us over many years. We were all fond of the old boy but times, and managers, must change.

A couple of weeks later on the evening of June 1, 1981, Tony and Terry were recording vocals in Bennett's studio, along with Allan. Perfectionist Bruce Welch demanded take after take, in what became a gruelling singing session, and nerves were jangling as the recording was finally completed. The guys thanked Bruce and said their goodbyes. Allan went home to his family, and Hicks and Sylvester agreed to wind down over a relaxing drink at a nearby hostelry.

Over the previous months Terry's outbursts had become more and more irritating and unsettling for us all and tensions had been building. In a diary entry a few weeks earlier I had written: '*Tony said to Terry, "Why do you hate Allan so much – and why does your wife hate the fuckin' lot of us?"*'

That quote gives an insight into life in The Hollies at that time. In the pub the drinks flowed and, sure enough, Tes began to strut his stuff. The wind-down drink developed into a wind-up rant, with poor Tony on the receiving end of Terry's fanciful tongue. He said that he was the most important member of The Hollies, and then went even further. He blurted out that The Hollies would be 'nothing without me'. Having given him more than enough rope, an exasperated Tony answered: 'Do you want to bet?' To which Terry replied yes, and foolishly held out his hand. Tony couldn't believe his luck and shook on it. The trapdoor dropped open and that was the end of Sylvester. Tony told me later, in his usual understated way: 'I just explained the facts of life to him and the conversation became a little heated.'

The fair wind of fate was blowing, and the good ship Hollies was about to chart a new course into the eighties. A couple of weeks later back in Brian Bennett's place, The Hollies three-way sounded as strong as ever. At the suggestion of producer Welch, a beaming Labi Siffre arrived and effortlessly sang top harmony alongside Allan and Tony, and 'I Don't Understand You' was in the can – although in my opinion, that's where it should have stayed. Maureen was with me at the session, and that night we stayed at Tony and Jane's house on Bywater Street. The following night it was chopsticks at Mr Chows, followed by a star-studded night in Johnny Gold's basement club, Tramp.

John Miles is one of The Hollies' unsung heroes. He is a great musician, composer and arranger. Witness Tina Turner's live concerts on TV and you'll see what I mean. There is Milesy playing guitar or keyboards while directing the powerful backing band that enhances Tina's dynamic stage show. On July 6 John, Tony, Allan and I were in Studio Three in Abbey Road to record one of John's songs, 'Carrie'.

Bernie had decided to call it a day. He'd had enough of music business politics and was in the process of opening a delicatessen in Nelson. I met him for a coffee a couple of years ago in his hometown of Clitheroe. Although he is no longer manning the bacon slicer, he greeted me by thrusting half a pound of pork sausages into my hand. When we got home, Sue, who had recently become my wife, cooked them for tea. They were delicious.

Anyway, back to Abbey Road. With bass player Alan Jones, Tony playing guitar, John Miles on piano and me on drums, we set about laying down the basic track. Veteran EMI recording engineer Peter Bown oversaw the session along with Milesy's tech guy, Mike Day. At first progress was slow but, importantly, we had met Mike, who would be crucial in the development of Tony's latest brainchild, and key to an exciting venture that would lead all the way to the West Coast of the USA.

Our 1981 hit record 'Holliedaze' came about because of the Stars On 45 craze. Some Dutch guys had produced a medley of Beatles hits recorded by sound-alike imposters and released it on a 45 rpm disc as a single. The short snatches of song were all the same tempo and rocked along to claps and a four-on-the-floor bass drum beat. These novelty singles were storming the charts, and any successful recording artist was fair game to the exploitative forgers.

Tony phoned me and said: 'It's only a matter of time. We could be next.' I agreed. Thankfully, a counterfeit 'Hollies On 45' didn't happen. We had a better idea, and I wouldn't need to raise a drumstick. We planned to use The Hollies' original master tapes.

On a day late in July, after my journey south, I was greeted by Hollies tech Simon Hart outside Euston Station. Simon knew his way round the city. In his earlier years he had driven a big red double-decker bus for London Transport. Si used to tell me about his adventures piloting the iconic eighty-seater Routemaster, cutting up boy racers who got in his way as he traversed the capital's busy streets for fare-paying passengers. Now he was behind the wheel of his red Golf GTI. The words from the Flanders and Swann tune ran through my head: 'Hold very tight please, ding-ding', as we scorched up Abbey Road in his scarlet sixteen-horsepower hot-shot Volkswagen and turned left into the famous walled car park. We headed up the front steps of the famous studios where recording engineer Mike Day, Tony and I went into a mixing suite.

I'd previously compiled a list of suitable Hollies hits, and studio manager Colette Barber had made sure the masters were sent up from EMI's tape vault in Hayes. Copies were made, but the songs varied in tempo and it was imperative that all the selected tracks were running at exactly the same beats-per-minute. For this, Mike Day used a vari-speed device to bring the chosen sections of tape up or down into one common tempo. He then cleverly spliced the songs of our choice together in what we considered to be the most appealing running order. It was a slow process, but eventually the chosen ones were transferred to a Studer 4-track tape recorder – possibly the very same machine that we had first recorded some of the same songs on back in the early 1960s. The three vacant tracks were filled with a bass drum and double-tracked handclaps courtesy of a LinnDrum machine.

Finally, 'Holliedaze' was mixed down to quarter-inch tape and was ready for mastering. And unlike the Stars On 45 guys, we had used original Hollies recordings in creating the medley. It was 5 a.m. on the morning of the last day of July when the three of us hastily assembled a bunch of our leftover hits for use on the flip side of the disc.

Outside, a new day had begun. The dawn chorus tinkled around a sleepy St John's Wood as the fading choral strains of 'He Ain't Heavy', the last track on the B-side, drifted down the corridor. Years of hard work had been melded into a couple of pop medleys. But we were struggling to christen the underside of that seven-inch circular disc of plastic. Then I remembered that George Martin had come up with a title for an earlier album of Hollies hits in the late 1960s. At the time we had considered the great man's cheesy suggestion just too corny. But now we were tired and in need of sleep so, by way of acknowledging Sir George, the B-side of our forthcoming hit single was given 'the fifth Beatle's' inspired title: 'Holliepops'.

Done. The tape box was labelled. It was 6.30 a.m. when Tony and I left the building.

A few weeks later 'Holliedaze' entered the Top 30. The *Top Of The Pops* production office phoned to ask us to record the show the following Wednesday, adding: 'Is there any chance of borrowing your old pal Graham from Crosby and Stills?' Why not? Tony phoned Willy who said: 'Send me a couple of plane tickets and I'll be over.'

Graham arrived from Los Angeles with his wife, Susan. Tony picked them up from the airport, and they stayed at his place on Bywater Street. The following day we were back in Abbey Road Studios. In the 1960s it had been found that certain chart-topping groups and instrumentalists were cheating the public by miming to another person's performance while appearing on *Top Of The Pops*. So, the Musicians' Union had decided to stamp out the immoral practice of deceiving the British viewing public, and no one was exempt from the Big Brother treatment. When an artist was due to appear on a major TV show and perform to a backing track – which was normal practice in those days – the whole process of making a record from scratch had to be gone through to satisfy the Union official in attendance. It was an expensive and demoralising process, especially as we were the guys who had actually played and sung on every Hollies recording, including 'Holliedaze'. We explained to our comrade the technicalities of splicing and creating the montage of songs. Thankfully, he understood, and we were allowed to use the same tape for our forthcoming on-screen performance.

At Television Centre we floated through a day of camera calls and cups of canteen tea. The two Salford pals, Harold and Willy, were having fun again. Tony and I, who in a previous life had been a pair of Dolphins, caught glimpses of the original Two Teens, as Allan and Graham became Ricky and Dane again for a day. Our dressing rooms rang with laughter and it felt good.

My mind flashed back to a grim Sussex Gardens Hotel, when all five of us shared the same scabies-riddled bedroom. I remembered our Ford Thames van with Harold and Willy sleeping on the floor after squabbling over who was going to snooze on the five-foot long red, spongy leatherette cushion. To us connoisseurs of comfort that cushion was known as 'the Snake'. Had that really been almost twenty years earlier?

A knock on the door brought me back to the present. We were led to our *TOTP* set, and the five of us – Allan, Tony, Graham and original bass player Eric, who I had invited to join us for the occasion – took up our time-honoured positions without any prodding from the attendant floor manager. I slid onto my drum stool and took up sticks. Youngsters, recruited as camera fodder, gawped as camera crews tried not to run over them. Incredibly, the presenter was Jimmy Savile, who had introduced us on the very first *TOTP* on New Year's Day 1964 in the old church on Dickenson Road, Manchester.

'The Hollies!' Magic time. Five cameras. 'Just One Look' and just one chance for me to hit the drums in the right place at precisely the right time. I was intent on making my playing appear real, just as I had done on TV shows around the world since the inception of the band. The art of deception had been honed to perfection. Our vocals were skilfully lip-sync'd by the three old hands up front as the cascade of Hollies hits was committed to video tape ready for nationwide transmission the next day, September 10, 1981.

We didn't see ourselves on the box that Thursday. No armchair viewing of *Top Of The Pops* for us. Audio International Studios had been booked and Graham tagged along, eager to be on the mic alongside Allan and Tony, singing his usual impeccable top harmony. 'Something Ain't Right' was the song, and he nailed it with ease. On those two special days in September it seemed as though he had never been away.

Thanks to the BBC and Graham William Nash, a West Coast chapter was about to unfold in The Hollies' book of tasty treats. *What Goes Around*, a new album of songs, was to be recorded at Rudy Records at the Crossroads of The World. Allan, Tony and I would soon be ensconced in the North Villa adjacent to the Sunset Marquis Hotel on Alta Loma, just off Hollywood's Sunset Strip. There we would savour the tropical gardens, occasionally watching hummingbirds flitting to and fro beneath the LA palms as we relaxed in the outdoor jacuzzi, followed by an occasional late night cocktail in the Polo Lounge at the Beverly Hills Hotel.

As Dee, the TWA air hostess had famously said: 'Fasten your seat belts. We're gonna party all the way... but shhh, don't tell the captain!'

Photograph: Dan Burn-Forti
Calligraphy: An Vanhentenrijk

Last Word...

'You can't buy this,' Hollies singer Pete movingly exclaims to the beaming standing ovation assembled before us. He's right. Getting high on the backs of the paying public is a selfish privilege. Maybe I should feel a twinge of guilt, and not overwhelming elation, as I pump the kick drum pedals and thrash my cymbals in support of Tony and Steve's elongated screaming guitar chords at the end of 'Long Cool Woman'. The atmosphere crackles as I jump down from my riser and run to the centre microphone, where I breathlessly proclaim: 'We are The Hollies. Thank you Salford, good night, God bless!' The play-off music swells, and I step back to stand shoulder to shoulder with my bandmates and take in the applause. After the fourth bow, I break ranks and half-sprint, half-float to my dressing room. I have nothing left to give after a two-hour performance. Now I need to get out of my wet stage clothes and shower away the sweat in readiness for my reward, a pint of good English ale.

As the hot shower cascades over my body, my mind flashes back in time to the highs and lows in my life.

The low: the death of my wife Maureen in 2009.

The high: meeting Sue, who later became my second wife in 2015.

I count my blessings.

Jesus – I'm a guy in his seventy-seventh year, I shouldn't be having all this fun.

Since the early 1980s The Hollies – Tony Hicks and I, assisted by Ray Stiles, Ian Parker, Steve Lauri and Peter Howarth – have navigated the tricky world of entertainment, steering our band through the unpredictable maze known today as the music industry.

Allan Clarke had suffered from voice problems for several years and had been advised by his doctor not to sing. We had tried to keep him going, but his final appearance with The Hollies was on Sunday, November 27, 1999 in Stoke-on-Trent. He came offstage and, without a word, promptly left the building. I wish him well.

We are indebted to our old friend John Miles, who had filled in for Allan earlier in the year. He effortlessly became our lead singer for three nights, and we all played out of our skins. Thanks to Milesy, we realised that there was life after Al. John was Tina Turner's musical director and unavailable for the long term, so the great Carl Wayne stood front and centre until his untimely death in 2004. But the show must go on and we had binding commitments. Then along came

Peter Howarth. For over fifteen years he has entertained us both on and offstage. We are proud to call him The Hollies' lead singer.

Seated in the bathroom of my home in the north of England, a few miles from where Tony and I started out as teenage rockers in our band The Dolphins, my eye is taken by my Hollies Rock 'n' Roll Hall of Fame statuette: *'For their Impact on the Evolution, Development and Perpetuation of Rock 'n' Roll.'* Next to it stands my Ivor Novello award, on which is engraved: *'For Outstanding Contribution To British Music.'* That'll do.

> Against the wall feeling down,
> Another gig another town
> Plumb the depths raise the roof
> It's now or never...
>
> Clear to the left the time is right
> Life begins at the start of night
> Take the stick force the pace
> And live for the moment
>
> Paid my dues I stop and stare
> I should know 'cos I was there
> My spirits trapped within theses walls
> It's now or never...
>
> Bare my soul, rev the heart
> Run the mile and soon we'll part
> I'll be gone before the curtain falls
> It's now or never... the moment of truth

It Ain't Heavy, It's My Story

There's a little piece of me in every theatre in the land
I left my mark and lost my soul
So much to give, only so long to live
We journey on we hit the highs
As the sun goes down… and the last chord dies

The Moment of Truth

THE END

Acknowledgements

Above all I must thank Tony Hicks. He and I started out as two teenagers with a passion for music and a dream that certainly came true.

Thank you Steve Lee Vickers for introducing me to literary agent Guy Rose, who in turn arranged a meeting with David Barraclough and Imogen Gordon Clark at Omnibus Press HQ. They liked my manuscript and editor Nick Jones helped me to put the baby to bed in readiness for the typesetting of this book.

Photographer Henry Diltz kindly provided the 1966 NYC Hollies images. Thanks to Ron Furmanek for making that happen. Our official photographer Rob Haywood also deserves a solid credit for his more current photos, and a special thanks to Rod Shields for his loyal support from 1964 to this day – not forgetting my best man and food taster, John Pratt.

Thank you

Bob Palmer	Ian Paice	Rowena Pratt
Mike Rutherford	Chrissie Marks	Gareth Pritchard
Alan Parsons	Vernon McCallum	Mark Crabtree
Rob Haywood	Stuart Nevison	Brian Westbrook
Layton Lillas	Steve Rigg	Del Roll
Alistair Thomas	John Elliott	Russ Quilty
Graham Nash	Robert Shakespeare	Rainer Haas
Samantha Luc	Dominic Snyder	Peter Ratcliffe
David Zonshine	Danny Handley	Jonathan Prevezer
Mark Nelson	Allan Clarke	Steve Lauri
Tim Chacksfield	Dick Beaumont	Tim Ramage
William Ludwig II	Bruce Thomas	Mike McCann
Ken Townsend	Julie Eyre	Andrew King
Simon Hart	Trevor Pickles	Ann Taylor
Craigie Zildjian	Spencer Leigh	Jack Wilson
Tina Clarke	Goldie Francis	Nigel Reeve
Sarah Hagan	David Hopkinson	Chuck Blashaw
Robert Haydock	Mark Jones	Mick Eyre
Hadrian Thorne	Ian Parker	Suzi Quatro
Chris Bryans	Chris Johnson	Sheila Bowen
Victoria Gascoigne	Darren Shaun	Derek Quinn
Phil Smee	Chris Hill	Steve Phillips
Simon Smith	Jerry Wilcox	Clem Cattini
Uli Twelker	Allard Britton	Peter Howarth
John Miles	Steve Rushton	Tony Brady
Lloyd Ryan	Alan Hydes	Donald Muir
Clive Seedall	Steve Perry	Lesley Haywood
Elaine Nash Connors	John Clarke	Simon Riley
Mick Spratt	Niki Haydock	Don Powell
Mike Handley	John Hanson	Barbara Smith
An Vanhentenrijk	Ray Stiles	Jimmy Jewell
Knut and Borgny	Janine Bannister	Joe Vickers
Andy Neill	Alan Coates	Pete Wingfield
Alan Clayson	Jim Duckworth	Tony Marsden
Arnim Kilgus	David Templeton	Robyn Alexander
Geoff Coles	Harriet Vickers	Ben Pratt
Ben Gascoigne	Jimmy Smith	Mike Heatley
Paul Hicks	Keith Bateson	Gray Bartlett

Acknowledgements

Geoff Muir
Margaret Storey
Steve Stroud
Pam Haydock
Ben Gonzalez
Barrie Sharply
Duane MDR

Wim and Ria Wigt
Lesley Pickersgill
Matt Fuller
Ray Lucas
Bonny
Denis Haines
Angus Mitchell

Brad Thomson
Alec Makinson
Paul Francis
Brian Bennett
Liam McCartan
Derek Royle